TWIST OF FATE

A JACK WEST NOVEL

DEANNA KING

ISBN: 979-8-9856982-0-6

Book Cover by NTLT Productions—Bada$$ Sci-fi/Fantasy Book Covers by Regin Tersaun

Proofread and edited by Sharon Jaeger

Published by Deanna King Writing

deannakingwriting.com

PRAISE FOR DEANNA KING

"Ms. King's novel reads like a good Netflix crime series—an engaging story with compelling characters making the reader want to binge from chapter to chapter. Best part of all: It takes place in Texas and really captures the diverse, yet unique character of the state."

~Samantha Calimbahin, Fort Worth Magazine

ALSO BY DEANNA KING

For my husband Travis—My life partner in crime, and my best friend.
Thank you for believing in me.

1

Spring 1955, thirty–six years ago

With nowhere to run, she started backing up. Pointed at her face, the barrel of a 9 mm seemed more like a cannon. God, she'd die in this dirty, dank storeroom.

"Pull the trigger. She'll be dead. We can go on with business the way we used to. Why are you waiting, Archie? Shoot the bitch!" JoAnn wanted her dead so she could have Jed for herself. This had nothing to do with business. She was in love with Jed—Celeste was in the way.

Archie's speech was slurred; he was drunk. "You took it all from me, you fucking bimbo. My mother never loved me, but she loved you. Why?"

"Archie, come on, you don't want to do this. Put the gun down, please." Celeste's heart was thumping so hard, she knew they could see it pounding under her shirt. Could she disarm him? Did she have the guts to try?

JoAnn shoved Archie toward Celeste and he stumbled. The

alcohol messed up his coordination, but he caught himself from tumbling head first.

"Stop pushing me, JoAnn, shit. I want this tramp to be so scared she pisses herself." Archie's words stilled slurred.

"Archie, please, I swear, I didn't know your mother would leave it all to me. What do you want?" Panic rose in her throat. Here she was, alone with two people who wanted to kill her. Was this how her life was going to end?

"I want what should have been mine, all of it—control. It's my time to be the boss. That's what I want, you stupid bitch." Spittle shot out as he screeched out the words. His face twisted up in an ugly sneer as he stared at her with glassy eyes. The idiot was not rational. Celeste would never relinquish her power to him. Sara had not wanted her simpleton son in control; the business would implode if Archie was in charge.

"Archie, be reasonable. Your mother wanted me to have control for a reason. You know I can't sign it all over to you." Celeste tried to keep the tremor out of her voice. She would not whimper. Archie was a coward. But he *was* waving a pistol in her face, and she wondered if he had enough drunken courage to pull the trigger.

Walking to the back end of the bar to find her, Jed heard the commotion in the storeroom.

"Hey, Celeste, what's going on back here? What's all the yelling about? I heard—" Jed saw the gum aimed at Celeste's beautiful face and lost it. He shoved JoAnn, sending her crashing into cases of beer, bottles shaking and clanking. The woman hit the concrete floor, sprawled facedown.

Jed rushed over and kicked Archie's feet out from under him. The drunk fell sideways and his hand holding the gun went up in the air as he worked to keep his balance. Jed grabbed Archie's arm, jerking it and disarming him in one swift move. The hard tug popped Archie's shoulder out of socket sending him to the floor in pain.

"You drunken bastard. How dare you hold a gun on her! What the hell?" Jed kicked him in the ribs and then grabbing the front of

Archie's shirt he hoisted his sorry ass up. Still holding his shirt, Jed began punching him like a doll on a rubber band, not letting go, punch after punch.

Celeste squatted and picked up Archie's revolver. Her hands were shaking, grateful the gun had not discharged.

Archie's nose was broken and bleeding when Jed finally let go of his shirt, letting him drop back down to the concrete floor.

The whore screwed up her face in fury, her eyes on Jed and Jed only as she pulled herself up off the floor.

"What the fuck, Jed? What about me? Don't you know what I would do for you? I'd do anything for you, *anything*, understand me? I mean it, *anything and everything.*"

"What do I want with a ten-cent whore? I overheard you, JoAnn, egging him on, you bitch. You wanted Archie to shoot her. I can understand his anger, but not yours. Get over here."

She took a timid step, and Jed grabbed her by the arm, pulling her close, so close he could smell the whiskey on her breath. JoAnn puckered her lips sending him an air-kiss. This was enough to send him over the edge. Taking his free arm, raising his fist, for the first time in his life he punched a woman.

"*No*, Jed," Celeste shrieked. "She's a girl, you don't, oh—" Her mouth dropped open in disbelief; he had hit her, and hard.

"JoAnn's a whore. She hasn't been a real woman in years. Besides, she threatened you, so she's getting what she deserves." He looked at the whore with disgust, and he spat on the floor.

JoAnn got up not bothering to wipe the blood dripping from her nose and the side of her mouth. "I see what the score is. I bow to the powers that be." She bowed to Jed as a Thespian actor bowed after act one. She turned to Celeste and repeated her bow, sneering. "It's up to you now, Celeste. You'd better not screw it up. If you do, one day you won't see it coming. And just like that,"—JoAnn snapped her fingers, and it echoed as she narrowed her eyes in hate—"a new boss will take over. When that happens, you'll be six feet under."

"Are you threatening me, JoAnn?" Celeste took a step toward the woman, ready to punch the whore herself, holding the gun up to show her the ball was in her court now.

The whore didn't flinch. With the life she'd lived, she'd been in worse spots. JoAnn let out a bitter laugh. "Nah, honey, ain't no threat, just fact. There are things said you don't hear, but I do. In my profession, there's a lot said. Call it pillow talk, and there's not enough power in your pockets to keep you safe right now."

"Get the hell out of my club, bitch." She turned to the man moaning, with a bloody nose and holding his shoulder. "You too, Archie, get out of my club—*now*." Celeste's voice quavered a bit; she hated showing them fear.

Jed took her by the arm and pulled her toward him, looking at the other two with contempt.

"Come on, Celeste, let's get out of here. You two pieces of shit clean up this mess, and then get the hell out of here."

Without another word, Jed walked a flustered Celeste back into the main room of the Crystal Barrel and up to the bar. "Skip, pour me two whiskeys, straight up." He looked at Celeste. "Are you okay, babe?"

Celeste's hand shook as she reached for the glass and took a drink. She wasn't a drinker, and it scalded her throat, hitting her stomach, and then warming her to her toes.

"Just shaken, that's all. I thought Archie might have the guts to pull the trigger since JoAnn was egging him on. Thank God you came into the store room when you did. No telling—" A single tear fell and then another as she let her fears ebb out.

"It's over now." He waved at Skip. "Give me another whiskey." Jed tossed back his drink, then turned and looked at her. "Celeste, honey, we need to get some more power behind us. A couple of rent-a-cops and a TABC agent on the payroll is not enough. What we need is some political power."

"We have Roger and he knows people. We know he employees the type of people who will work with us in our kind of business. Plus we have Ken." Her hands still shook a little. Jed pushed her glass toward her. "Drink," he told her.

Taking another sip, it burned, but her nerves were settling.

"Celeste, Roger is a shyster and scum, plus he's Archie's friend. His people are a joke. As far as Ken is concerned, we keep him out of the business. He can't be connected; if he is found complicit he can't represent us, so it's imperative he steers clear of our other businesses."

"Jed, I'm not worried about Roger's people. We have the money to guarantee their loyalty. There are a lot of ways we can play this to our advantage. I just have to grow a set of balls, that's all."

Her nerves were fine now, her resolve must not be broken, and the wheels began turning in her head.

CELESTE MASON HAD WORKED her way into power. She had been careful, yet daring, developing the business, establishing connections with people of means, power, and money, and it had been easy since money garnered money. There was no way she could've known what would happen. The dominoes were set in motion with nothing to stop them from falling. Once Sara Sutton had the angel of death sweep her way, complete control was handed to her. It was then she became a woman marked for death.

"IT MAKES ME SICK. He has such puppy dog eyes when he looks at her." The dark-blonde-haired woman put a Virginia Slim between her cherry-red glossed lips and waited for Randy to light it. JoAnn inhaled, held it and then exhaled, and a heavy stream of smoke floated out and encircled her head.

"She's a pain in the ass, but she has nice ass. Her rack ain't bad either," Randy said as he clipped receipts together. He punched a key on the register, opened it, and slapped the receipts under the cash drawer.

"Huh. My ass is nicer and we've got about the same size boobs, although I think mine are a little bigger. I'm betting ya couldn't tell us apart in the dark." With a bit of force, JoAnn stubbed out the half-smoked cigarette.

"Uh-huh, both of you are about the same height and weight, and from behind y'all sorta look alike. There is one difference though; you have a tickle in your ass that she doesn't have. Besides, I'd bet my last dime she ain't no virgin, which you definitely ain't. Shit, Jo, you ain't been a virgin since you were fourteen." He slapped his palm on the bar and gave her a wink.

"Fuck you, Randy, you had a piece, and you liked it, so back off. I don't even make you pay for it, either. Hell, even in the dark and under the covers, you'd be able to tell which girl was which. I can guarantee it."

"Jeeze, take it easy, Miss Fire-in-her-panties. God, you act like you run the show and you don't. If I were you, I'd take off in a flash like you do your pants. Get back to work. Celeste and Jed are headed this way and you don't wanna piss either of them off, now do you?"

She angled her head to one side and saw them out of the corner of her eye. "I'll see you later, Randy." She wrinkled her nose and blew him a kiss before turning around to leave.

JoAnn sashayed away from the bar, passing Jed with a smile and she let her red-tipped fingernails lightly slide against his shirtsleeve.

"See ya later, doll?"

Jed flipped his arm, tossing her fingertips off, narrowing his eyes. "Not me, JoAnn, Randy yeah, but not me, ever."

Celeste tried to ignore her, but it was hard. The woman made her butt loads of money or she'd kick her to the curb. Another important issue was the whore recruited more than half of the other girls. If JoAnn walked, they might too.

"I cannot stand that whore." Jed disliked all the girls, but he hated JoAnn the most.

"Yeah, I don't care for her myself, but she makes us money. The other issue is Randy, the dumbass. He's just a horny man in a candy shop with a zipper for a revolving door. JoAnn gives him all the free candy he wants." Celeste's voice was clipped.

Jed looked over at the bar, watching Randy. "Come on, babe. Let me buy you a glass of water." He knocked on the bar. "Simpson, two ice waters."

Randy filled two glasses with ice and squirted water in both then set them down on napkins in front of Jed and Celeste.

"Randy," Celeste began, "you ought to give it a rest and stop with the freebies, and if you don't, I'll get Sarge to kick your ass."

"Hell, boss, if they give it away for free and you don't lose money, what do you care if one of 'em gives me some on the side? I call it a job perk since we don't get health benefits or retirement." Randy flicked the bar towel in the air slapping it on the bar, using it to wipe up nothing.

She gave him an icy stare. "Randy, what's with the attitude? Cool off before I get irritated." Her eyes never left his face as she picked up her ice water and took a drink.

He stared at her, then at Jed, and he shrugged. "Jed—"

"Listen, Randy," Jed cut him off. "Just because your old man is a cop doesn't mean you have carte blanche with the girls or anything else. All it takes is one phone call and you're gone. Understand what I'm telling you?"

"Is that a damn threat?"

Before Jed responded, Celeste leaned into the bar. "No, it's not a threat, it's a *promise*."

Jed laid his hand on her arm, but she flipped it off.

"Randy, this is my show, my business. I can have you kicked out of the door before you blink. You got that?"

"*Sure thing, boss*," Randy's voice oozed with sarcasm. "Just to warn you though, word is some people have it out for you, so be best to watch your back."

"Are you issuing me a threat, Randy? If this is a threat and I find out you are involved, your sorry ass will be mine. Is—this—clear?" She enunciated the last three words; tiny spit particles sprayed the air.

"No threat from me; I'm just saying, that's all." What was he thinking, talking to her this way? It'd be better for him to back off before she hired someone to whack him. Nope, she wouldn't, because his old man was a cop, for Christ's sake.

Celeste knew what his undersized brain was mulling over.

"How about I talk to your old man? Betcha he'd straighten your ass out. He had a profitable deal going on here, and he wouldn't want to lose it all just because his son was a major screw-up, now would he?"

Randy had been shooting his mouth off to anyone he could get to listen. Gossip traveled fast in their circle. He backed away from the bar, scowling.

"Keep my old man out of it."

"Tell you what, Randy," Celeste said, "how about you do your job? I pay you good money for what you do besides bartending, and part of your pay is shut-up money. Be best for you to keep your mouth shut. If I get wind of any threats to me and find out you're involved, your dad being a cop on my payroll won't make a damn bit of difference, you hear me?"

Randy locked eyes with her. Ever since she gained total control, this tiny woman had grown balls the size of Alaska. Hell, if he wanted to, he'd be able to break her skinny neck in one snap. He smiled at her, envisioning doing just that. With a knock on the bar top, he nodded.

"Got it, boss, anything you say." A faux smile, his teeth clenched.

She stared him down before speaking. "Go check to see if the bar-backs have the new kegs to install."

Randy called for Pete to come man the bar and he went to the back, cursing Celeste under his breath the entire way. He hated both of them, her and Jed. One day he hoped to prove how much he hated them. Besting them would be satisfaction, damn close to the satisfaction JoAnn offered him.

Jed laughed.

"What's so funny?"

"Celeste, you are a tough bitch. I think you are even tougher than Sara. You gonna tell his old man he is messing with you?"

"Not yet. Do me a favor, have someone monitor Randy. I know he is gonna cause us trouble. He thinks he can get away with anything cuz his old man is a cop. Right now we have enough to worry about with that sleaze ball attorney, Roger and his crybaby sidekick, Archie. And Simpson's as bad as his son is with the whores, but his being a cop benefits us. Randy is as useless as tits on a bull." She blew out a long breath.

"With the few cops we have on the payroll, Simpson and Bullard are the most reliable. I just wish we hadn't let Simpson talk us into bringing his fuck-up son, Randy, on board."

"Jed, Sara is the one who took that chance. It was her call. She is still in charge, but I'll be damned. Randy should have brains enough to realize I am Sara's other arm. All I have to do is say something to her and he's gone."

"Randy has been trying to get in tight with Archie and Roger, so that is an issue we need to watch; and, what about Scottie, Celeste? How do you figure he is gonna fit in?"

"I'm not sure, Jed. I haven't figured him out yet. Sara is friends with his uncle from up Chicago way. At least that's the story. Scottie is here learning the business from her, or I heard tell he was in trouble and she took him in. She never fully explained it to me. After meeting him, my money is on he was in trouble and needed to leave Chicago."

"I don't care for the guy, but if he fits in with her plans, and she wants him here, then fine by me."

"He seems okay, and he and I get along fine. But with Sara's health failing, all I know is Archie is next in line. Jed, if he gets control, I am outta of here, because I won't work for that pissant. He'll have the business run into the ground in a year. After that, what he'll have left is three failing bars, and nothing else."

Jed was just as much aware of this as she was. Everything Sara built up with the whores and the gambling would end. The jerk was a hothead. It wouldn't surprise him if one of their competitors whacked him.

CELESTE CLOSED HER EYES, recalling those years as if it were yesterday. Remembering the day Sara Sutton died of heart failure unexpectedly. Six months later Archie shoved a pistol in her face in a drunken rage, because the old lady left everything to her—the bars, the land, the corporation, the house, everything. The only thing his mother left to him was a small fifty-thousand dollar pittance. Sara's instructions had been that Celeste took total control at once. This was the start of so much immense hatred, from so many sides.

Archie wanted complete control. Roger the shyster wanted to be his sidekick to wield power. Scottie wanted her to be indebted to him; and he wanted to gain ultimate power in this business. This tangled web equaled death, and there was no way she could have ever predicted the ending.

LATE ONE EVENING, as Celeste was leaving the Crystal Barrel, three thugs grabbed her and dragged her to the rear of the lot. They pushed her between them, roughing her up. She fell to the ground in the ruckus and one of them kicked her in the ribs. The heaviest of the three picked her up off the ground and the skinny, tall one subdued her, pinning her with one arm, covering her mouth with his nasty, calloused hand.

"You're a tiny thing. If we keep this up, you're gonna get hurt, or worse, you understand me? So, back off, bitch, cuz this job ain't for a woman to control."

He took his hand off of her mouth and the heavy dude flicked her in the cheek with the back of his beefy hand. "Yeah, and if you blab to anyone about this, we'll come back and finished what we started."

"Can't promise what might happen to you next time, either. Now, back the fuck off, and let someone else take over," his thuggish cohort threatened.

The fat leader backhanded her again, only this time he sent her sprawling to the ground and the three of them took off for their car. Celeste overheard one of them say, "Rog will be happy we scared her," just as the car door shut.

Sarge had just opened the back door looking for her when he saw her lying on the ground and the three men speeding away.

"Shit, Celeste, I told you to wait for me. Jed is gonna kill me for not protecting you. Did you know those assholes?"

She dusted off the dirt, wiping the blood from her lips. "No, but one of them said 'Rog will be happy we scared her.' You think he meant Rog, as in Roger Stockard?"

"He's the only Roger I know; you know anyone else named Roger?"

"No, I don't and the Roger I know as in Stockard is tight with Archie. You think they are both behind this?" The possibility of both scumbags being behind this attack pissed her off. "I wanna talk to Scottie."

"He's still here in the back, let's go find him." Sarge walked her back into the club and went to find Scottie for her.

One week later, the Houston Chronicle headlines read:

Two Gunned Down on Richmond Avenue: Attorney Roger Stockard and a man named Archie Bowers. Very few details, no witnesses, or anyone offering any leads—the police were baffled.

"You got a two for one, Celeste," Scottie bragged. "And I won't even charge you for the other douchebag."

Two men both dead–well she'd ordered a hit on one, but both dead didn't bother her in the slightest. Yet, was she ready for the consequences?

One night five weeks later, Celeste had another near miss in the parking lot of the Silver Moon. A truck came out of nowhere without lights, aiming straight for her. Jed shoved her out of the way so hard she went flying, crashing to her knees, spread-eagle, face first on the asphalt.

The truck sped away before Jed had the rational thought of getting the plate number because he was worried about her.

"Oh my God, Celeste, are you okay?" He helped her to her feet.

Her jeans were ripped at the knees and a trickle of blood ran down. She had scraped her hands from skidding on the asphalt.

"Damn it, Jed, that was no accident. Did you get a look at the driver?"

"No, I didn't, but the passenger looked like Randy Simpson."

She didn't miss a beat. "Mother Fucker, if it was Randy, you can bet your ass JoAnn is involved. Those two have become thick as thieves." She needed to get this under control before she ended up dead.

JoAnn was vindictive for one reason, and that one reason was Jed. She was positive. The jealous whore wanted Jed for herself. Not able to get the man she'd set her sights on, she had ended up with a pussy named Randy. Now that JoAnn was stuck with Randy, this meant she was just as dangerous as he was as well as the others who wanted her, Celeste Mason, dead.

2

"Celeste, have you been listening to a word I've said?"

"Yes, Ken, I have."

"It's a legit business venture, and if the bar's businesses do poorly, then the new company will continue to grow. It would be a very easy transition from the bar businesses to the restaurant supply business. We can start with the three clubs you own as first customers."

"If you feel it's the right move for us financially, then let's do it—whatever you think is fine by me."

She was not engaged in the conversation; Ken saw that clearly.

"If we all agree, Ken, set it up on your end. Use the south-side warehouse, the one closet to the Silver Moon for supplies." Jed shuffled the papers back into the file and handed it back to Ken.

"Uh-huh, sure, Jed. Whatever you say is fine." The woman was preoccupied, which was not normal in the course of a business meeting.

"Where are you, Celeste? Because you are not here?" Jed nudged her foot with his under her desk.

She took a folded piece of paper from the top drawer of her desk and handed it to him. "I'm here, that's where I am."

Bitch, watch your back. You think you are safe but you aren't. Several people don't like the way you are running things, and, if you know what's good for you, you'll leave town and not come back.

"Where did this come from?" Overwhelmed with anger, Jed crushed the note into a ball.

"Found it under my door this morning. The whole crew was here last night after we left. It could have been any one of them. This is the third threat letter I've received in the last three months."

"What? Why didn't you tell me about the others?" Jed was irritated at her for keeping this hidden from him.

"I don't know, Jed. I guess I didn't want to act like a scared little girl. Roger and Archie *had* been my biggest threat, but they're both dead. It has me puzzled, since we finally got Randy straightened up. Who would want me out? Our business is booming, and solid, and people seem happy. Plus, we are not encroaching on anyone's territory, sharing the wealth you might say. Shit, gambling and whores, Houston is big enough for all of us and then some."

"Uh, Celeste, I need to leave, okay?"

Ken needed to stay out of the dirty side of the business—it was imperative. The door clicked shut. They were alone.

"So, why does someone want me out, Jed? I mean, yes, I've made a few enemies, but this feels different."

"Different like how? Maybe Randy and JoAnn are just messing with you again? They could be just trying to scare you. I wouldn't put it past them."

"No, it goes deeper. I think someone on the outside is trying to muscle in. They want my whores and my bookies, and more, is what I think."

"More? Like more what? You talking about someone wanting to add the drug trade to our businesses too?"

"Yes, I do, and one word comes to mind. Mob."

"Celeste, do you mean Scottie? We know his family has mob ties up Chicago way. Do you think he is the one threatening you? He's been loyal up to now."

"Jed, he's been itching to get in deeper, and the family ties stretch for miles. But I have no beefs with Scottie. We get along okay, so I can't see that he wants me dead. What I think is he would like to take control, but not kill me."

"Alright, babe, how should we handle this?"

WITH CLOSED EYES, she recalled how things had changed. It had been over 25 years. She wanted out, he wanted in. This she could make happen, but she'd never be *out*. The one thing he'd never see would be her behind the scenes, still wielding the reins of power. All she was doing was taking a hiatus until she was ready to take over again. Her past played out in her mind like a well-scripted movie.

"THE PLAN IS I need to disappear, and he takes over. I talked to him, and he's sure there's a contract out on my life. So it's best if I relinquish power to him."

"He's a bastard, Celeste. I am sure Sara had no idea he could be a threat to you."

"Well, power is an aphrodisiac, and Scottie is on a high. If he wants it, then we can sell out. He has influence up north, and damn, I won't fight it any longer."

"Sell out, are you crazy?"

"He'll just think he's in control. We have him by the short hairs because of the Richmond shooting. You and I know he was the shooter, and we have people who will say they saw it. With the powerful people in our pockets, this won't be a problem."

"How do you intend to stay in?"

"I won't sell him the buildings or the land, Jed. I'm keeping them and putting them in your name. He can run the *business,* but he'll have to pay you a percentage. Scottie has to use our legal company for all bar supplies, and he can use the trucks for his drug transport. It's a win-win. So if I'm dead, he gets what he wants, and he won't even realize I'll have unseen control behind closed doors. All Scottie will be is a front man. And, another good thing is I can stop working at that damn ratty boutique as a cover. I hate that place with those goodie-goodie girls."

"What if he doesn't go along with it and the contract on your life stays in force?"

"I've written a letter and have it all set up, so if something happens to me, his ass will be burned. Besides, he knows the one person who saw him in Richmond has already spoken to the police, and I'm going to offer him a deal."

"Well, if it's JoAnn you're talking about, I'm all for frying her ass; can't stand that whore."

"If the people up north think I'm dead and I make Scottie a deal, he can't refuse. I don't see why it can't work."

"How will you fake your death so they'll believe you are dead?" He wanted to hear her plan. He was sure she had worked it out to the smallest detail.

She explained her plan to him.

"It might work, but one question—why pick him?"

"Because Ken told me he's a rising star. I say we get him in our pocket, and if we do, Scottie will think he has him in *his* pocket too."

Jed was in awe. This woman's mind was sharp. It was the reason Sara had left her everything.

"Then let's get you killed off before someone does it for real."

She picked up the phone. "I'll call Scottie and tell him to meet us in an hour."

"WE GOTTA DISPOSE OF HER, TOO." Scottie wanted to tie up loose ends. "What if there was a way to get rid of her and me?"

Scottie looked at her as if she had two heads, then looked over at Jed.

"What's she talking about?"

"Why don't you ask her? She's sitting right there, and she was asking *you* the question."

Scottie looked back at her, waiting for her answer.

"You want the business, and your goons up north want me dead—tying up a loose end I figure. There are so many other loose ends, but I guess if they get me, then the others won't talk, and they'll have to be loyal to you. I hafta disappear, and you are afraid JoAnn will point a finger at you for killing Roger and Archie. Have I left anything out, Scottie?"

"That about covers it."

"So if they *think* I'm dead, this will satisfy you?"

He thought about it for about two minutes before he bobbed his head in a brief nod.

"I'll take that as a yes. Also, if anything happens to me in any way deemed unnatural, the dominos will fall, and not in your favor, understand?"

"Is that a threat?"

"No, Scottie, it's a promise. Here's the deal: I help you, you help me, or we can both burn in hell. I don't care one way or another anymore."

"What's your plan?" He had no problem with her being alive. He liked the woman, and if Jed were to disappear, he'd move in on her.

She told him the plan, she told him who, what, and why. Scottie took the bait and was in for the idea.

"Jed, make the call."

Jed dialed Ken's office. The young whippersnapper attorney answered.

"Hey, dude, how would you like a freebie?"

"Whatcha talking about, Jed?" The arrogant young attorney propped his feet on his pristine desk.

"I figured you needed some relaxation. You can have JoAnn tonight; free, all night long, no time limit."

He knitted his brows. "Free, why free and why all night long? What do you have up your sleeve, or should I ask what does Celeste have up her sleeve?"

He sat up. This was the first time they'd offered him *free, and an all nighter*. Warning bells went off. There had to be a catch.

"Can't we do a nice thing for you? Ken told us you've been working long hours and have had some tough cases." Jed tried to sound offended.

"No. There's a catch, so what is it, Jed? And don't lie to me."

He did not care to be indebted to anyone. The rumors were blackmail was part of SS Corporation's success, and he wanted no involvement. Lord, he did like the whores; they were worth every penny, especially JoAnn. One thing he was cautious about was covering his tracks. He couldn't let his wife find out. It would ruin him. Without her support, he could never get to where he wanted to be. And he needed his father-in-law's political ties. Oh, but the warm feeling rising behind his zipper, as he thought about JoAnn and what she allowed. It was too much not to accept.

"Scare her a bit, teach her a lesson. She's been giving us a bit of trouble, and I want you to go over the line more than normal." Jed knew the whore and her tastes.

The man at the pristine desk let loose a throaty chuckle. "Overboard, with JoAnn, hell, Jed, she *is* overboard in the sack."

"So I've been told; never had a taste for it myself. Some men don't have any problems paying big bucks for what she does, or lets a john do to her."

The man on the other end let out another crude laugh. He loved what this whore allowed a man to do. The kinkier and more dangerous it was excited her too. JoAnn could make him cum harder than any woman he'd ever fucked, and she gave back as good as she got.

"Sure, Jed, she's worth every dollar she charges, but hell, if I'm gonna get her for free—well fuck yeah, I'm in for the entire night." He got a woody thinking about it.

Jed hung up the phone.

"The ball's in your court now. You call her, and then it's all set."

Celeste didn't hesitate because she needed JoAnn dead. She guessed she was really a cold-hearted bitch. Just remembering the day in the storeroom—when a drunken Archie had a pistol in her face, with JoAnn behind him, begging him to shoot. It was her incentive. If JoAnn had been holding the gun, she'd be a corpse right now.

She picked up the phone. "JoAnn, this is Celeste."

THE MOTEL WAS SEEDY, off the beaten path, and perfect. He threw back his third straight Bourbon as she stripped, and then lying on the bed, she inviting him in, and he took charge. She thought he was done, but he had other ideas.

"Get me another drink. I'm going to taking a piss, and then I am coming back to fuck you again."

"Can't wait," her reply low and husky, and she watched his tight backside walk into the small bathroom and the door shut. When he was out of sight, she put the envelope of coke in his glass. It was triple the normal snort, and she poured whiskey over it, stirring it with her finger. Celeste told her it was a favor for Jed.

"Get the man high and once he passes out, call Jed. He'll take care of the rest."

Celeste swore to her if she did this, Jed would do something nice for her, and she'd step back. JoAnn desired Jed with every fiber in her being and if this was what took to get her man, she would do it.

JoAnn would do anything for Jed. Her one worry was Celeste. Was she really going to take a step back?

JoAnn wasn't afraid of taking chances. If this was how she got Jed, she needed to make sure she did a great job. She took another envelope out, poured more into the drink then dumped the rest onto the table and snorted it through a rolled up one-hundred-dollar bill she'd got from her last john.

"Powdered courage, JoAnn, you don't do that. Why tonight?" He sauntered back into the room, taking the glass of tainted Bourbon from her, then chugging it.

"Coke always makes me feel sexier." A sexy low laugh bubbled up, and she sat on the edge of the bed, crossing her naked legs.

After pouring a second healthy shot, he tossed the entire drink back and then pushed her on her back, telling her to scoot up to the headboard. Pulling her arms up he cuffed her hands to the metal headboard. He gagged her with a silk scarf and picked up his belt. With slow, deliberate moves, he slid the belt up between her legs and after a few passes, he hit her with the belt, softly at first. As the cocaine began affecting him, he whipped her with more aggression, causing red welts to appear on her legs. JoAnn's laugh was muffled, as she gurgled; the pain pleasing her abnormally. Something he himself would never understand, but happy to be on the giving end of this type of sick pleasure. He took the belt, cinching it around her neck, pulling her head up toward him, and yanking the gag out of her mouth.

"You like that? You want me to fuck you again?" The words rose from deep within his chest in a bear-like growl, the high from the cocaine making him invincible and mean.

She panted; her own snort of cocaine had her feeling no pain. "Yes, yes, get the scarves and tie them together, just like you did last time. I want to be delirious."

The woman's sexual fetish of scarfing was unreal. In his life, he'd met no one, man or woman who liked autoerotic asphyxia, and she'd been a woman who craved the feeling and begged for it. He unhandcuffed her and made her roll onto her stomach, then he re-cuffed her to the metal headboard. Knotting the scarves together, he formed a slipknot that fit over her neck, affixing the other ends to the small metal headboard posts so when she arched her neck and pulled, so did the scarves, tightening around her skinny white throat. He enjoyed doing her on her stomach because entering her from behind gave him control, and he could fuck her harder.

"Pull the scarves tighter. Last time the scarves never tightened." She pouted with a big huff. "I didn't get my jollies, but you did." She was a lunatic, one he'd never understand. But fulfilling her wishes, any time, made him a happy horny man.

With a hard thrust, he entered her. Pulling the end of the scarf he began driving into her, and with each thrust, he pulled the scarves harder and harder, his eyes closed. The only thing he felt was euphoria. It was at least five minutes of hard driving sex, and he didn't notice if she was getting off or not. He didn't care if she came or not. His satisfaction was important. Hers did not matter.

Sweat rolled off his brow, the salt stung his eyes, and he dropped hard on top of her when he had finished.

"You get your rocks off, bitch?" He panted out a laugh as he as spoke to the back of her head. She was quiet. Why was she pissed at him?

"JoAnn, did you get off or not?" He reached up and uncuffed her, then turned her over. Was she was pissed off, giving him the silent treatment? It wasn't the first time she had acted this way.

No one had ever come off a high like that so fast. Her face was lifeless, her eyes bulging; he had gone too far. Holy Christ, she'd asked for it. He felt for a pulse. Had she just passed out? No pulse. God, now what was he going to do? Panic gripped him as he reached for the phone.

"It's me. I have a problem. You hafta help me!" He tried keeping the alarm out of his voice.

Briefly, he told Jed what had happened. If they helped him, he would pay whatever they asked. He paced the room, not looking at her, and unable to leave. What was taking them so long to get here?

Jed knocked on the door. "It's me. Open the door."

His face was pallid. "I'm not sure what happened. Oh God, I mean, she asked for this. I'm going to prison! I can't go to prison!"

"We'll handle it; sit and be quiet." Scottie shoved him toward the bed. Sarge followed him in.

When the camera came out, he became violent.

"What in the hell, what is, oh no, you're not doing that." He acted as if he was a wild animal caught in a trap. "You bastard, uh-uh, no, don't do that."

The big bald man held him back and, with one punch, knocked his ass out. It felt good to hit the bastard. After Jenna had told him what he made her perform, it angered the crap out of him.

"Lay him on her, like that. Put the scarves in both of his hands, but be careful. Now move back and let me get the pictures."

Jed watched as Scottie took photo after photo, getting every angle, then he stepped back.

"Get his clothes and the clothes Jenna gave you, Sarge, then drive the car over here," Scottie barked out orders.

"Jenna already has it out front and waiting."

They took the whore's lifeless nude body into the bathroom.

Scottie took his .38 special and put a hollow point bullet in her skull. "Now whydaya do that, Scottie? She's already dead, man." Sarge thought that was overkill.

"No face, no way to identify the body." Scottie was satisfied with the job.

Now she was no longer a worry to him. She'd been the one person who knew that it was him that night on the streets. Why she hadn't ratted on him was a mystery. He was convinced of two things now—he'd never have to be indebted to a whore, and no worries he'd be blackmailed.

There had been little spattered since her heart was no longer beating. Particles and bone had blown out of her head; they wiped most of it off then redressed her in clothes that Jenna brought to them. Jenna stood at the door, handing the car keys and clothes to Sarge.

She saw feet on the bed, but not the owner. Sarge was purposely blocking her view. There was a man crumpled on the floor. At first, all she saw was the torso of this naked man. He moved slightly, and a tiny gasp escaped her lips. She recognized him, squinting to see if he was breathing. Jenna let out an inaudible sigh when she saw his chest heave. Sarge backed her up from the doorway, and with his hand on her shoulder, he turned her around to get her to leave.

"Take my car, Jenna, and go home. You didn't see nothing, understand?" Sarge warned her.

She fumbled with the keys, trying to get them into the ignition. Something dreadful had happened, but she wasn't sure what or to whom. Whose feet were on the bed? Fear rose in her throat. Jenna had no idea if it was all planned. All she was sure of was since she was a whore too, she could have been the woman lying in the room. It was time to quit the business, and Sarge needed to keep her safe.

Once they'd dumped the body, they drove back to the motel to deal with their *pal*. He was out cold, and they took the young lawyer out of the room. They stuffed him in the car's trunk and drove the fool back to his place, and tucked him in for the night. He would have one freaking headache when he came to. The dumbass would remember most of it, and he would be calling.

3

Present Day

F ake elephant skin cowboy boots, Wranglers, and a light gray
sports coat, the only thing missing was a hat to give Jack West
that Texan look. The bottom edges of his jeans were getting damp as
he strolled over the dewy grass toward the paved road. After walking
a quarter of a mile, he turned right. Another 300 feet in and he
turned left. After 71 more yards he stood in front of the concrete
bench adorned with angels around the edge. He sat and lowered his
head, whispering a short prayer, and then raised his head with a sigh.
No matter how many years passed this still haunted him.

The headstone was a soft variegated gray and black. It stood two
and a half feet tall and was two feet wide. A large *W* was carved into
the top center. Centered beneath the W were a football, a star, and
praying hands. Below this was the name, *Cole Arron West—
Wonderful Son and Brother*, his birthdate and date of death.

Even when he wasn't at the cemetery, he saw this headstone. All
he needed to do was close his eyes. Each chip, crack, or impurity of
the marble, and the curve of every single letter, painted a picture in

his head. It had been eighteen years since he'd lost his best friend in the world. His older brother Cole was in the wrong place at the wrong time, a random victim shot dead in a gang drive-by. The area they hung out in was not in the gang district; someone wanted his brother dead. There weren't many random murders. Ninety-nine percent of the homicides he'd worked ended up being spur-of-the-moment killings, the motive often being jealousy or out-and-out rage and hate, or money. Plus each victim knew their killer, which made this even less random. He'd seen very few premeditated murders since he'd been on the force.

Cole's murder was deliberate. Something always bothered him about this shooting, even before he entered the police academy. His brother's case, unsolved, lingered in his thoughts. This had been the very reason he'd gone into police work. It was his drive to find the person who pulled the trigger, getting justice for his brother.

With a more than negative outlook toward gang members, it became his nature to profile anyone who even looked like a thug. His anger festered. This rage-filled attitude led him to various reprimands in the department and several soul-searching and police counseling sessions early in his career. Counseling helped him learn to squelch the negative attitude and do the job, making his brother proud.

There continued to be anger, but he kept it in check, never letting on how he felt about particular types of people. He was always searching for an anger outlet. As time passed, he realized putting every ounce of energy into the job worked best for him. Big brother Cole might have told him to ease up and try to focus more energy on his life. Have fun, laugh, get a girl or something, and don't let your work control you. God, he missed his big brother.

With both arms propped upon his knees, his hands clasped together, and for the first time, as he sat alone in this silent cemetery, he addressed the headstone.

"Well, big brother, there's no new news. I wish I could tell you I've got justice for your senseless death, but I'm working on it. But, bro, it may never happen, but I won't ever give up."

He closed his eyes and leaned back. Truth was he was nowhere near getting any answers. Jack worked Cole's murder book at home when he had the time. After this many years, the pages were tattered and fading, but he never wanted to quit. Most days, he put his brother's case aside to do the police work the people of Houston depended on him to do. All of this was a kind of vindication in his heart for his brother's senseless death. Each solved case with a solid conviction made him feel like he was there for a purpose. He hated that saying. Things happen for a reason. There was no *reason* for his brother to die young, no *damn reason.*

The sound of crunching gravel caused him to turn his head and glance over his shoulder. A car was approaching. Long, sleek, and black. It was the funeral director's car. He'd been there for only an hour, but he knew from past visits how mere moments slipped away into oblivion. It always did out here, so peaceful and serene. He might have enough time to get a bite to eat, as long as the morning traffic cooperated. It was time to go. He had to go to work.

Surveying the area as he stood, Jack shoved his hands into his pockets. It was the best place for his brother to rest. The grounds were nicely maintained and groomed. Magnolia Cemetery was not considered a large graveyard in Houston, but it was beautiful, a six-acre parcel of land and by far smaller than Glenwood and Washington Cemeteries. It also was a key landmark since it was the resting place for a very important person who'd been part of his life.

His parents chose this cemetery since it was near their home. They wanted to be near Cole even in death. Their house now sold, his parents were retired and living in Florida. It felt like a hundred years ago when he lived between Bunker Hill Village area and Piney Points Village, born and raised there a lifetime ago. He moved to Deer Park after his mom and dad moved to Florida. Until then, he stayed close to them, in a nice apartment a stone's throw away. It was convenient since his mother was constantly baking, and home-cooked meals were at his fingertips. Oh, how he missed home cooking and his parents.

After a search for a few months, he got a decent deal on a three-bedroom townhome in Deer Park. It was all he needed and not too much yard work. The townhome needed no improvements, and it fit him and his lifestyle. If luck was to shine on him one day, and a special woman came into in his life, it would be perfect for the two of them. His home was located close enough to Beltway 8 and Highway 225, and was roughly twenty-five miles to the station. Nice area. A few renters, mostly owners, it was a quiet neighborhood.

Houston's Magnolia Cemetery was near the station, so it was never an imposition for him to visit his brother's grave. There was no excuse not to visit and pay his respects or just talk to Cole. He made a promise to his brother on the day they laid him to rest, and his promise was he'd never let him be lonely, ever.

Deep in thought, he again heard the crunch of tires as the funeral director's car was pulling away and another truck headed up the path. Loaded with a green funeral cover, tent and chairs, they were setting things up for another sad day for an unknown family.

As he stood, he skimmed the three tombstones in front of him. Jack had researched his older brother's neighbors. Familiar with the graves on either side, he turned to his right to look downward at the headstone. An old woman who died at age eighty-eight lay buried. Della Roseanne Crayton. His assumption of why she'd passed was because of her advanced age. On the left lay a younger man, Russell Edward Washburn. His gravestone carved with *Loving Husband, Father and Brother*. Oddly, he investigated Russell's cause of death and found out he'd succumbed to pancreatic cancer.

Both graves were adorned with fresh flowers in the vases attached to the bottom of the stones. He admonished himself for not getting flowers. "Sorry, big brother. I'll make it up to you." Words said toward his brother's grave marker.

He then glanced right. "Della, you angel, have a wonderful day." Then he turned to his left. "Russell, my man, I wish I was acquainted with your family. I'd visit your kiddos for you, but I'm sure you are peeking in sometimes." Jack stared at Cole's headstone. He smiled. Not a heartfelt smile.

As if on perpetual rewind, his brother's unsolved murder ran through his mind again. Cole's case might go unsolved, but he'd keep trying. Assuming all those who might have been involved were thugs, dying young or incarcerated because crime became their life, or perhaps they moved on to a different life. This he doubted. Once you were in, you were in, with no way out, because this existence was for life or until death. Drugs and the hard lifestyle they'd chosen warped their brains. Dying young was another sad certainty. Misplaced loyalties meant no one would ever talk. It was at most a hopeless case for law enforcement officers. Not him, though, not Detective Jackson West. He was a man who never quit.

Jack peered again at his brother's final resting spot. "Okay, bro, gotta go get some morning Wheaties, but now I eat them as an Egg McMuffin, or sausage and egg, depending on if I splurge. After my Wheaties McMuffin powers me up, I have to go fight crime. I'll be back as soon as I can."

He saluted his brother goodbye and turned to walk back to his older black Dodge Ram. In his truck, he turned the key and came up with an idea. "Cole, you can hear me wherever you are. I promise to make up for missing the flowers. If a case doesn't keep me too busy, I'm gonna bring you a surprise."

Jack was not a lunatic; he just missed his brother that much.

As he headed to the station driving on the Loop, he grumbled. Traffic was congested, like always. Stuck driving five miles an hour, he was stopping and starting every few minutes. Up ahead, he saw flashing lights and one lone fire truck, with half dozen tow trucks. As usual in the bustling city of Houston, the tow truck drivers swarmed in droves. They arrived first on the scene, even before the police or any other emergency vehicles arrived. It was as if they lay in wait and were equipped with radar, which guided them to each fender bender in the city within seconds of the crash. Each driver waited to put his or her business card into a hat to see who got the job; it was craziness like this at each accident.

Detective Jackson West was going to have to sit in the slow, nonmoving traffic like the other regular people. He slipped his phone from his pocket clicking on contacts. Scrolling through, he found the number for Dawson Luck, hit call, waiting for his Bluetooth to fire.

Dawson answered on the third ring. "Hey, Jack, what's happening?"

"Hey, partner, listen. I am on the Loop right now, and it's a parking lot. I see the tow trucks working, but I'm going to be here for a bit. We have anything new going on?"

He heard paper shuffling and Dawson breathing. "Lucky, you still there?"

"Nah, we haven't pulled a new case yet, and I am finishing up the report from the last case."

Dawson Luck was the best paper-pusher partner he'd ever had. He did adequate paperwork, but he hated doing it.

"Get here when you get here. All you can do, right?"

"Will do. Tell the captain I am on my way in and what my delay is. See you when I see you."

No McMuffin at Mickey Ds today. Stale donuts and break room coffee would be breakfast, and better than nothing. Man, he thought, what a cliché cop breakfast.

No new case yet, no new murders; but it'd be short-lived. It was Houston, after all. Maybe his captain would let them work on his brother's cold case. Nah, it was dreaming on his part because he worked his brother's case whenever he was not on another case and Davis stopped him. Cole's murder was Jack's obsession, and it had clouded his judgment. Very proficient at his job, there were times his gut would talk to him like an inner voice, but it never said a word about his brother's unsolved case. Cole's crime scene photos tugged at his insides. Now he wished he could just *un-see* them. A regretful decision, one he could never take back. As time went on, and over the years, the pictures were no longer of his older brother, just pictures of a puzzle, and he was searching for the missing pieces.

Twenty minutes passed, and the traffic moved, albeit sluggishly. It took another five minutes for the traffic to have a decent, normal flow. Jack was up to forty miles per hour, yippee. It took him another half hour to get into downtown. After parking in the police parking garage, he took the service elevator up. Cutting through the front reception offices he walked into the Homicide and Major Crimes Division. After a quick stop at the break room, he grabbed two medium-sized Styrofoam cups, filled them with coffee, grabbed a stale donut, and then walked through the side door of the sixth floor.

It was a large room with multiple desks facing each other in pairs. File cabinets sat on either side of the desks. Jack sat across from Dawson, and there was a short partition between the desks. They'd been fortunate to be closer to the back; it gave them just a hair more privacy. Jace Severson and Xi Chang shared the area with them. There were four more pairs of desks, and when most of the fellas were there, it was noisy. If your desk was in a corner near the rear of the room, you had a coveted spot in the homicide room.

Jack's boots made no sound on the dark gray and black Berber carpet as he headed back to his work space. Dawson's back was to him, and he was deep into typing on his computer.

"Morning, pard, here's some sort of fresh coffee." Jack set the cup in front of Dawson.

"Thanks, Mom, I am happy you're here to take care of me."

"This is where the caring stops. Get your own sweetener."

"Mmm. Nope, like mine black and strong, like my women." Same reply as always.

His partner, Dawson Luck, a transplant from the Arizona Police Department Robbery Division, was on the cusp of being a narcissist. Lucky stood at five foot nine, with a big nose and big feet, and eyebrows resembling a long black caterpillar. When he either frowned or concentrated, it appeared the caterpillar was trying to fold in half. Lucky thought he was gifted with *game* and considered himself a ladies' man.

The first time his wife showed up at the station, the fellas drooled. Their mouths gaped open when she told them she was Mrs. Dawson Luck. Vivian was gorgeous. The entire station wondered what in the heck she saw in Dawson. It was his *big feet*. They'd howled in laughter. He was one lucky S.O.B. With the last name Luck, *Lucky* was a fitting nickname, more fitting when the fellas saw his gorgeous wife!

Jack recalled a time when Dawson was feeling macho and so full of himself. His partner got his butt kicked by a feisty black patrol cop named Cassandra Sparrow. It was friendly teasing and the female officers took it in stride. Dawson's bantering was innocent, and no one considered any of it as sexual harassment. Dawson was very careful to not cross that line. He loved his wife; he'd never be stupid enough to jeopardize his marriage or his job. One day, he caught Cass in an unpleasant mood, not up for his sassy mouth.

She'd had a crappy day on patrol. With her patrol partner, Amy Cordova, they had been working out their frustrations on the wrestling mats. Detective Luck, without thinking, made a simple girlie remark. Cass looked up as sweat rolled from her forehead and a dark expression crossed her face. She didn't care for Lucky, not for any real reasons. He just rubbed her the wrong way.

"Listen, Dawson, you bring your big nosed, big-footed self over here." Cass scowled, one hip jutted out. At five foot six, and a hundred thirty pounds, her body toned and muscular. She was in great shape. Cassandra Sparrow, the sixth child out of seven brothers, and she had learned to outsmart them, and outmaneuver them.

Dawson beamed at her. "You talking to me?" His DeNiro accent was horrible.

Cass crooked her finger inviting him to join her on the mat.

"Sure, butterfly, I'm coming." And with a wink, he moseyed over to the mats.

On the mat at the ready, she took him down, not just once, but three times. She was fast, she was smart, and she had brothers bigger than her she could wallop. Dawson was a piece of cake. The others stood around watching the show, and the third time she pinned him they applauded her.

Cass took a bow. Dawson submitted and gave way with the sweep of his arm. "You, Cass, are a better man than me."

With a smirk on her face, Cass gave him the once-over. "You best be remembering that, Detective Luck."

They shook hands. Both parties left the mats, and Dawson Luck headed to the men's locker room, prepared for the onslaught of razzing from the guys. It would go on for days and Jack learned his partner could laugh at himself and not get sensitive about the joshing. They hadn't been partners for a long time and he was still learning stuff about Dawson every day.

When he first made it to the Homicide table, Jack's partner was Frank Windom. Frank was an excellent partner who taught Jack all he knew over the years. He had been in Homicide for twenty-seven years and planned to retire in three. He told Jack he was glad to end his career with a partner who cared as much as he did about the job. Jack admired his mentor, happy he had three years to learn from him. Two years later, Frank dropped dead of a massive heart attack, leaving a large void in Jack's professional and personal life.

"West, Luck," Captain Yao called from the hallway, "ya'll come to my office."

The captain's office was next to the squad room, a medium-sized room with a wooden desk. Two oversized bookcases along the back wall were filled with files, books, a surplus of whatnots, gifts, and a spattering of small framed pictures of family and friends. It was obvious the captain was not a neat freak.

Papers cluttered his desk. There was a lateral four-drawer file cabinet sitting inside to the left of his doorway, piled high with case folders, books, binders, and other means of information, bagged or boxed. On the floor beside the desk closest to the window sat several evidence boxes, closed up with yellow or red evidence tape, with a clipboard on top and a sign-off sheet.

Their captain nodded at the two empty chairs, motioning for them to have a seat while he finished his phone call. Lucky took the seat on the inside next to the window and West took the seat nearest the door. The wooden armrests were scarred with age and the blue cloth seats faded from years of being in direct sunlight. West and Luck watched the captain flip through papers on his desk, listening, nodding, and interjecting a yeah and uh-huh every few seconds into the phone.

Captain Davis Yao: an American-born Chinese in his early forties, married with two daughters. He dreamed of leading the homicide team in a town as big and sprawling as Houston, and he'd succeeded. "Absolutely, I'll take care of it. Of course, Darrin, we can have lunch next week. Sure, sure, call me later to set up the date." The captain dropped the phone back into the cradle.

"Chief Pratt wanted me to tell you both that you did excellent work on the Griffin murder case."

The case had been tough emotionally on all of them. A fifteen-year-old girl murdered by another minor who was short of being an adult—five months shy of turning eighteen. What a great way to celebrate a milestone birthday.

"I want you each to work on a cold case. The cold case unit is short staffed. Chief Pratt wants us to assist when we can. If nothing new pops up, it may have to go back to storage, but dig deep because the unsolved case closures have dropped. It would be nice to get a few old cases closed for a change. But, that said, this is Houston and I suspect your time will be limited on these cold cases. However, not if, but when, a new case comes in, set the cold cases aside. If time permits, you can pick them back up and work them on the side. You both know how that works. Half the time my detectives are working two cases at a time, sometimes even three. Boys, it's sad to say that Houston is job security for us in a morbid way."

Jack knew there were no truer words said. Houston was not just a melting pot of people; it was a city fraught with criminals of every kind, from dope pushers, thieves, cybercrimes, and murder. Nope, evil never slept in his fair city; so working two and three cases at a time would bust your hump, but as a cop in Houston, it was just a common part of your job description.

The captain's glasses slipped to the end of his nose as he scanned the papers he was holding and then peered up at them.

"Here are the two I want you to work. You'll get the files in an hour, which is when I expect to have your current case reports all nice and neat and on my desk, right?" His eyes went from West to Luck.

"You bet. I am almost done with the last of the reports, sir. I'll have them on your desk before that." Dawson bobbed his head. Lucky, meticulous, his drive to keep the paperwork in order, and Jack had no complaints, letting his partner kick him to the curb with paperwork.

"Okay, guys, that's all I've got for now." Captain Yao dismissed them.

Jack and Davis Yao had grown up in the same neighborhood until Davis's family moved into Houston Proper. Over seven years had passed, and they accidentally ran into each other at the station. Jack was a second-year patrol cop, and Davis four years in Vice. No one knew they had known each other when they were kids. Yao was his boss, and he thought everyone might think he was showing favoritism, so they tried to keep this info quiet. It hadn't mattered. As time passed, everyone found out. Hell, what were they thinking? They worked with detectives.

4

"Done. Now, I take this in and get them to file it, and then our part of the Griffin murder case is wrapped up." Dawson hit save and print.

"Good deal." Jack stood up, stretching his neck. "It's quiet in here without 7-11."

7-11—they were an odd and funny pair. They had gotten the name 7-11 because of Detective Chang's first name. It was Xi pronounced *Ghee* with a ZH sound as in *zhee* but spelled with an X as in the Roman numeral eleven, XI. One detective jumped on that, and his nickname *Eleven* had been born. Ghee and Jace Severson became partners, and the same detective who had given Xi his nickname boomed with laughter.

"That's funny, Severson and Eleven, oh boy, now we've got a 7-11 for real." The whole group busted out laughing, even Severson and Chang. They embraced the nickname, Team 7-11.

"Detective West," a female voice sounded. Jack, standing with his back toward the side door, turned to see one of the department's file clerks standing there. She was an older black woman, rather short and plump. This clerk had been with the HPD in Files and Archives for nearly thirty years. If anyone needed anything at all, all you had to do was find Miss Flossy, Florine Millie Carter-Jackson-Albright. She had been divorced once and widowed twice. Flossy pushed a cart in with several large binders piled on top. These were the cold cases Davis had wanted him and Dawson to work.

"Yes, that's me." He gave her a dashing smile. The woman's face lit up with a dazzling grin. She'd recognize this handsome cowboy detective by his front side or his backside; he was the epitome of a Texas hunk.

"You know, I know'd it was you, Detective Jack. Cuzin you can't ever hide from Miss Flossy. My, my, my, you is too good-looking for this place. Why isn't you a model? That's what I always say." Tsking, she pushed the cart closer to his desk.

He blushed, as he always did, and she let out a full-bodied laugh.

Jack skimmed over the pages on the clipboard Flossy handed him and signed off on a file. He and Dawson were given cases from the late 1980s. He grabbed the file and read the name: *Mason, Celeste* A.

"That there's a case that needs a solving," Flossy remarked. Jack had heard tell Flossy read many of the unsolved cases; they intrigued her, and she always dreamed of being able to put an investigation to bed.

"I hope you can help that young woman cross over to the light. You think so, Detective Jack?"

"Miss Flossy, who knows? We might do just that." Jack stared straight into the snappy brown eyes of a woman who was a firm believer of the Lord, the devil, and the *other* side.

"Be praying you do." Flossy stared at him, then gave him a mischievous grin, turned, and pushed her cart back out the door.

Jack took the binder, set it on the file cabinet, and cleared room on his desk. With a small pad and pencil for notes, he flexed his arms, cracked his knuckles, and flexed his fingers, getting ready.

It was now 11:45, his coffee long gone, and he needed food and coffee. Then he could begin his read. Jack would be at it for a while because it was who he was. He headed downstairs to grab a Subway sandwich, which was conveniently in the lobby. Cops liked it because it was a close place to grab a bite to eat when you were knee deep into an investigation. His preference usually was to drive to Antone's and grab a couple of Originals—subs ready-made and delicious. Today, though, he'd settle for Subway and break room coffee. Food to hold him over for a while, he hoped; he wasn't sure how long he'd stay and read. Sometimes he got caught up and forgot the time.

Lucky was walking back toward his desk as he was leaving. "I'm going down for a sub, you want something?"

"Grab me salami on rye with hot mustard, would ya, and a Diet Coke. There's a twenty spot in the first cubbyhole." Dawson nodded his head sideways to his own desk.

"No problem. Salami on rye, hot mustard—the usual," he repeated.

"I'll be back in twenty." Jack walked behind his partner, ignoring his suggestion of grabbing a twenty out of his drawer.

A sub, a drink, and chips, lunch for the workingman. West and Luck both set up ready to eat and began the intensive reading on two of the town's unsolved murder cases. At the top of page one, Jack read: "Mason, Celeste, case number 081286, Unsolved."

The report called in on the unknown body August 12th, 1986. Celeste's story had begun over 34 years ago.

He read for a few hours, getting through a few of the preliminary reports and a couple of witness statements, but stuff in the binder was in an unorganized mess. His bladder was singing a tune, and he was tapping his boots in time. He needed a break and a coffee refill, but took a detour to the facilities first.

In the men's room, he bumped into the Tornado, Vice Detective Rick Tormo, who primarily worked with the Gang Unit. Not much younger than Jack. Rick was medium height, five foot eleven, and weighed 205 pounds. The man was in decent shape because he worked out in the station's gym at least four days a week. Jack figured with his muscles as toned as they were, and on the Gang Unit, he had to stay in shape. Good chance he had to keep up with boys half his age who were gang members. Houston had its share. Rick tried to be comical, always trying to make the fellas laugh, but not always successful.

As a Gang Unit detective, he thought Rick's personality was too sunny. Since Cole's murder, his views were jaded. Jack didn't fault the man for trying to see the best in everything. The issues at hand, he felt, were troubling in vice. The crap Rick dealt with and what these low-lives did to Houston and its residents were enough to keep a man's psyche in a dark gray place with little sunshine. Houston's gangs kept rising in numbers, and becoming more vicious. Most of the things they perpetrated set the hairs on your neck afire and your blood boiling.

Rick was married, with two kids, and was nearing 11 years with Vice. Jack was aware of Rick's aspirations to get on the Homicide table, but there were no openings. With a good-humored frame of mind, saying he'd stick it out with the Vice Unit until retirement in twenty or thirty years.

"I enjoy the fact I don't have to wear a suit and tie. Man, I can wear jeans with holes, a T-shirt that says Father of the Year, Honorable Mention, and a ball cap." Then he would spurt out a laugh. Rick, a man with energy and excitement about him, a whirlwind on the job, so the fellas in Vice dubbed him the Tornado. The nickname stuck.

Finished washing his hands, Rick looked up to see Jack in the mirror behind him. "How's it hanging, Jack?"

"Long and hard, Rick, long and hard." Jack's brows waggled lecherously. Rick was in Vice. It was the expected comeback.

"You fellas have any new stuff going on these days?"

"Same ole, same ole. Scum bags out there peddling drugs, threatening to pop a cap in someone's ass. Gang graffiti gone wild, women and teenage girls going wilder, you know the story. Although, I'll say I haven't put in as much O.T. as usual. It's okay though. I get to play with my kiddos before they go to bed, and it has been rather nice. Look, I'm late for a department meeting, so I'll see ya."

He waved off and pushed through the swinging door. Jack's bladder reminded him it and his feet were playing a duet, and he headed to the urinals on the other side. As he stood there taking care of business, he thought about the Tornado. Rick was always in a rush when he was nearby. He acted more in line of a tsunami when he was near, ready to blow off and out of sight as fast as he could. It was because he'd badgered Rick to death regarding Cole's case with questions on top of questions. Hell, if he were Rick he would have run from himself too. Rick had been a kid too when it had happened. What more could Rick know than he did? Next time he saw him, he'd apologize for being such a pain and a nuisance.

Back at his desk, he read the first written report from back in 1986 on the day the body was first found.

It was muddy, undeveloped land, behind an old rundown motel called All Occasions Motel. Poorer, sleazier kinds of tenants lived there. Jack was familiar with the neighborhood, and nothing much had changed. The bad places in Houston stayed bad, got worse, or were just a whisper of a ghost, and no one needed any reminders. The pictures he pushed around showed pictures of the area back in 1986. Jack conjured up a general picture in his head of the vicinity of things not in each photograph.

The parking lot was full of potholes and rubble, filled with beater cars running or not. Behind the old motel sat fifteen acres of semi-wooded and marshy land. It was not fenced off, not exactly. A chain-link fence divided into a separate five acres leased to a local construction company. The padlocked gate touted a sign: POSTED: No Trespassing—Private Property.

The surrounding area littered with trash and debris from the tenants' trash which had blown around, in or out of the overfilled steel dumpsters in the back. Empty Miller High Life bottles and crushed cans of either Budweiser or Schlitz beer littered the fence line. Next, he moved on to the statements made by the boys who had found the body, creating pictures of the story in his head as he read.

Four boys had discovered the victim's body in the marshy region;

they had been four-wheeling. There were trees and brush covering the entire vehicle. Covered in brush, in a slight ditch, what they thought was a hill turned out to be a car they bounced off when they saw the taillight sticking out.

Slumped over in the driver's seat was a woman, seat-belted in and lifeless. The driver-side window partially opened. It had rained a few times yet the inside of her vehicle had not been soaked. Her clothing: the only sign the victim was female. What hair the woman once had had fallen out, and the corpse was small. All of her fingertips were cut off, and someone had shot her in the head, blowing part of her face off. Add in decomposition, and her own mother wouldn't know her.

It scared the four boys who'd found the body half to death. After Tully Cranston, the motel owner, called the police, mass chaos erupted. A side note said Cranston had paced back-and-forth muttering under his breath. "This is going to hurt my business or kill it altogether, no pun intended." They didn't appreciate his attempt at humor. Why this statement was on the report was anybody's guess.

He flipped to the decedent's identification. One Texas driver's license issued to Celeste A. Mason, age 33. Height, five foot three and a half. Weight one hundred one pounds. Eye color blue. Hair color dark blonde. The green 1973 Ford Pinto registered to Celeste Angelina Mason of 1753 Chimney Rock Road, Unit 293, at the Gulf Bay apartment complex. Ownership papers had been in the glove box, the car bought and paid for. After a search of the glove box, they found nothing to help in the case—no real clues. There had been a few receipts and old registration paperwork, all in her name. A purse found in the car yielded no advanced info on the deceased, no pictures in a wallet, no telltale information that confirmed or questioned the identity. The decedent's clothing, the report stated, yielded no forensic evidence. Their victim's fingertips were missing. No way to get her prints. In addition, the girl evidently had never been to a dentist or at least no one had located any records. Something niggled at him regarding the shoddy work done on this investigation and the lack of effort the investigation team had put toward solving it. Who had wanted this poor girl dead and why?

Jack continued to read, but the story had begun way before this.

Thirty–four years ago, at the HPD

Simpson, with his partner Pete Bullard, met with their captain discussing the Mason case. The body found, decomposing beyond recognition; her fingertips cut off. All the identification found in her car and purse led them to the conclusion this was Celeste Mason; they had no doubts about it. There was no murder weapon, no dental records to compare, and no one had ever reported her missing.

"Ain't any leads, Captain, don't know where to go with this one," Bullard said.

"Nothing at all, not even one tiny lead, not a hair, nothing? That's what you're telling me?" Captain Horacio Harris eyed them over his black-framed glasses which had slipped a hair and sat on the tip of his bulbous nose.

"Yes, sir, that's what we're telling you. No one reported her missing. She ain't got any parents. The dead gal had a job in Sharpstown, no real friends, and we questioned everyone we could, but have come up with zilch." Simpson said.

Bullard leaned back propping his foot on a chair by the captain's desk.

"Not a clue why anyone would want to murder her. She worked at a clothing boutique and did some waitressing. People claimed she wasn't close to anyone. She was a loner, I guess." He cleared his throat nervously, and then straightened up once Captain Harris glared first at him, then at his foot resting on the chair.

"Well, here's the deal, you two clowns. Someone wanted her dead, and I suggest you dig deeper, find out more, do something, damn it, for a freaking change. That double homicide on Richmond

Avenue last year ain't solved either, even though you had a prostitute who says she witnessed the entire hit, now she ain't anywhere to be found. Detectives, I want you both to get your sorry asses out there and detect." Horacio Harris's face went beet red.

"Yes, sir, we'll do what we can." Bullard knew this was a lie. When news hit around the clubs that Celeste Mason was dead, everyone felt the need to be on high alert.

5

J ack leaned back, closing his eyes. It was a slow read. He built a more concise report in his head, filling in the blanks as best he could. With a rolling movie in his mind's eye, he filled in the story with his own ideas of what might have happened. It wasn't all fact, not by any means, but this is how he did it. Being on the job this many years you took facts, added a few calculated guesses and some fiction, which was oddly stranger than the truth, and you could paint a picture to see.

Celeste Mason, a poor lady on the wrong side of the tracks. Had she been a working girl who had a pimp that got carried away and lost control? The sad thing was nobody reported her missing. She had been unaccounted for over seven days. It's what the police report presented. The M.E. report affirmed she had been dead longer than a week. It was tragic, because if those four boys had not come upon her, she might still be out there and no one would have been the wiser.

He continued to read. Why her, and why did not one person miss her? The proprietor of the motel, Tully Cranston, hadn't known the girl. He had lost no tenants, and all rent payments were current.

Cranston, not knowing the woman nor did he have any information. The old man was listed as a dead-end witness.

There weren't any witness reports. Nobody staying at the motel saw or heard a thing. It was bit odd. But considering the type of establishment this was—one renting rooms by the hour—most of the clientele would prefer to stay out of a police report. The dicks who worked the case, Bullard and Simpson, had both retired years before. A card for Bella's Boutique. The only lead which'd been useful, but not promising. When they questioned the manager who owned the boutique, she told them Mason had worked for her.

He read about her position at Bella's Boutique. A no call, no-show after three days the reason for her termination, the report stated. It wasn't their policy to check on staff; therefore, they conveyed nothing to the police. One young woman recounted she was a bit of a loner and quiet.

Angie Wilcox told the detectives Mason did not associate with her coworkers. She was too busy working nights at the clubs to socialize.

The next statement he read was from her coworker, Wanda Forsythe.

"Celeste was always secretive. We all knew she worked at a dance club, the Silver Moon, three nights a week. It was a country-dance bar. There was another nasty place called the Crystal Barrel. Sometimes she worked there too. It was one of those scummy places. And there was a topless roadhouse. Same people owned all three clubs, but she never waitressed at that place." Bullard noted in her statement.

He scanned the other employees' statements, and they had not talked to her much. They did not work the same shifts or even run with the same crowds. Then he referred to the manager-slash-owner's statement. All she'd stated was Celeste was a quiet worker, giving her no trouble. She was the assistant supervisor and closed up two nights a week. The girl kept to herself. She was shy with the customers. Recently, Miss Mason came out of her shell more, which the owner attributed to her job at the bars. The no-call, no-show was a huge surprise. Celeste needed all the hours she could get. She never missed a day and welcomed the overtime.

"Poor thing I think lived payday to payday. It was a shame she had not gotten a real chance in life," Bella reported to the detectives.

He researched Bella's Boutique. It had closed its doors eight years ago. Well, that was a bust. There were five names associated with the store. This dead girl had to have known over five people, and where was her family? A damn needle in a haystack. He pressed his lips together.

A financial statement disclosed the poor woman was—broke. The deceased's bank records didn't raise a red flag. She had been at Bella's for over five years, but not always a full forty hours, the owner reported. That had to be why she needed the part-time job. Something bothered him about this. What he understood was waitressing was a lucrative job for a girl who was young and pretty. Was she too shy or inept? Waitresses he'd been friends with claimed you'd make money if you put your ass in gear and made it successful, and it was fun.

He would have to check into these part-time jobs, not expecting to get much, but one never knew what small detail might come out. The people who went bar-hopping back then were now in their fifties or sixties at least, and how would he find any patrons from that far back? Again, a bunch of needles in several haystacks. Anyone he found that worked there when she did would be better than finding no one. He never second-guessed any minor clue. Jack would turn over the tiniest pebble if he thought it would solve the case, and tie it up in a nice neat bow.

He focused on the bars. The best place to meet the wrong person at the wrong time. Did someone stalk her and then kill her? His initial thought was she had an ardent admirer, and she had not felt the same. However, the report said no sexual assault had occurred. Not all murders involving women were sexual, but he figured ninety-nine percent were. Why hadn't they at least done a rape kit? It wasn't as if these kits didn't exist, and who had made the call to forgo this type of forensics?

Back then, by that seedy motel there had been no malls, no chain stores, just underdeveloped land. The road crews had nothing but that small bar to hang out in and drink. The Crystal Barrel had always been a dive. He moved on to the next bar she'd worked at, owned by the same person. This one was more upscale. The Silver Moon, a nightclub inviting the local cowboy in for a beer and a dance with the cowgirl of his choosing. Someone had bought it and renamed it The Station. It was still a well-oiled business, booming with every wannabe cowboy, and the place to meet that next one-night stand love of your life.

Her job at the Silver Moon had been waitressing. He surmised she did the same at both bars. Wanda Forsythe mentioned a topless bar, but evidently she had never worked there. She might have met her murderer at a club, which created a ton of suspects. As far back as the case spanned, it would be pointless to find these people. Chasing names of ancient bar patrons, how could he with zero names, anyway? This was yet one more frigging needle in three damn haystacks, on top of the half dozen he already had. He groaned at the thought.

Her life was bland. She was not flamboyant, and she did not have a trove of friends. This Mason woman had no other extracurricular activities creating any other avenues for him to explore. What was he missing, and why hadn't anyone cared if this sad young woman, with no money and no social outside life, lived or died?

He would have to dig into her past harder now, harder than the detectives had done in the beginning. Damn it, a needle in a stack of needles. This might prove impossible, but Jack was no stranger to impossible because it happened in Houston, Texas every day.

6

"Hey, Lucky, I drew a shitty case. Not much to go on, so I'm gonna have to dig, but where to start, I'm not sure. How is your own read going?"

"It's about a missing hooker, JoAnn Cutter, and listen to this, her street handle is Princess Lay-Ya, spelled L-A-Y-Y-A," he hooted. "Says here she had something to do with another incident, a material wit, and she disappeared."

"What case was she a witness on?"

"A couple of guys got shot at point blank range, and she'd been at the bus stop across the street."

Dawson was being vague, but Jack figured he was reading and was preoccupied.

"I'm going to head over to forensics. I want to take a peek at the autopsy reports on the two dead men. Who knows what might pop? You gonna be around?"

"Not sure yet. I might do some canvassing, try to find people who knew my vic to talk to. Tell Bennie howdy for me."

"Will do," Luck called back as he reached the side door, waving at Jack over his shoulder.

Ben-Gay, like the arthritis cream. Bennie Guay, Chief Medical Examiner for the city of Houston going on eleven years. It was clear to understand how he earned his nickname. A short Italian with very dark features, not the usual handsome Italian, he was average. His brain though, was way above average. Dynamite comes in small packages, and he was a whole case of dynamite packaged in a five foot five, 130-pound body. The entire precinct had howled in merriment when they all found out he had to stand on a small step stool to do an autopsy. The decedent had been a rather large man with a chest and stomach protruding out so far it had been hard for him to dig into the man's insides. Bennie had cursed all of them; of course, it was in fun. However, he reminded everybody Beethoven and Genghis Khan were five foot three, and Picasso five foot four.

"Therefore, you bozos, I am in an exceptional class of short, famous men."

The man had been a child prodigy, graduating high school at fourteen. With an I.Q. off the charts, his dream was to be a neurosurgeon. While in medical school, he had the chance to do some intern work with the HPD in the coroner's office and fell in love with death. Forensic science intrigued him. The job of saving lives was important, but there were plenty of smart doctors graduating in considerable numbers from Johns Hopkins and Stanford Medical Universities. He was fascinated with the puzzles of death, natural or not. This type of challenge stimulated his brain, and he loved mysteries.

Jack got back to his cold-case still thinking about Lucky's. This unaccounted-for Princess Lay-Ya was dead. If she was a material wit for a shooting, someone might've gotten rid of her. He figured his partner's case was a no-win situation. Without a physical body, you couldn't prove it was a murder and this might be unsolved missing persons forever. A lot of these type cases stayed unresolved. There was only one way to spin their stories: kidnapped, killed, and gone forever.

Back flipping through his murder book, he wondered if Detective

Bullard or Simpson were alive. Next step, he'd check with HR to see if they were breathing and had an address or phone number on file. They'd both chucked it in for retirement, but he couldn't be sure of their current status in life, or if they were alive. Jack dialed Personnel.

"Yvette Rogers, Personnel, can I help you?"

"Yvette, Jack West. Hey, do you have time to look up a couple of old retired dicks for me?"

"Now Jack, if I had time for old dicks, then I'd—" she barked out. She was raunchy, but it was what endeared her to over ninety percent of the men on the force.

Hell, they were all on the perverted side, and they attributed it to the job. Half of them were still dirty-minded teenagers. It stands to reason; they were men. Yvette was a good egg, though. He liked her. Yvette was a young black woman who was as spunky as they came, and smart. He guessed working with male cops all day was like working with a passel of foul-mouthed truck drivers. It was a fact that most of the men didn't have the proper filters when talking to the women who worked in the office. The women either accepted it or didn't without voicing it to keep peace amongst the ranks. Yvette was one of the few who accepted it good naturedly.

He snickered at her almost-joke. "Bullard and Simpson would've worked at HPD some twenty years ago."

"Uh-huh, I heard of the Bull. Rumor was he was tough, and sometimes mean. Let me do some checking and get back with you, okay, Jackrabbit doll?"

"Call my cell if you don't reach me at my desk, Yvette."

"Yes, sir, give me a few minutes. I'll see what I can dig up for you."

She hung up, and Jack turned back to the crime scene photos again. It was never a pretty sight. The other issue beside them being gory was that pictures did not always capture the small things your eyes did at the original incident. All he had was pictures. He could not turn back the clock, so he would make the best of it.

Next, he moved to the body dump, since it had not been

determined where the murder had taken place. That was a total mystery. They had gone to her apartment but had found no evidence a crime had occurred. Yellow crime scene tape roped off the area; he saw in the background a thick brushy marsh area with lots of trees. Her body lay dead, left in her car to rot away, and no one would find her—at least it's what her killer hoped. Debris scattered all over the large vacant lot, all kinds of trash and garbage. If not for those boys, it might have been years before someone found her remains. Her bare bones then would have been harder to identify. There had been an extraordinary amount of rainfall days before those boys had stumbled on her dead body, and unfortunately, footprints, tire tracks, or other traces of evidence washed away.

Next, he took out the pictures of her body. Jack had looked at his share of dead bodies. He hated it, but it came with the job. He thought briefly back on when he had gone with his parents to identify Cole's body. Cole was the first dead body he had ever seen. He had been the fool, adamant screaming brother who had needed to see firsthand. He shook it off and resumed going through pictures of another dead soul, a perfect stranger, but he would get to know her better during this investigation

She had been fully clothed, no signs of tearing or ripping of any garment, apparently no sign of her being sexually assaulted. Again, he went back to the fact no rape kit was processed. What made the investigating detectives so sure a sexual assault had not occurred, and why not at least check?

The shot to skull was at close range. Cause of death described as being made by a large caliber gun, a hollow point .38. CSU reported there had been no great amount of body fluid or bits and pieces of brain matter in the vehicle, other than what had been transference. Her Ford Pinto was not the murder spot. If her killer murdered her in the automobile, there would have been nasty spatter inside the vehicle. The clothing was free of blood-spatter. If she had been wearing those clothes when she took the bullet, her brain would have splattered all over them. He couldn't see it; someone shot her head off then redressed her. Blowing off a face was very personal. Her killer cut off her fingertips, postmortem. Why had they done this? The driver's license showed it was Celeste Mason. She had not shown up at the Boutique for her shift, and no one knew where she was, so it had to be her body, or that's what the reports showed.

What had the reason been for killing her? There was no evidence of a robbery; she had nothing on but costume jewelry. Why had someone wanted her dead? Motive, he needed a flipping motive and what he had was zilch.

He scanned over the cataloged items listed that were in her purse.

Items in victim's purse:

One fake leather purse, color black. Contents: One Chap Stick, compact with mirror, one small red comb and brush. One women's wallet, black, with three dollars cash and eighty-five cents in loose change, a driver's license, social security card, no photos. Three keys—all on a plain key ring. Six individual packages of condoms.

Three keys: car key, apartment key, and the third key to the boutique where she supposedly worked. She was a supervisor, makes sense. The unopened condoms in her purse...he found odd. All the people the detectives questioned said she was a shy, keep-to-herself young woman, and reportedly no boyfriend. Why would she carry condoms?

He went over the items again. The condoms and the lack of photos in her wallet niggled at him. It was nothing, probably just reading things into things, so he passed it off, and continued studying the crime scene photos.

She had been wearing pants and a plain blouse with a jacket, all from Bella's Boutique. The owner, Bella, confirmed they were clothes sold in her store. There were several scarves stuffed in the pocket of her blazer, silk scarves that did not match her other clothing.

Bella had stated the victim was found in the same clothing she had seen her wearing on the last day she worked.

These small things brought up more questions, and he felt something wasn't right. This was more than it appeared. What had been the killer's motive?

Her dark-blonde hair gathered in a ponytail, or what had been left of it, had come loose from an elastic tieback. The decomposition sped up because of the heat and humidity, normal Houston weather. He learned from the number of years on the job these environmental phases, and sepsis sped up the decay of the corpse. It had not been determined how long she had been out there. No definite date or time of death. It had been an educated guess.

The phone on his desk rang. "Jack West."

"Jackrabbit, this is Yvette; I found the information you needed, doll face. Peter Ballard died last year."

"Sorry to hear it. They don't tell everyone when they have services. Damn, that's a shame. What about Ian Simpson? Did you get a lead on him?"

"Uh-huh, he ain't dead, but he's in a home for people with memory issues. He's got dementia, I'm only guessing though, might be Alzheimer's."

West wondered if the old guy would remember anything. "Jackrabbit, you need an address or a phone number?" Yvette sounded impatient.

"Yeah, give me his address."

It was a nursing facility in south Houston, in between the Deer Park area where he lived and Friendswood. He thanked Yvette, and she gave him a girlie laugh.

"Whatever you want, Jack, it's yours, and I mean that." Then she snickered before she hung up. He wasn't sure, but he figured he was blushing at her implied remark.

Ian Simpson—he needed to take a stab at talking to him. One fact he'd heard was people with dementia remembered things from long ago and forgot things which happened five minutes before. A short follow up with him, then it'd be crossed off his list.

Jack thought back on Celeste's purse contents again. A strip of condoms in her purse was strange. No pictures in her wallet bothered him. There was still a ton of the murder book to review. Forensic reports to comb through. Jack needed to leave the office for a while, and he needed coffee. Dawson was back, and he'd resumed his reading. He guessed it had been a short visit with Bennie. Jack closed the binder, slipped it into the top file drawer, and locked it.

"Lucky, I'm heading out. I'd like to visit with a few people while it's daylight. I'm not coming back, so catch ya tomorrow."

Lucky waved at Jack but kept reading.

Jack snatched his suit-coat, wrote himself out for the day, waving as he passed the captain's door. After a quick trip to the break room to grab a cup of rather thick coffee, which had been cooking on the burner since morning, he exited through the back stairwell. It was 3:45. Taking the stairs two at a time, he exited through the back hall, and headed to officer's car pool to check out means of transportation.

Destination, Waller, Texas, to talk to a woman the deceased worked with at a club named the Silver Moon. He decided he would take the department vehicle home and leave his truck parked at the station. On his way in tomorrow morning, he'd stop and get rubber hip boots. When he showed up out there with the photos, it would be the same muddy place as before 25 years ago. It'd rained daily for the past nine days. Wonderful Houston weather, it rained some days harder than others, and sometimes it was a humid drizzle for three seconds. No matter for the detectives working a case, any wet weather sucked.

7

J ack took the Loop west and then twisted around until he was headed south. Traffic was not too bad, at least not yet. He took the notebook and flipped it open to the address: 1220 Arcadia Place, Waller, Texas. His best route would be to take I-10 to FM 359. One thing was for sure, the address was not on a sidewalk-lined street or even a paved street. Jack traveled all around Houston, the city limits, and the outskirts, but he'd never been to Waller. He sat back and drove, hoping she was home.

A pit-stop at a mom-and-pop convenience store, Carter's Stop and Grab, he bought something to drink; he was parched. A balding man waited for him at the front counter. He was wearing a painter's canvas jumpsuit and standing behind the cash register. On his left, a woman sat on a stool working a crossword puzzle book.

"Hiya, what can I do you for?"

He set the 16-ounce water, a bag of hot fries, and a Butterfinger on the counter as he fished out his wallet. "Pretty hot today, huh?"

"It sure is, Officer."

Wondering what his tell had been, his brow rose.

"Anything specific give me away?" He handed the old man a ten, waiting for the old guy to ring him up so he could be on his merry way. But the old geezer stood there holding the ten-dollar bill, looking at Jack. The dude in no hurry at the rate of speed he moved.

The old dude let out a rather hoarse old man's cackle. "Ain't no tell, saw your sidearm, udder wise I'd a not known."

"Very observant, which I'd say is a good thing if you have late hours here."

"Yep, I'm on it and yep we got late hours."

The old goat handed him a handful of change and his receipt and then walked to the back, not saying another word.

By Jiminy, when he was finished with business, he was done. It made no never mind to Jack; he had places to be and no time to chit-chat. He politely said goodbye to the woman whose head was stuffed in the crossword puzzle book. She gave only a slight nod acknowledging she'd heard him. His mom taught him to have manners. He always used them, even if the other party didn't acknowledge.

FM 359 was only five miles, and he spotted it straightaway. A sign made of fence slats. Painted in bright green with the words, *Welcome to Waller*, then in silver and underneath, *hey we aren't big, but come on in for a visit, anyway.*

He made a right turn off of the interstate, hitting gravel a hundred feet in. So much for paved roads from this point. He blew up dust as the tires crunched the white rock road, and through the cloud of dust, all he saw was land on either side of him.

It could be no one lived on this FM road any longer, a useless trip. There were no houses in sight for the next three or four miles. He was about to hang it up and turn around when he spotted the trailer park off in the distance. There were twenty or thirty trailers spread out, dirt roads between them. No sign was up, but it didn't mean he wasn't in the right place. He pulled the black Dodge Charger into the drive. The car no longer black but more a shade of ash, like a crop duster showered it with a load of commercial pesticides. A couple of little old women were sitting on the porch of the first trailer he came to. Jack rolled down his window after letting the dust he kicked up settle a bit.

"Ladies, excuse me, I'm trying to find Arcadia Place. Am I in the right spot?"

One of them shook her head but didn't say a word. She was sipping a glass of iced tea through a straw. The other one was a rather heavyset black woman wearing her housecoat and completing her ensemble with a head full of pink sponge rollers.

"Nah, sir, it's up the road a piece. You gots'ta have mo' money to live up that way." She crossed her flabby arms.

"Yeah, what she says is right. Only two places up there, you can't miss it. If you take a left by the old green truck and go about a mile, youse gonna see two trailers about a half a football field apart. Just who are ya looking for, mister?" She pulled at her long-faded dress which half covered skinny and very white legs. The old lady looked up at him revealing several missing teeth.

"I'm trying to find 1220 Arcadia Place. Do either of you know if Jenna Berrie still lives there?"

"Uh, yeah, she does. Is she in trouble?" The toothless, skinny white female leaned in to hear him.

"Nope, I just need to talk to her."

The directions given were for him to look for an old green Ford truck. He smiled. *Only in Texas*, he thought.

"Thank you, ladies. I hafta say you being out here saved me from going door to door, and on such a warm day, too."

He waved, rolled up the window, and he cranked up the air then put the Charger into reverse, driving away leaving more white-colored dust behind him.

Damn, the country roads were long, and on a hot Texas day, the road grew longer. Were those two women positive about the directions? Just as he was about to turn back, he saw it. There it was—the aged green Ford truck. A ton of scraggly weeds grew in it, around it, and through it. A missing hood without a motor, but there were doors. Surely they'd been rusted shut. The tires were flat and had become part of Mother Earth again. Thank goodness for the old ladies and the truck, since there were no signs, street or otherwise. He turned the Charger into the drive, kicking up white chalky dust with every rolling inch of his tires. Jack felt like he was eating and breathing dirt.

He saw two trailers and one had a sign hanging on the gate of the chain-link fence that surrounded it: *We are 11, not 12.*

The other trailer had to be number 2012 Arcadia Place. The way the neighbors advertised their address got a smile out of him. There was a car and a beat-up Jeep sitting to next to a small double-wide. He hoped he found someone at home.

Jack took his suit coat off the passenger seat, opened the door, shook it out then put it on. He patted the inside pocket feeling his notebook and pencil and then checked his Glock, unstrapping it, being prepared. No partner with him way out here. It would take too long to get back up. Staying on the offensive, better than not.

A single vehicle on gravel created enough noise to start dogs barking. No barking dog, none, and he found it odd. Everyone owned mutts out in the country in Texas. He stepped up on stairs built of wooden pallets. They'd constructed a nice and roomy porch with handrails on both sides. Someone took the time to sand it and put on a coat of redwood paint and varnish to fancy up the place.

As he reached the top step within range to stick his arm out and knock, the front door opened. A slim woman nearing her sixties, with dark shoulder-length hair streaked with gray, stood there.

She crossed her arms with a resolute posture. "Whatever you're selling, mister, I am not buying. Don't need any pamphlets on saving my soul. I'm not interested. Have all I need and a Bible too."

Jack guessed she'd not seen his gun when he put on his jacket and he was entertained with the idea she assumed he was a door-to-door salesman. This was a first. He always got made—everyone knew he was a cop.

"No, ma'am, I'm not a salesman. I'm Detective Jack West, with HPD. I want to ask you a few questions about a former coworker."

Oh sure, she beat the salesmen and Bible thumpers off with a stick out here in this overpopulated area. It was hot standing in the sun wearing a suit coat over a long-sleeve shirt, and he was worn out from driving.

"Do you mind if we go inside and talk?"

"Proof, let me see some identification." The woman stepped back shutting her door to give him enough room to display his badge.

Good grief, now she exhibited caution. This lady was a ninny. Just because it was daylight did not mean only nice people were active doing God knows what. It would have been safer if she'd called out first, asking him to state his business and brandishing a tire iron in her hand for protection.

"It looks genuine enough." She let him into her trailer.

She pointed to a sofa decked out in a daisy pattern and looking a bit worn. "You can sit there."

He sat but did not make himself comfortable, as it would have done no good. As his butt hit the thin cushion, he felt the springs give with his weight, not just give either. They tried to poke a hole in the seat of his pants. Jack shifted his tail end over an inch adjusting, sitting closer to the edge, and the poking springs disappeared.

"Can I get you water or something?" Her voice vaguely monotone and flat, she acted uninterested in why a Houston detective was calling on her.

"A glass of ice water would be nice, thank you."

His bottled water empty, and it was rare for him to take offered refreshments, but he was dry-mouthed. Besides, it was Texas, and hot.

The semi hospitable woman handed him the glass, then she backed up, taking a seat across from him in a worn-out cloth rocker recliner, and she began rocking.

Jack took a big drink, and the cool water felt refreshing, clearing out his dusty throat. She waited for him to tell her why he'd come, but he didn't jump right in on purpose. He wanted to make her nervous.

Jack took out his notebook and pencil, took his time, and then looked at her, pencil in hand ready to take notes.

"You worked at the Sta—uh, the Silver Moon sometime back in the eighties, correct?"

"I did a long time ago, and you were fixing to call it the *Station*. Someone said the name had changed. I worked there for about three and a half years, give or take a few months here and there."

"You were you acquainted with a Celeste Mason?"

"Acquainted, yeah, I guess."

"How well did you know her?"

"Not very well, but I liked her and so did the other girls who waitressed, but only a few of us used to be close friends. There were a lot of girls who worked together. We all tried to help each other, like a sisterhood. I was sad someone murdered her, but I didn't cry because you know I wasn't close to her."

Most women cried at the news of death, or shed a few tears, especially if it was someone they'd known. He'd guessed he was wrong, or this woman was one without a heart.

"Do you recall if Miss Mason had a boyfriend?"

"Not really, I don't think."

"Not really. Either she did, or she didn't. Which was it?"

"Most of the guys liked her. She was pretty, I suppose, but I don't go for women. Thing was, she was standoffish about men. A bouncer, Jed, sorta made sure nobody bothered her."

Jenna pulled a leg up under her but kept the rocker going with her other foot. "All she thought of was business, never fun. But—" she stopped.

"But, but what, Miss Berrie?"

She sat there thinking. Crap, she was getting herself into uncharted territory. Even back then, the police never questioned her about all of this, and she was now very uncomfortable.

"Celeste didn't have a boyfriend, that's all."

That answered the question about the condoms. No boyfriend—

no sex—no need for condoms. Then why have some if she had no use for them?

"What *can* you tell me about Miss Mason, other than this?" Jack felt like he had driven all the way out here for nothing and he wanted something.

"Let me think." She put her finger on her lips and sort of patted them, nodding her head and hm-ing as she did so.

His agitation level rose a few meters. He shifted in his seat, making sure not to restart the spring action under the thin cushion, and just about then, the front door swung open with a bang.

"Jenna, who's fucking parked in our driveway?"

A big man, well over six feet tall, topping in at close to six feet five walked in the door. Jack stood six one but sitting, and with this gargantuan standing at the door, he felt like a midget. The man possibly weighing 300 to 350 pounds, dressed in a black leather biker vest and boots. He was a well-built man who looked big enough to kick his ass. It would be a good challenge, but Jack would have to pass today. A tattoo of a nasty-looking snake wrapped around his neck, another intimidating feature. Jack stood and offered his hand.

"Detective Jack West."

No handshake, a stare was all he got from the very large bald-headed biker dude.

"You're parked in my drive and my buddies are bringing over a flatbed trailer, so you hafta move your car."

"Are you Jenna's husband?" Jack prodded for a name. Surprised the man wasn't wondering why a detective was at his place.

He broke out into a deep belly laugh. "No, man, but she wishes. We live together in sin and all that implies." He winked.

"Nice to meet you, uh, hmm, not Jenna's husband." Jack extended him his hand again.

The big dude grabbed Jack's hand. "Name's Max Renner, but everyone calls me Sarge."

"Max, I'll be happy to move my car. Then it won't be in your way. Jenna, I'll be back."

He followed Jack out. "Once your car is moved, go on back in." Sarge left, heading for the back door of the house. Not once turning back to watch as the detective moved his car out of his driveway. Damn it—this was not good, Sarge flung open the door to his workshop, frowning, not good at all.

Notebook at the ready, Jack sat on the sofa ready to continue his line of questioning, still wondering why this man, Max Renner, hadn't asked more questions.

"This bouncer, Jed you mentioned, what's his last name?"

"Logan." Jenna cringed. It just popped out, and she didn't want to tell him anything of any importance.

He took his notes—Jed Logan, bouncer at the Station.

"To your knowledge was there anyone who might have wanted to hurt Miss Mason or want her dead?"

"Uh-uh, heard nothing like that, least wise no one ever said."

"Did you go to her funeral?" He wasn't even sure why he brought this up, but an expression crossed her face he didn't ignore. She hesitated; her mouth opened then shut.

"Well, did you or not?" He repeated the question.

"No, I don't do funerals. It's creepy."

"Yes, they can be. Were there any of the other girls in your little sisterhood who might have attended her services?"

Jack played on the sisterhood remark, and he wondered if anyone was the dead woman's friend.

"How would I know? I didn't ask, and I didn't go." She huffed, pulling her leg out from under her. She set her other foot on the floor and began rocking the chair faster in a nervous state.

"Girls talk and I figured if you were friends with the other girls they would've said something."

She ignored his remark. "Detective West, is there anything else you want to know?"

"You and Sarge, have ya'll been together for a while?" Now this was okay to talk about.

"Almost thirty years. You know, Detective, I don't even care we aren't married, cuz we're common law married. It means the courts figure we're married too."

"Wow, thirty years. My, that's a long time. I'm guessing Sarge must have known Celeste too."

Her mannerisms spoke volumes. She was fidgety and shifted in her seat. Jack sensed her hesitation to answer the question.

"Uh, uh, he, uh, he didn't hang out with the girls, it was just me and him."

"So I take it Max met her." Jack was not letting up; she was clearly lying.

"Yeah, but only a few times, because I was jealous, so Max stayed away from other girls."

Jenna cast her eyes to her bare feet, not meeting his stare. This woman was lying. Her body language said it all but he let it go for now.

"Okay, so, Miss Mason was alone, no real friends, is that what you're saying?" He let his tone sound accusing to goad her into more information.

"Well, she had an old lady friend. This old lady was a rich distant relative from what I'd been told." Jenna pursed her lips wishing the words were back in her mouth, unsaid.

"Her first name was Sara, didn't know her last name."

Jenna realized Sara had died, and the detective could not talk to her, much less find a Sara with no last name.

Sara, how many women named Sara could there be in Houston, holy cow. This sucked.

"Okay, so let's go over this one more time. Miss Mason didn't have a beau, and no family. Poor girl must have been lonely. I heard she was a good-looking girl. Most attractive girls have friends. Was she mean?"

"Well, no, she didn't act mean, or she wasn't mean to me. I suppose she was pretty in a scrawny way. But she was very shy."

"Hmm, I've never met waitresses who were timid. I mean, as a shy waitress how did she make tips? Waitresses can't be too shy in the work they do."

"Ahem." In a nervous gesture, Jenna cleared her throat. "Well, um, uh, what I meant was that she was shy with men and the dating thing. She was an okay waitress, I guess." She tried to crab-crawl her statement, revising her answer to fit the question.

"No one ever missed her once she went missing? She was a no-show at the boutique about a week before they found her body. Strange, don't you think, Jenna?"

"I am sorry someone killed her, really I am. That's all I can tell you, Detective."

Jenna stood up, walked to the door, and opened it. "I've got stuff to be doing, so are we finished with this question answer crap now?"

Jack thanked her and left. He had a strong gut feeling there was more to this story. Jenna Berrie was holding back and he might have to tackle her again. What he needed was something to tackle her with. He climbed into the dust-covered Charger and backed out of the long driveway. Not wanting to cut the interview with Jenna short, but it was in his best interest to leave before Max's friends showed up. They were just like him, and one of 'em would be okay to tangle with, but a dozen more would be suicide. Not tempting fate was a good motto, and as a cop, perhaps it was his only motto.

His timing had been near perfect, as he passed the old blue Ford hauling the flatbed trailer and gave them the standard finger wave as everyone did in Texas. Man, he was hoping they all thought he was a salesman. No need for them to know he was with the HPD. He figured they would ask who he was and maybe big ole Sarge would tell them to mind their own motherfucking business. His lips turned up in a big grin. He could hear him saying it now.

JENNA'S HANDS trembled as she picked up a pack of cigarettes, trying to fish one out. She fumbled with the package of matches. He watched and then took the package out of her hand, striking the match for her, and lighting her cigarette.

"Ain't no way they can implicate you, Jenna, so don't worry."

"Sarge, I know the real truth and what if, oh God." She dropped onto the tatty couch and took three deep consecutive drags and then crushed out her half-smoked cigarette. Her eyes teared up.

Sarge picked up the phone. A man answered on the fourth ring.

"Got some bad news. The damn case was reopened. HPD is working cold cases, and this one came up."

The person on the other end exhaled a heavy breath. "After all these years, are you kidding me?"

They talked for a few more minutes, and he hung up.

"Who were you talking to?"

"*Sarge.*"

The name Sarge meant trouble. She'd been dead for over three decades and didn't want her murder solved, not now, or ever.

SOMEWHERE ABOUT FIFTY miles west where enormous stately homes with well-groomed lawns stood and money dripped off roofs, a man poured a stiff drink. He sat at his great solid cherry wood desk, took a swig of the bourbon, then set his glass on a coaster. Why did he want to torture himself with this awful past?

The pictures were vivid; the color had faded only a little. Damn, he was in better shape all those years ago, with muscles. Glancing down at his biceps, unlike the flab he called arms these days.

She had been the best whore he had ever encountered, and why she consented to his whims, he'd never know. He was a mean bastard back then, and he loved sadomasochism. The blow and the booze had carried him to a place of no return. Covering up his mess had been the start of the end of him. Now another judge would bring down the gavel and declare him, Judge Troy Wolff, guilty.

He had heard HPD was working unresolved cases whenever they

could, and he had worried this one might come up. Never in his life did he hope fresh homicides kept this case unsolved. Here he was, hoping for murders. Did more people have to die to keep him covered? Shit, he was a monster.

He picked up his glass and swallowed it in one gulp. It burned, but he didn't care. It was the best bourbon money could buy.

8

Traffic sucked. He was sitting behind a senseless wreck with a half a bottle of water, a bag of chips, and a Butterfinger. No caffeine meant he needed to eat sugar. He unwrapped the candy bar, took a bite, then punched in the number, hoping Dawson was at the station.

"Luck, Homicide Division."

Lucky sounded as beat as he was feeling right now.

"How's it going? You ready to go home?"

"Flap Jack, I'm wasted on reading all this stuff. Reading makes me tired. Are you headed home?"

"Uh-huh, trying to get off the Loop and get on 45. There's an accident blocking two lanes. Jiminy Christmas, man, all I have done is spin my wheels, but hey, I did just get started. How's your read going?"

"It's going is all I can say. This chick, Princess Lay-Ya hoochie-coochie-momma, JoAnn Cutter, was a good friend of the Houston PD. Her solicitation jacket was quite impressive and gross at the same time. She had some other charges too. She wasn't just one track minded. I'm about to head out, but let me update you on my busy missing hooker."

Jack felt terrible for holding him at the station, but he'd be lucky, not just the nickname either. His calling him meant he might miss a lot of the traffic he'd normally hit on the way home. Dawson lived somewhere between Beaumont Place and Mount Houston or the general vicinity. No matter where you ended up on the Loop, you were bound to have an accident to deal with. Hell, he had one this morning to start his day off on the north Loop. Here he was stuck in another one on the furthest end of the southeast part of the same damn Loop. It was crazy.

"Here, listen to this. Ms. JoAnn Cutter arrested for drug possession with intent to distribute twice. The charges dropped, and she got off scot-free. My guess is she knew someone who was a fixer. Anyway, there were indecent exposures, drunk and disorderly; a half dozen parking tickets, unpaid. Funny, they are still unpaid, with useless warrants out for her arrest. You believe that, Jack? And get this; pandering. Bad enough she sold herself, but she was tricking out other women to boot. This—I can't call her a lady, cuz she ain't one— this *gal* associated with way too many bad people, and it got her killed, dude, not missing. She's dead-in-the-dirt killed. Whatdaya think, Jack, I should be looking for bones, right?"

"Didn't you say she was a witness to another case? What was that about?"

"A double homicide from over thirty-six years ago, over off Richmond Avenue and it's an unsolved case too, by the way. It was an attorney, no big law attorney, small potatoes, and some friend of his. Reports say they had been leaving the attorney's office early in the morning, around three a.m.; and why they had been in his office at that hour was another mystery. My missing person reported she saw the whole thing, but then couldn't describe the shooter or the car. You know, I am wondering if whoever it was got to her too. The shooter even took the time to get his spent shell casings, which meant he was taking his time. If he was so nonchalant about it, like a tortoise in a race, why couldn't she give the cops back then a description?"

"Where was your wit, close by, what's the deal?" He stepped on the brakes as traffic slowed again.

"Off Richmond, used to be a three-story brick office over there, bulldozed to the ground some while back. There's a big tanning salon there now. She was at a bus stop on the opposite side of the street. Told them she was meeting a friend who worked at a place called the Naked High Heel, a skin shop, topless bar back then. There are still plenty of skin shops on Richmond Avenue. New names, different girls; at least I hope there are different girls. Can't imagine the same girls being there twenty-five years later, can you?"

Picturing what these women would look like now. Old grandma type women with gray scraggly hair and saggy yellow skin and wrinkled like prunes. Wearing a G-string, no top, and trying to balance themselves on six-inch stilettos. Most men would have puked at the thought, but it made Lucky laugh.

Topless bars or any types of sexually-oriented businesses were not Jack's idea of fun. He opted out when any of his bawdy friends back in his youth wanted to hit the topless bars and get what they had called a "dance and a whiff." Nope, it wasn't his thing.

"In her statement, it says she told them she had finished work, and her john had dropped her off. It was almost three a.m., and her roommate that worked at the Naked High Heel was meeting her. It was a Tuesday night, the streets weren't busy. The uniforms canvassed the area. Back then, there was an old hotel and a small apartment complex with plenty of residents, but none of them were talking. Both of the buildings are gone. She was alone at that bus stop. There was another bus stop not more than a block away. Four people were waiting for a bus and no one saw or heard a thing. Guess they were all too afraid to talk."

Lucky had a point. The apartment tenants should have heard the shots. He was sure someone *peeked* out a window. In certain neighborhoods, people didn't snitch out of fear: it was the same now, better to mind your own business and not get involved; nothing had changed. Jack had to admit her lifestyle wasn't the safest.

"You know, Luck, you might be right. You may not be looking for a breather. I'm betting its bones. Who were the detectives on the case back then?"

Dawson thumbed through the papers. "Was, uh, Detectives Bullard and Simpson who worked the case."

His gut tightened. They were the dicks on his cold case. Was this just a coincidence? He decided not to mention it, not yet anyway. Heck, the detectives back then, just like now, worked several cases at once, so it might not mean a thing. Just because the same dicks were in multiple cases didn't mean one had anything to do with the other. Jack caught the tail end of his partner's comment.

"—besides, I want to blow off the phone and head home to my beautiful wife and dinner."

"Sure, Lucky, have a good one." Jack disconnected the call.

There was an end in sight. A car and a small pickup had banged into each other. The tow trucks were all fighting to be hired. What had caused the accident was anyone's guess, texting or tired, on the phone not paying attention—they all fit. Sometimes he'd worked traffic, an occasional event, or something of that nature when he had been a patrol cop. Jack appreciated the uniforms. They were always the biggest help for canvassing a large area or for backup, but he preferred homicide—always would.

AFTER HE PUNCHED the snooze on his alarm, he rolled over, closing his eyes, wishing he had another few hours to sleep. Lord, he had stayed up too late, nursed a few too many beers. He'd flipped through his brother's murder book; hoping something might jump out and either grab him or hit him square in the face. Neither the grabbing nor hitting or jumping occurred, and he opted to catch up on his recorded shows, shows he was terminally behind in watching. He didn't fall into bed until 2:00 a.m.

Showering, shaving, and dressing took a mere thirty minutes. He grabbed a large capped metal coffee container and filled it with half of the pot of coffee. Jack grabbed the keys to the Charger and headed out the door. He had wanted to beat any 8:00 a.m. traffic but missed his window since it was after 8:00.

Jack hopped on Highway 225, deciding to drive to the station first. He'd buy rubber hip boots on his way out to the body dump site later. No accident, fender-bender or otherwise, had slowed him, just congested traffic, and that was normal. He arrived at the station at 9:30. Dawson beat him there. An empty Starbucks cup on sat on his desk. Lucky working on a cup of break room coffee, with his head stuck in his case file, with a bag of Cheetos next to the empty Starbucks cup.

Jack set his metal mug on the desk.

"Hey, you knee-deep into the old case, pard?"

Dawson peered up, grabbed some Cheetos out of the bag. "You want some?"

"No, thanks, I'll grab a breakfast burrito lunch or something on the way out later." He wasn't hungry with the coffee from last night and the few beers sloshing around in his gut.

"Hey sorry, I didn't ask you about your case last night, Jack. How'd it go?"

Lucky emptied the bag of Cheetos, crumpled it, then tossed the bag toward the trashcan and missed.

"Crap, I missed the can." He stood and did a fake-out jump and slam-dunked the wadded-up bag into the can.

"There's two points."

"Glad your team scored." Jack closed his eyes and counted to five.

Lucky annoyed him more often than not. "Sorry, Jack. What did you get last night?"

"A bucket full of nothing, and an achy back from driving, that's about it for now."

"Wasted time, I hate that."

"Me too, but I'm inclined to think I wasn't getting the whole story from this Jenna chick."

"You know eventually things come out in the wash. I'm betting something will pop up."

"Hey, Luck, have you ever been to the Crystal Barrel?"

"If that's the one over off Southwest Freeway, it's a dive. I've heard some of the biker gangs hang there. But no, I've never been in the place. I prefer upper-class bars, you know, like piano bars and clean sports bars." Dawson Luck hated dive bars.

"Me neither. My dead girl worked there, and at a place called the Silver, uh, the Station, it used to be the Silver Moon. What say you go with me one night and check out this place, the Crystal Barrel? You think that wife of yours will go along with that?"

"Vivian will be okay with it. She has to be. I'm a detective. It's my job. Sometimes she gets upset, and pouts, but I put her in her place." Dawson Luck was joking and quickly added, "You know I'm lucky to have such an understanding and beautiful wife."

Jack wouldn't argue, nor comment, as they both went back to reading files of yesteryear.

Reading all he wanted to read, no fresh case had come in and it was nearly noon. His stomach growled, so he hit the street and stopped by a fast-food joint.

"Lucky, I am going to head out. Take a ride out to where they found my dead girl's body. First, I have to go buy hip waders since we've had all this rain. I'll call you later, update you on my status. If a fresh one comes in, call me. I'll come back to the precinct, or you can text me the address."

"You got it, partner."

Jack signed out, leaving Luck alone in the squad room.

FISHERMAN'S HAVEN was a smaller store, not like the other sporting goods stores he shopped at. He just needed the hip waders and nothing more. He didn't want the whole getup because he didn't care for fishing.

"Yah sure yah don't want a Pflueger Trion Reel and Rod combo? We've got some fantastic sale prices this week. If you're a Zebco man, have some 808 series you might like. Couple that with some nice lures. I hear the fish are really jumping in the Gulf Stream." The old angler started ringing up the rubber hip waders.

"Just the waders today, but thanks." Jack took out his wallet, paid, and then stuck the receipt in his wallet. The department might not reimburse him, but hey, he'd use it as a write-off for work expenses on his taxes. It was one thing he learned when he'd watched the movie *The Shawshank Redemption*. If you used it for work, you might write it off as an expense. He wondered if it was even worth it.

He waved adios to the avid angler who owned Fisherman's Haven, took his new waders to his truck, and tossed them in the seat behind him. His mission was to head to the spot where they had found the body in August 1986. It might be a wasted morning. He was sure there was nothing to find, but it was how he did things.

The old no-tell-motel was still there, and it wasn't seeing mega action. A few cars sat in the less-than-standard parking lot. The vacancy sign stated that there were plenty of rooms by the night, by the week, and by the month. Jack only imagined what the rooms looked like inside. The outside needed more than a coat of paint; it needed a coat of "cover up the ugly" or better yet, a demolition team.

As a courtesy, he stopped to check in at the office. He parked his truck next to a beat-up Ford Fairlane and an old ratty Chevy pickup that had seen better days. The front office smelled stale, and the floors were gritty. The ashtrays were full of cigarette butts, and the sliding glass was gone from the front counter.

"Morning, Officer, can I help you?" The older, unkempt man behind the front desk greeted Jack, grinning with a bare minimum of teeth left in his mouth.

Jack wondered if the old man had teeth in the back and if he ate solid food at all. The old guy was rather skinny.

"I see you have the nose of a bloodhound, sniffed out the law pretty darned fast, huh?"

Jack leaned over the counter, glancing at the paperwork the old geezer was working on.

The partially toothless man cackled, or perhaps it was a squawk as a hen or a rooster made because of the number of years he'd smoked Lucky Strike cigarettes. There was a crumpled, empty pack sitting on the counter and a new pack stuffed into the front pocket of his maroon-and-white-striped, short-sleeved shirt.

"Nah, when you have been renting rooms as long as I have, you know Johnny Law with or without being badged. I just knowed, that's all."

"You still rent rooms by the hour?"

"Are you hunting for somebody, or just nosing around, cuz I got work to tend to and no time to waste gabbing here with you."

The old toothless man turned snippy. Whom he rented his rooms to was nobody's business. Yeah, sure, hookers frequented his place, but, hell, he was no one's judge.

Jack badged him, explaining to the old geezer why he was there and what he wanted.

"Out of courtesy, mind you, I don't want someone to come out back and bring a shotgun, now do I?" His lips turned up a bit as he gave the slovenly old man the eye.

The old motel owner glanced at his badge, then at Jack.

"I'm Tully Cranston. I was here that day the boys found her, you know." He became pensive thinking back on the incident, remembering how he hated that such an awful thing had been discovered close to a place he called home.

"Do you recall any of your rooms in a mess, back then I mean?" He was sure the rooms were less than sanitary now and smelled. Crap, the sheets might be the same ones on the beds from three weeks ago. Not a place he'd venture staying overnight.

"Nope, nothing was out of order here at my place, can't help ya there."

"How far back do you keep your records?"

The old man scratched at his gray stubble and lowered his eyes. "Hmm, let's see, there's a pile of boxes stored from fifteen years ago. Might be longer. Who knows what I got? I ain't much of a neat freak, and I ain't that organized either. There're all kinds of shit—uh, pardon my language—I boxed up to keep. I stuffed papers with papers, and there are at least, oh, I reckon about thirty years of boxes."

"Are they easy to get to?"

Tully let out a loud hee-haw. "Yep, at least what the rats ain't *eht*, I guess. Got 'm stored in my son's old barn. Not much telling what kind of shape they'd be in after being in there all these years."

Well, he wasn't ready to rumble with rats, or dig into sixty years of misfiled, unkempt paperwork, but if at one point he needed to, he'd do it. It was doubtful anyone even used real names when they signed in on the register. Jack was looking for a snipe on a snipe hunt—when you knew there was no such thing as a snipe.

"I'd like to talk to you when I get back. Will you be here?" His voice brought the old man out of his coma.

Tully waggled his head. "You bet. Sure, sure, I'll be here. I own this joint, and it's mine free of debt. Times aren't as good as they used to be though, you know?"

"So it seems." Jack gave the old place a once over. "So it seems," repeating himself, walking out the door, ready to find the body dump spot from 34 years ago.

Tully watched him walk out and wondered why now? Too many years had slipped by. Who cared any longer? He scratched his head, took out his fresh pack of cigs. The old guy tapped one out and stuck it between his lips. He flicked a Zippo lighter open against his thin thigh, lighting what his grandson called them, the end of his cancer stick. He inhaled deeply and then let the smoke curl out of his nose and then the rest out of his puckered lips.

Tully thought it was odd. It had been thirty-four years, and no one had ever come back to ask him any more questions. Hell, it either had happened right behind his place or had ended up right behind his place, and nobody questioned him about a goddamn thing. Why not? Kiss my foot. If they hadn't been interested back then, why were they interested now? He crushed the nub of his cig out. The police were not interested. Or they were always twenty years too late. Made no difference to him as long as they didn't get in his face regarding what he rented rooms for; he rented rooms, and that was not illegal, now was it?

THE AREA WASN'T AS horrible as Jack figured it would be, although it was bad enough. It had rained nonstop for five days, so the marshy places were marshier, and any parcel of land which was a gully or low-lying became pure mud and sludge. There were no roads, no paths, just land, weeds, and muck. Any path was now washed away. He slipped off his boots to pull the waders on his feet. Well, crap, he hadn't factored in his boots wouldn't fit into the feet of the waders, so he wore just his socks. He needed a pair of crappy tennis shoes stored in his truck for days like this.

Pulled up over his dark brown Khakis, he hooked the suspender straps of the rubber waders over his dress shirt. Jack grabbed several pairs of rubber gloves, plastic evidence bags, and stuffed them in the front bib pocket of the waders. He took out copies of the pictures of the crime scene, folded them, and stuffed them and his cell phone into his pants pocket inside the waders. Grabbing his keys, he locked the truck, dropped the keys in his other pocket, and took off to find the spot the boys found her body.

From the pictures, he recognized the general spot. Jack prayed that the overgrowth and recent rains were not hiding any critters, mainly snakes of any kind. Even sticks resembling large or small snakes of any kind had him jumping. He had no fear facing a hardened criminal staring down the barrel of a sawed-off shotgun. A snake, though, it was the one thing which could make him sweat profusely and have him screaming like a five-year-old girl in pigtails, running for the mountains. He had his gun, and he'd shoot to kill, asking questions later.

The pictures showed the same section of land, with more weeds. The small creek was ankle-deep. He waded in, walking over to where the killer ditched the car. He found a long thick limb, thanking God it was not a snake. Using the limb, he spread the tall grass and sifted through for no real reason. The elements had destroyed evidence, buried under twenty-five years of sludge and mud. Hell, what did they even miss, and just how did they miss it? They had the car and its contents. He didn't know why he was out here, except to see the area, conjuring a picture of what could've happened. This spot—had it been convenient for the body dump? Her murder did not happen in the car, so where had the murder scene been, and why dump her body out here, and in her own vehicle?

Jack passed the long limb through weeds again not expecting to find diddly; there wasn't any trash this far back. The sun hit something, and it reflected a nanosecond. Bending over, he took the limb swishing it over the mucky area. It was a faded Budweiser can. He took the limb he was using and decided what the hell, why not? He wasn't a bad golfer, but he wasn't good either. Besides, he hadn't been to the golf range in more than a year, and he was a play around at it kind of golfer. A practice shot and no prying eyes. Picking up the beer can he laid it on a soft pile of wet grass. Holding the long limb like a seven iron, he did the golf butt wiggle. Bringing the limb into a backswing, he smacked the devil out of it, watching it soar across the short gully.

God that felt great. He needed a tension release. Maybe letting off steam by whacking golf balls at the driving range was a good idea. Shooting his gun was another way his tension could be relieved, but, undoubtedly, he needed something more physical. He needed an outlet to work off steam and get back into better shape.

Jack surveyed the stretch of land, wondering if the dead girl ever stayed at the no-tell-motel or if her killer stayed there. Was this a convenient place for the perp? Shaking his head, there were too many unanswered questions.

Tully stood at the desk watching Jack drive into the lot. He figured the detective didn't find squat. The motel owner took his coffee-stained mug, poured his eighth cup of coffee, and emptied the full ashtray. A fresh Lucky Strike hanging from his lips, he waited for the detective to walk back into his dirty, smoke-filled lobby.

"You have any luck out there in the mud and weeds?"

"Nope, lots of the same mud and weeds minus the car and the body."

"Coffee, Detective, before you ask me questions, which you are gonna do, right?"

He raised an eyebrow. "Mr. Cranston, of course I've got questions, probably some of the same one the detectives asked you back when it happened."

"Well, I ain't got nuttin' to hide. The other ones, the dicks, er, s'cuze me—*detectives*—they never came back. I saw them twice. First time was when it was called in and they talked to the boys who found the body. Second time they showed up to ask me questions about my place and the people here. Afterward I never saw 'em again."

Jack wondered why they hadn't attempted to come back to do a follow-up on their investigation. Notebook in hand, his cell phone chirped. The name came up—The Precinct, so he answered.

"Jack West."

"Hey, it's Luck. We've got a new case. Where are you?"

"Place called All Occasions Motel over off Southwest Freeway."

"Come to the station and get me and we'll go together. Our vic isn't going anywhere and CSU is already there."

"Okay, be there in twenty or thirty, depending on traffic."

Tully stubbed out his burned-to-the-nub cigarette. "Gotcha a new case, do ya?"

"Yep, we do. Are you here most days?" Jack flipped his notebook shut.

"Yep, I live in the side room over yonder." He jabbed his thumb toward the back. "Here day and night. You can come back anytime, if you come back, that is."

"We have to work the new cases first. This case is only on the back burner for now, *my* back burner." His eyes bore into the man. "I'm like a pit bull with a bone, meat or no meat. I don't let go easily."

Tully faintly bobbed his head, tapping out another cigarette from the near empty pack. "Good, glad someone's working it, wasn't worked hard enough before, leastwise, that's my opinion."

"If there is any reason that I need to come back, I will. Thanks, Mr. Cranston."

"You bet, Detective, any time."

Jack left and headed to HPD to get his partner and head off to another crime scene.

9

L ucky gave him the address, and Jack whistled. "Wowzers, pard, crime in a high-dollar area, haven't had a high-dollar neighborhood to work in for a while."

Ignoring his high-dollar area comment, he buckled his seatbelt. "You eat lunch yet?"

"No, and I'm starved." As if on cue, Jack's stomach rumbled.

Dawson Luck chuckled. "So I hear. If you'll stop over at Jersey Mike's on Yale Street, I'll spring for the sandwiches and chips, cuz I hafta eat."

Although he was craving a Chili Cheese Coney from James' Coney Island, it was closer but too messy and not driving food, so Jersey Mike's it was.

Food eaten on the run. Wrappers stuffed in a bag, Jack drove into the wealthier community, the enormous stately homes of the rich and powerful. He searched for the telltale signs of mayhem, coroner's car, black-and-whites, and a mob of people all standing on or near the crime scene rubbernecking.

Glen Cove was a residential area for the rich, new or old money. What atrocity happened here? When the street ended, Jack turned into the large gated drive that guarded a massive house. With a beautifully manicured lawn, the house reeked of money. Jack had seen these homes when he looked for his own. It was "dream-looking." Large, luscious homes with four and five bedrooms, four baths with a pool and hot tub, a game room, even a media room. Kitchens that would delight the most experienced chef to the mommy homemaker baking chocolate chip cookies for her kids. How could bad things happen to rich people? He reminded himself how great his life had been. Not rich in monetary ways, but rich in spirit and love. Then one fateful night someone had taken his brother from him, and his idyllically middle-class life had shattered. It happened to all lifestyles, poor, rich, middle-class, successful or not, smart people and stupid people. Murder and mayhem did not discriminate.

A uniformed officer had the area taped off, and a few other officers were backing off the onlookers.

Cassandra Sparrow stood at the front door, letting allowed personnel only pass.

"Cass, you and Amy were radioed the callout?"

"Yes, sir, Amy and I rolled up at twelve-fifteen. The housekeeper called it in. She cleans on Monday, Wednesday, and Friday. She's in the front room with Amy right now."

"What's the story?"

"We met her at the door and the poor woman was crying and speaking in Spanish so rapidly we thought she'd hyperventilate. Amy took her statement. She translated while I wrote since I can't speak a lick of Spanish. Housekeeper arrived at the house at approximately eight-thirty this morning. She always starts downstairs and works her way upstairs. She went upstairs around eleven forty-five and that was when she found the body in the master bedroom."

"Took her over three hours to get upstairs?"

Cass gave him a look. "It's a big house, Detective West, and she evidently does a thorough job. You'll see how immaculate it is when you go inside. When she gets upstairs, she always begins in the back, which is the Stegwig's bedroom, and works her way to the other side.

When she went into the bedroom, she saw clothes strewn about, which wasn't normal for the misses. Drawers pulled out and a large jewelry box upturned. The contents were scattered all over the floor. She started picking stuff up, and that's when she saw the *first* body."

"First body?"

"Yes. She ran back downstairs, grabbed her cell phone, and dialed 9-1-1. We did a sweep, then headed upstairs. We saw the woman on the bedroom floor, and Amy checked the bathroom and found the second body, a man. Both were dead. The victims are Mr. and Mrs. Stegwig. The housekeeper IDed them. No one was to be home when she worked today. We searched the entire house and found nothing amiss. Just the three rooms were touched, from what we could tell. The master bedroom, the bathroom, and a room across the hall used as an office. The desk was ransacked and papers were everywhere. It could be a robbery that went haywire, but I don't see it."

"Yeah, why?"

"Look at this place. Lot of things to steal, maybe the perp had expected no one to be home and didn't have time to complete the job. The dressers were ransacked, and the jewelry was dumped all over the floor, but nothing was taken."

"And?" he prompted her.

"In a small cabinet, there were four guns. They weren't loaded, the clips were full, but none of the clips were in the guns. Guns are in demand, primarily by gangs. So guessing this might rule out a gang crime."

"Was any money missing?"

"Housekeeper said she never saw cash lying around, so she wasn't sure. The cash from the man's wallet on the nightstand was gone and the woman's purse dumped out, her cash gone too. It appears to be a murder/suicide, or someone wanted it to look like a robbery. No note was found though, so hard to tell what happened. I guess, Detective West, it would be your job to deduce if it's a robbery gone sour. CSU is in there now, and the videographer is filming, you know the usual rigmarole; they've been at it for less than an hour."

"How long has the housekeeper worked here, did she say?"

"Eight years, and she knows this house inside and out. Poor woman is nervous. I'm sure she's worried she'll be implicated."

"The neighbors hear anything?" He walked around the house and didn't see the garage; must be a rear entry. On a corner lot and a sprawling piece of property meant no one heard anything. He'd have the uniforms canvass the area.

"Lots are big, so this isn't an area with zero lot lines. One neighbor, a Ms. McGovern, who lives next door, and she's in the main living room. She's pretty shaken up."

"Someone go get her, or did she just show up?"

"She is what you call the neighborhood watchdog, came over here on her own volition, checking it out to see what happened. That was when an officer approached her and then contained her."

Lucky walked up, and Cass half-smiled. Personal feelings about the man aside, this was business, and she conducted herself like a professional.

"Detective Luck." Not a trace of dislike at all entered her voice.

"Officer Sparrow, your callout?"

"Yes, sir."

"Anyone home or is it just the vic?"

"Two vics, Detective Luck. It would appear to be a robbery gone sideways. The housekeeper called it in, but no one else is in the house. CSU is sweeping the place right now."

"Where are our victims?"

"Upstairs."

"Anybody call Bennie?" The medical examiner's car was nowhere around.

"He's on the way. CSU and the videographer are in there. Medical personnel arrived on the scene, but since the vics were both dead, they left as fast as they arrived."

"Thanks, Cass. Lucky, let's get in there and get a look-see for ourselves." Jack put paper booties over his boots, pulled on his rubber gloves, and walked into the house. Dawson Luck followed suit and walked in behind him.

Cass was a first-rate patrol cop, smart and keen on details. Someone should keep their eye on her because she was a future shining star. Jack saw a definite spark in this patrol cop.

The house was indeed immaculate. A large entryway into the home opened up with double-paned glass doors encased with a swirling design of metal that protected and decorated the doors. The front foyer was adorned with expensive, very elegant Spanish marble tile, high ceilings, and a beautiful chandelier overhead.

You didn't just see the money, you smelled it in the air. A small antique table sat inside the entrance, a basket filled with Godiva chocolates and fresh flowers in a vase on top. *Who still put out fresh flowers?* he wondered.

The staircase was wide and winding; it grabbed your attention right away. The metal staircase handrails were a replica of the metal design on the main doors.

Jack saw a formal living area to his left and a formal dining area to his right. It was all very elegant, with sophisticated touches and expensive furniture. He figured the entire house was just as impressive.

"I am going upstairs, Lucky. You go interview the housekeeper, then meet me upstairs."

"Yep, I'm on it."

Lucky took off for the formal living room, and Jack headed upstairs.

Mr. and Mrs. Marcus Stegwig lay dead, one in the bedroom, the other one in the bathroom.

The woman's body was fully dressed lying on her left side. Her left hand was near her throat, and her right arm draped over her breast. She was wearing an exercise outfit, a yellow T-shirt, and stretchy exercise pants, white socks, and tennis shoes. Her T-shirt was saturated now in dried blood that had pooled under her upper torso. She had taken a bullet to the neck. Her hands were covered in dried blood; she'd grabbed her throat. Jack wondered if she had bled out, or had she drowned in her own blood.

"Detective West," Loren Taylor said, "Too bad we have to meet up like this, huh?"

Jack bent over the female murder victim. "Yeah, it is. Who's here with you?"

"Cheech is." Loren took a picture of the area behind the dead woman.

Vince Stoner, the other person from the CSU department, everyone called him "Cheech" as in Cheech and Chong, *stoner* heads from the seventies.

"The other victim is in there." Loren pointed toward another doorway leading into the bathroom.

"Okay, I'll go in there in a moment."

"Hey, where's your sidekick, Lucky?"

"He's talking to the housekeeper; he'll be up shortly."

Her body had bloated, and fluid was leaking from her nose and mouth. No rank smells yet. The room was exceptionally cool, so decomp was slower. He had seen several dead bodies. She'd been dead for over forty-eight hours.

There was bruising on her right thigh, and from what he could see on her right arm. Jack wondered if there were matching bruises on her left arm. He'd worked a few domestic violence calls, seen similar bruising on women aggressively grabbed by spouses or boyfriends. Fingerprint powder dusted the place; Loren had already dusted for prints.

"So, you get any prints outta here?" He surveyed the room.

"A few, undoubtedly most will be of the dead couple's since this was their room, who knows? The housekeeper runs a tight ship, not a speck of dust anywhere. Until today, that is. We'll get her prints, to double-check against the prints we find. The man's wallet, her purse and wallet, we've bagged and taken back to the lab. To be honest, I'm not hopeful."

Jack walked back to where the second decedent lay with Loren right behind him.

"Not many prints. But we found what we could, and we'll match them to the decendants and the housekeeper. The room was cleaner than I had expected. It was all wiped down. That's why I'm not hopeful about the purse or the wallets. I gotta hunch the perp wiped them down too."

Dead—Marcus Stegwig sat, his back against the claw-footed bathtub, his body semi-slumped. A swollen face with blood which oozed and dried, and mixed in with brain matter, splattered all over the right side. Both arms hung downward, his eyes lifeless. The dead man wore expensive dress slacks and a light purple shirt. There was a bullet hole in his right temple. The bullet had exited the left temple and left a tiny exit hole. The shot was a straight through and through.

For all intents and purposes, it appeared to be a suicide. He crouched in front of the body. No gun. Where in the hell was the gun? No gun. Then it can't be a suicide. Was there any missing cash? If so, then it had to be a robbery gone wrong—or was it staged?

"If it was a real suicide and someone found them, then took the gun—" Mumbling, thinking that was a one percent chance, and he doubted that one-hundred percent.

"No gun to compare it to, but it's a .22 caliber. Maybe this was an execution. Or it might have been a suicide, if the man was right-handed. Look where the casing landed," Loren pointed out. He looked over his left shoulder, following Loren's finger.

A .22-caliber shell casing lay to the right of his body about four feet out next to the toilet, marked with an evidence marker.

"It had to have bounced and then hit the top of the vanity cabinet, then bounced back and rolled, stopping at the bolt that secures the toilet to the floor. Shell casing, but no gun."

"Loren, you already said that. No gun, then it couldn't be a suicide. Obviously, you can't shoot yourself with a loaded finger."

Two victims with bullet holes in them was all the evidence he needed to know that a gun had been there.

"You find the slugs?"

"We took one out of that wall next to the doorframe." Loren pointed at the wall. "Since he was sitting at this end of the tub, that's about where it would have hit. I am surprised he didn't keel over, against the wall more slumped over. The slug was barely stuck in the doorjamb. I'm also amazed it was a through and through. A .22 caliber bounces around, it hardly ever exits."

The spot was marked where the slug had been. He crouched next to the hole and glanced back at the body. The bullet trajectory fit one of two things: he killed himself, or his assailant made him sit against the tub before executing him, and none of it made sense.

He scooched over and hunkered in front of the body, his back to the vic, and he held his hand up like a gun.

"If I were to off myself, the casing would eject out to my right. Up and then over about four feet. Because, there is no other way for it to go. It would have bounced, hit the wall, and bounced back this way."

Jack assessed the area before speaking again. "But, say I am the doer, and I sit here, and you are there."

He had Loren switch places with him. Jack squatted next to Loren, pretending to have a gun in his hand holding it to Loren's temple.

"I shoot you in the temple. You fall over toward the left. If I have the gun at your right temple, your lifeless body will not end up in a straight-up upright position. The body is going to lean over a little. Even if a doer off'd him, he would have fallen over some; this vic is sitting too upright. What did the killer do, sit him upright after he shot him, or hold his right arm to keep him upright when he shot? The human head is heavy. A shot in the head would make his head snap, would have caused him to be unbalanced and he would have leaned a little."

"That seems reasonable. Look at the burn marks around the wound. The entry point left a black and gray abrasion ring, gunpowder burns, and if you will notice, the gun barrel left a markedly visible impression." He pointed with his gloved hand. "A starburst shape, see? This tells us the gun was held to his head like so." Loren placed his hand against his temple as if he were holding a gun on himself, his forefinger touching his temple. Whoever shot him had the gun pressed hard at his temple. This is a tight area. GSR would settle everywhere, and the shooter would have the bulk on his hands, or whoever was holding the gun."

"Uh-huh."

The bathroom was small, smaller than a master bathroom would be in such a majestic house. It had one toilet, one sink and countertop that was not lengthy, and the claw-foot tub.

"This is the master bath?"

"Hell, no, this must be his bathroom. You know, the man gets the smallest bathroom and closet. Back over there, where I thought a closet was, is a larger bathroom. A separate vanity area and the wife's makeup all over a double sink countertop running the near length of one wall. There is a massive rock shower with twin shower heads, and there is an enormous walk-in closet. This shitter must have been his, or the one the wife made him use. My guess is he wanted to do himself in here."

Jack regarded the body, and what did not fit was how he was sitting. It made no sense either way, suicide or murder. Gunpowder burns were on his temple. The gun was up against his head—on his own volition or not, it was hard to say. "If he were a suicide, he would have GSR on his hands, and more than just a little." He squatted and peered at the bullet entry for a second look-see. Glancing at the dead man's right hand, he saw blood, but not much.

"If he off'd himself, there'd be more blood on his hand. The blood spatter would be on the right side of the body. Don't see spatter where it should be though."

"You'd think so, wouldn't ya? There's blood on his hand, but not as much blood spatter as one would imagine."

"You swab him for GSR?"

"Sure did, look what I have here." Loren held up a small plastic case. The label read, *Instant Shooter Identification Kit.*

"Nifty, what is it, new toys for CSU?"

"What's going on in here?" Lucky walked into the bathroom.

"Loren was fixing to show me a new toy he has. By the way, you let the housekeeper go?"

"I have her contact information and told her to call if she thought of anything else. Stoner fingerprinted her before she left."

"Great. You can tell me what she told you later."

"Guys, if I can interrupt, let me tell you what I have here," Loren said as he got into a squat, setting the case next to him.

They watched as Loren got all CSU'zy with his new toys.

"It is a binary test kit. You use the sticky tab swab called carbon tape particle collection device. First, you get a sample bag and seal it to take to the crime lab, then they can use the SEM-scanning electron microscope test for GSR; that way, they have evidentiary evidence."

"I've heard about these. When did CSU get these to use?"

Loren didn't respond; he was busy with the kit. He guessed CSU must have gotten a budget increase.

Loren Taylor continued his lesson on how to use the kit. "Now I dry swab his hand like this and use the propriety L.E.T. swab and then use this chemical agent."

Loren went through the motions conducting the test. Jack and Luck stared at the swab Loren had sprayed. Five minutes elapsed and a blue reaction on the swab appeared.

"Nitrocellulose is present. That's what that blue reaction means; there are small spots and specks. This means it is highly probable that this man here fired a weapon. Not to mention that his shirt reeks of GSR and there's no weapon anywhere close, or even in the room. I don't think he shot himself, then went and hid the gun either, do you?"

Well that was a hundred percent unlikely, so yeah, where was the freaking gun.

"Anybody find a note?"

"No, and it made me wonder. What if he thought before he killed himself, a note wouldn't be necessary? He does her, and then he kills himself. Let's say he killed his wife, and someone offed him afterward. I mean it could happen, I guess. I can't see that it was a robbery gone sour."

"Why not?" Lucky bent over the male victim.

"This house, I mean, you can see their lifestyle and there are plenty of items to steal. If they surprised the perp, then he killed them, he could have robbed the place. Heck, the jewelry alone could have been stuffed in an empty pillowcase."

Loren made a point. So what happened in this room? The three men stood pondering the situation for a short minute, then walked back into the bedroom where the woman lay.

"Loren, what's your take on this?" He gestured at the dead woman. He already had his own idea of the situation. Viewing it from another person's perspective gave him ideas. People didn't see exactly the same thing the same way, and another view was sometimes helpful.

"Hmm, well, with the shot in the throat I figure she was standing about here." He stepped to the side of where the woman's body lay. "She took a full frontal shot. If it was a straight shot to her thyroid, she would have died almost instantly; that's the M.E.'s call of course. All the blood on her hands tells me that her hands went up to her neck, an automatic reaction."

"Lucky, what do you think?"

"That's a reasonable explanation, Loren, but did you see the blood smears?"

"What blood smears?" Loren stooped over her, searching for the smear.

"There, by her right hand, next to her pinky and ring finger."

Jack hunched over. "Good catch, Lucky." A smear that resembled the toe of a shoe and Jack looked at her right side, then back to the blood smear.

"Hmm, looks like her killer nudged her to see if she was dead. There's a small spot of blood on her shirt that seems to be nowhere near any other bloody areas. The killer musta set his foot here, close to blood that was pooling under her."

They all bent over staring at the smear.

"Check for blood on the other victim's shoes. What about the blood spatter on the shooter? If the dead man in there had been the shooter, what'd he do, clean up and change shirts before he took his own life?" Jack's brow crinkled. That would be dumb.

Loren hunkered to view the blood smear better. "Well, damn, I didn't see it. Fellas, I know I took pictures of it because I snapped her at every angle and close-ups. Man, I can't believe I missed that."

He hated missing things, and he hardly ever did. Loren looked crestfallen, and Jack couldn't help but laugh.

"Loren, it happens to all of us. No worries, man. You're one of the best. Shit, I missed it too. Lucky got—well, lucky. Besides, Bennie would have had all of our backs."

"Are you are you three girls talking nice about me?" Houston's top-notch M.E. walked into the room.

"Bennie, long time no see. They have you locked up at the morgue day and night. Betcha it's nice to get out in the sunlight."

"I get to leave my hole and get out from time to time. By the way, where's Cheech?"

Vince Stoner had come up behind him. "Hey, Doogie, I'm here. They called for the best, and I came running."

"Christ, Cheech, how many times have I asked you not to call me Doogie? I'd rather you call me Shorty." Bennie hated the name Doogie Howser.

"I'm sorry, can't help myself." He winked at Bennie. "Jack, I'm done across the hall. There wasn't much to find, but who knows, huh?"

"Yep, who knows?"

The M.E. looked at the body of victim number one. "Where's vic number two?" Bennie looked up at Jack.

"In there." Jack pointed to the bathroom.

Bennie trotted off to see what that situation was.

"Did your guys locate bullets or casings in here?" Lucky leaned over the dead woman, glancing up at where he thought the bullet would have gone.

"We found a slug in the windowsill on that wall." He pointed it out. "We extracted it and bagged it. It's pretty flattened, the windowsill is thicker wood."

Jack walked over to where the circle marked the spot where CSU dug out a slug.

"The casing is right here."

Dawson Luck walked to where the casing was marked and then turned around.

"I'd say she was standing by the window, by this chair, her back to the window. The shooter had to have been standing right about here."

He moved over a few feet from the fireplace hearth.

"She took a frontal shot to her throat. Maybe they were in a heated argument. If he had the gun in his pocket, and she walked over here, he would be behind her. She turns around—*blam*. If that were the case he would have been close enough to put one dead center into her chest. Why'd he shoot her in the throat?"

"Well, that's a good question." Loren nodded.

Lucky continued. "The bullet, small caliber, went straight through. If it hit her in the spinal cord at just the right angle, she died instantly, or she aspirated in seconds. No evidence of a struggle either."

"She either knew her shooter, or it was the biggest surprise she never saw coming." Jack frowned.

"Okay, dudes, gonna help Cheech finish up."

"Thanks, Loren. Any more ideas come to mind, let us know."

With that, Loren Taylor took off to help his partner wrap things up for the CSU unit.

Bennie Guay took charge of the bodies. CSU was finished, but Jack West and Dawson Luck's work had just begun.

Standing in the hallway, her body was visible. Jack glanced back. "Damn shame. What'd the housekeeper say?"

They moved out of the doorway when the assistants with the body bags and gurneys appeared. Bennie was being his short, bossy self. "Hey, not yet, don't move a thing until I say you can, you hear?"

Luck watched him work as he answered Jack.

"She confirmed she's worked for the Stegwigs for eight years. Said they were nice people. The lady, the Mrs., spoke Spanish, and that made her more comfortable with her employer. She worked when they were out of the house. But a few weeks ago, the woman had been home on Wednesday when she arrived at work, which had surprised her. It happened last Wednesday and the Wednesday before that. She was dressed in nice clothes, not her usual gym attire."

"Did she say why?"

"She's not the intrusive type, but she asked her if she had a job now. Mrs. Stegwig had told her no, she had a very important meeting."

"Who with? Did she say?"

"Nope. Like I said, she minds her own business and left it at that. That was last Wednesday, five days ago. She told me the woman had a decent size bruise on her right cheek and her eye was getting purple; someone had smacked her hard across the cheek. The housekeeper asked her if she was all right and the woman said she was fine, it was nothing. I asked her if she believed that and she told me no because she knows what it looks like when a woman gets hit by a man. She has a sister-in-law that went through the same thing."

"Alright then, let's go see what else we can find out from the neighbor. Okay, we're headed down. Talk to you before you leave."

Bennie gave them an above-the-head hand wave. He was bent over the dead woman, all his attention on the job.

10

B oth the bodies were bagged and on gurneys as the medical examiner's assistants waved adios to both Jack and Lucky.

"You guys gonna be here a while, huh?" the newest member from the forensic lab remarked as he helped wheel out the second gurney.

Jack inhaled and exhaled; it was going to be a late night. Lucky pouted. Cripes, this messed up his date night with his wife.

"Date night?" Jack grinned when he saw his partner's face.

"Hell, I live with that bodacious, scrumptious woman, but I sure enjoy date night."

"Hey, pard, you have a woman. I haven't had a date in months. I've been too busy. Besides, who would want this ragged, rough, old cowboy?" Jack heard someone clear her throat behind him.

Cass stood there smiling, her white teeth contrasted with her light chocolate-brown skin, and she put her hand up to her mouth to hide her smile.

"Cass?" Jack turned to face her.

She did an inward laugh, pressing her lips together before she spoke. "Gossip in the secretary pool in the department says otherwise. There are quite a few of the ladies who say you are, hmm

—how do they say it? You are a tall drink of water on a hot summer day." A huge grin covered Cass's face.

Jack blushed three shades of pink. She saw it and got him out of his embarrassing moment. "Oh, and the neighbor is waiting to find out if you need to speak with her. She said she has things to do this afternoon and doesn't have all day. Her words, not mine."

"Come on, tall drink. Let's go talk to the neighbor, get her while she's fresh." Lucky waggled his caterpillar eyebrows, as Groucho Marx would have done.

"Don't start, Lucky." Jack's face now one shade of pink and fading. He left Lucky standing there with a huge grin.

Cass grinned, and she and Lucky did a fist bump—were they bonding? Who knew?

He put his hand out. "I'm Detective West, this is my partner, Detective Luck. We're sorry to have to meet you this way, Ms. McGovern. I hope you are up to a few questions."

She was shaken up. Her face pasty-colored, her eyes puffy from crying, and he knew she had zero plans for the afternoon; she wanted to go home.

"Tell you what, how about we go get some fresh air?"

Ms. McGovern stood. She was unbalanced and wavered, and he took her arm to steady her. Any other time Jack would've chalked it up to her advanced age, but today he added in shock.

"Thank you, I'd like that."

She walked to the front not once looking back or toward the stairwell that led to death, death of people she had known. He walked behind her, making sure she didn't topple over.

"Do you recall the last time you saw Mr. or Mrs. Stegwig?" Jack began, notebook in hand.

"I believe that would have been Thursday evening. I waved at them both. They had gotten home about fifteen minutes apart, about six or six-thirty."

Then the Stegwigs were alive on Thursday, at least at six-thirty p.m.

"Ma'am, do you know where their son," Dawson Luck referred to his notes, "Sean Stegwig would be right now?"

"Of course, he would be at work. He has his own company doing IT work. Now, what did he name his company?" She put her right forefinger on her mouth, trying to recall. Jack was a patient man, and he waited.

"It is on the tip of my tongue, Red something. No, wait, the name's Red Hawk Tel-Com. I think it's short for Telecommunications."

"Red Hawk Telecommunications—never heard of it." Jack scribbled the name.

"He started this company about ten months ago. His father helped him and now—" She trailed off, her hand to her face, clearly distressed.

"Ms. McGovern, were the Stegwig's having any personal difficulty?"

"Like what? I mean, I don't know about their finances, but the wife, Marta, occasionally talked to me. She always said I was a good listener, and that every so often it's good to talk to someone, you know?"

Jack and Dawson both nodded a sympathetic head-tilt bobble. "What did you and Mrs. Stegwig talk about?" Lucky prompted, taking the lead.

"About her and Marcus fighting, and sometimes she updated me on her daughter Shayla who lives in Dallas."

"And were you aware of what they argued about?"

He saw her face flush, then turn beet red. She hesitated and then pursed her lips in a tight, thin line. That was when Lucky knew Jack needed to take over, so he did his "look." Jack was a better people person; Lucky at least knew his own shortcomings.

"I understand you don't want to betray a confidence, but Marta Stegwig has had the worst of all betrayals. Someone took her life. Our job is to put the pieces together to get closure for her family and for the community. We have to get all of our facts, and that means getting any information to help us solve this terrible crime. Do you understand?"

The older woman's eyes teared up. "Marta was talking to a divorce lawyer. Marcus didn't know it yet." The old woman puckered her face in thought. "Since he's dead, I guess it's okay to tell you. Marcus was mean to her and hurt her. Their son Sean didn't live in the house. I'm guessing he did not know his father was hurting his mother, or he didn't care. He was daddy's boy."

Lucky chimed in. "The son, do you remember when you saw him here at home?"

"Sean, uh, let me think. I saw him, or rather *heard* him come home Thursday night. Friday he went to work, or I suppose he went to work on Friday, but I didn't hear his motorcycle. Late Friday night, my cat was mewing, and I had to let her in, and I heard him open then close the garage, or I guess it was him. Sean didn't leave or I would have heard the motorcycle or the car."

"He was in the house Thursday and Friday night, then?" Jack jotted down a note.

She lifted her shoulders. "I'm not sure. He lives in back. His dad converted their pool house for him. It's his private apartment. Marta said Sean wanted to feel as if he was on his own, but they supported him. She said they saw him on weekends, but rarely. If he showed up on Saturday or Sunday, sometimes they'd eat together. Breakfast, lunch, or dinner, but this depended on Sean and if he wasn't with his own friends or the few strange friends he had. Those family meals were very infrequent, and Marta told me he didn't have any real friends." Her nose crinkled in disgust. The old woman wasn't exactly fond of the boy.

"Was he around this weekend, after you saw him on Thursday?"

"I am not sure. I was at my daughter's and she picked me up around six Saturday morning. She comes to get me one Saturday a month so I can see my grandchildren and spend the day with them. I don't drive as much as I used to, just short distances, and she lives in Pasadena."

"Yes, ma'am, now, back to Sean Stegwig—after you got home, did you see him again?"

"Oh, I heard him leaving about six a.m. this morning; I guess he was off to work. He drives a beat up old car sometimes. But today I heard him leave on the motorcycle, it's loud. I don't always hear the garage door open even though it is on the same side as my bedroom. I am an old woman, and my hearing isn't like it was in my younger days. But it's that damn motorcycle. Dear, oh dear, please pardon my language." She covered her mouth with her hand and blushed.

Both detectives smiled. If that was the worst bad word she ever uttered, this woman was a saint compared to most others.

She held up a finger, thinking. "I heard the garage door on Saturday night, come to think of it, but I didn't hear the motorcycle. Sometimes he took his father's car, a Lexus, very nice. Sean takes his father's car when he has a rare date and not his old car, the one that needs a paint job. He wants to impress the girls."

"One more question, and then we'll let you go. I am sure you're ready to get home and try to relax."

"Yes, I'd like to go home."

This was tough on her. Perhaps her daughter needed to come get her and let her stay a few days, not just one full day.

"Was Mrs. Stegwig seeing another man? Did she confide in you?"

"Not sure, but Marta talked about her fitness coach. His name is Rob or Robbie something. He's a trainer over at the Crestview Gym. I think that's the name of the place."

A trip to Crestview Gym would be their next stop. Less than forty-five minutes later, she had told them all she knew. She had Jack's card and she would call if something came to mind.

"Ms. McGovern, it's the small things that can break a case when you don't think it matters. Call me anytime no matter how trivial you think it is. And, ma'am, be sure to lock your deadbolts when you are at home. We have no idea what we are dealing with yet."

"Oh yes, of course, I always do." There was fear in her eyes as her now upstanding neighborhood, violated in the worst possible way—two dead, murdered or not—would plague this community.

They watched her walk next door, disappear into her own house, more than sure she had dead-bolted her front door.

"Nice old lady," Lucky said as he closed his notebook and put it and his pen into his inside breast pocket.

"Too bad she lives right next door to such an awful mess. Come on, Luck, let's go see Bennie before we leave. Then see if we can catch the guy Rob or Robbie something at Crestview Gym and then head over to Red Hawk Telecommunications to make a death notification."

"Jack, I'll get them back to the morgue. I agree with Loren. If there were a gun, it would be a murder/suicide, but no gun." Bennie shrugged. "Then I can't say. But neither of these victims got up afterward and disposed of a gun. The bullet impact print on the man's head says two things—someone held a pistol to his head and blew out his brains, or he did it himself. Or the shooter moved the body into an upright position. The shooter had the vic sitting there and wanted it to look like suicide, but then why take the freaking gun?"

"There were bruises on the female's upper arm—did she have one on the other arm when you moved the body?"

"Yes and yes. She had one to match on her left arm, as if someone handled her roughly. I could tell it was old bruising by the discolorations. She had some bruising on the left side of her face, you couldn't see in the position she was laying. Someone slapped her or backhanded her; her cheek was purple with a tinge of yellow. The bruising wasn't more than a few days old, and it's not because of lividity. Whatcha thinking, that her old man did it?" Bennie put the question to him.

"That's quite possible since the neighbor and the housekeeper said the same thing in their statements."

Bennie shook his head. Domestic violence was everywhere—rich, poor. It didn't matter what your station in life was.

"Tell you guys what, when I have something useful, how about I call you?"

"Yeah, call us when you've got any news."

All of them had stuff to do, stuff which detectives and medical examiners did routinely, just like breathing.

"I HAVE the address for Crestview Gym; it's not that far from here," Lucky said.

"I guess we can get that over with."

"Why, you thinking he's a dead end?"

"He could be her man on the side, but my gut instinct says he's not our man."

If it was one thing Dawson Luck knew about his partner, his gut did some of his best police work.

Crestview Gym was an elite high-class gym, custom fit for the higher-dollar member. It featured all the regular equipment: treadmills, elliptical machines, weights, and every type of body-working machine known to humankind. The gym also had two regulation-sized tennis courts and a full-sized basketball court. The special features were a mineral pool, a Jacuzzi, aromatherapy steam room, a wellness studio that taught yoga and Pilates, with topnotch instructors. Personal trainers hired out at one-hundred-fifty an hour, and membership fees were an annual eight grand. That was a bargain, since they had a private cocktail lounge with a five-star Sushi Room.

"Wow, Jack, the other half live pretty darn good, dontcha think?" Lucky gave a low whistle.

A buxomly blonde with a twenty-inch waist wearing gym shorts and T-shirt advertising Crestview Gym, sporting a name tag that read, *Tillie*, met them at the front desk.

"You gentlemen interested in a tour?" She flashed a brilliant smile.

He flipped out his badge. "No, ma'am, I am Detective West. This is Detective Luck. We're from the HPD. Is there a trainer here who goes by the name Rob or Robbie?"

"Oh my, is he in trouble?"

Lucky stepped in using what he thinks he has—his *game*—and smiled.

"No, ma'am, we just need to talk to him. Is he here?" Lucky leaned in over the counter getting closer to her, and that's when Jack shot him a disapproving look.

She giggled nervously as she stepped back avoiding any more close contact with Detective Luck.

"Yes, he's here. I'll go find him."

"She's some kind of looker, ain't she?"

"Better than your wife, you think?" Did he have to remind his partner how lucky he was, sans the name?

Lucky cleared his throat, embarrassed.

"Nah, Jack, no one is as beautiful as she is, but hey, I am human, aren't you? Or are you the man of steel? Doesn't a honey like that get your blood churning a smidge? Hell."

"Not an inch, bro, not an inch. I like my women to know the capital of Texas is Austin and not Houston. Or if I ask if they've heard of Monty Python, and their response is, is that the name of my big snake, then nope, I'm not interested at all."

Jack wasn't sure why, but he kept Gretchen a secret. It would please the heck out of his partner and the other fellas, too. He liked this woman a lot. She was the reason he went to the Lone Star. But he hadn't even held hands with her, let alone kissed her or taken her on a date. Jack decided he needed to remedy that, and soon. He heard voices coming up, getting him out of his Gretchen trance.

"Officers, I'm Rob, Rob Mahares. What can I do for you?"

"Is there someplace we can talk?" Jack didn't want this news to spill out for everyone to hear.

"Yes, in my office. I'll come around there. Give me a sec?"

In less than one second, the man had jumped up on the front counter, then jumped over and stood in front of them.

He was about five foot eleven, with not an ounce of fat. A dark, thick head of hair and a tan Jack was sure he paid for. Gym shorts displayed bulging thigh muscles and calves that looked as if they were made of steel. His bodybuilder-type tank shirt revealed arms bulging with muscles, and as they say, he had fully loaded machine guns for biceps. The veins protruded as if they were going to burst under his skin. His muscles were that tight. Jack eyed him, thinking he had to be on the juice. Some men had pumped up muscles, no liquid enhancement needed, and they worked hard to achieve this look. Since he was a trainer, he opted for *not* for the juice.

Lucky stepped back and out of the man's way as he led them to a side office. His eyes bugged out and his big fuzzy eyebrows rose onto his forehead, making him look preposterous. Jack ignored him.

Rob Mahares sat at his desk. "Now, how can I assist you?"

"Are you acquainted with a Marta Stegwig?" Lucky took the lead.

Jack was all right with this. He knew Lucky needed the practice. "Yes, I'm her personal trainer. Why?"

"When did you last see her?"

"That would have been last week, was a Tuesday, but I can check the electronic sign-in to confirm. Why, what's going on, is she all right?" His voice had taken on a demeanor of actual concern.

"What was the nature of your acquaintance with her?"

"I have been her personal trainer for about five years now, nothing more. Why?" His eyebrows came together. "Hey, do I need an attorney or what?"

"No, sir, you're not under arrest. We're following up on a witness's statement that you were acquainted with Mrs. Stegwig. She and her husband were both found shot to death today and we—"

Rob cut him off mid-sentence. "You're kidding. Oh my God, oh my God," he repeated.

"No, sir, we don't kid about these things." Lucky continued the questioning. "Mr. Mahares, can I call you Rob?"

"Uh-huh, sure, Rob is fine." He was in shock.

"Now, Rob, being her trainer for five years, I image you got to know her well, is that correct?"

"We were friends." He bowed his head, shaking it sadly. "Were, as in past tense, which has an awful ring, you know?"

"Yes, it does. Tell me about your friendship with Mrs. Stegwig."

"She and I talked about our lives, and about our problems. I am—was—like your therapist or bartender would be. I keep your secrets. Marta was having some problems at home. She and her old man were fighting."

"Did she say what they fought about?"

"She said Mark would get aggressive when he drank. She tried to stay out of his way. I'd seen bruising on her over the past year at irregular intervals and she would just wave it off. She'd been unhappy the past year, and last month she told me she was going to see a lawyer."

"Was she seeing someone on the side?"

Rob wasn't stupid; he knew where this was going.

"Listen let's get something straight here. First, I would never compromise my job here at Crestview. It's the best job I've ever had. I've been here now for almost nine years, and I have a cash investment in the place. I would never jeopardize that. Second, I am seeing someone. I never mix work and pleasure and you can call *him* to confirm."

Dawson Luck tried to keep the surprise from his face but failed miserably. Jack showed no signs of surprise by the admission that Rob Mahares was homosexual. He knew you should register nothing on your face, always keeping your facial canvas as blank as possible.

"That surprises you, Detective Luck? Why, because I work out and have a build like this, you know, *buff*, and I am a trainer and everything?" Rob looked at him with a tiny eyebrow raise and winked, and held in his laugh.

"I don't know, I guess it does, that's all."

"To each his own, Rob, we don't judge," Jack jumped in. Crap, Lucky had been doing well with the interview, until now.

"Marta was very comfortable talking to me. I was no threat to her, as far as relationships go."

"Did she ever discuss other problems with you, like money or her kids?" Jack now took the lead edging his partner out.

"She didn't get to see to her daughter as often as she liked. She lives in Dallas. Her son, he was a horse of a different color, and no, Detective Luck, he was straight." He grinned at Dawson Luck.

"What makes you say this about her son, Rob?"

"He was his father's son. Sean hated her. Evidently, he hung on every word his father said, more like he hung onto his wallet. I'll tell you the money was from Marta's family; Marcus had no money before he married her. She helped Marcus create the money he had, but she was the financial backbone. She told me her son was hateful to her, but then again I didn't witness it. Is that what you guys call hearsay?"

"Yes, it is, and I'll take all the information you have because you never know what other stories people may tell us that corroborate with your hearsay. Rob, I think that's all for now. You have no plans to leave town, right?" He was sure this man was not his perp, but this was his standing spiel.

Rob Mahares let loose a genuine laugh. "Cop talk—*don't leave town.* Yes, I watch *Law and Order* and *Criminal Minds,* Detectives, and I'm not leaving town. I work here five days a week and my off days differ from week to week, but they have all my contact info."

"Can we get that info from you now or should we ask the blonde up front?" Lucky piped up.

Jack closed his eyes with a teeny head-shake. His partner was a maniac.

"Mr. Mahares, please give me your home address and your phone number so I can reach you, and here's my card in case you remember something."

JACK STARTED THE TRUCK, a little aggravated by his partner.

"Lucky, you know better than to care one way or another about the sexuality of a person and never act shocked."

"Shit, Jack, that took me by surprise, and, uh, I apologize about the comments about the blonde chick that was out of line. We're working on a case and I should be more professional, sorry."

That would work for him until it happened again, which he knew it would.

They left Crestview Gym, satisfied Rob Mahares was not a viable suspect.

"Off to find this Sean at this stupid telcom company Red Hawk. The address is, uh, over on Bissonnet Street, I mapped it. The building is in a strip center near the corner of Bissonnet and Highway 6. Are you familiar with the area, Jack?"

"Yes, there's a Starbucks and a Panda Express and across the street is a pharmacy, not sure which one though."

"What do you say when we're done, we grab a bite before we head back to write up our kajillion reports?"

"Yep, right after we do a death notification and question this kid."

Jack headed to do a deed he didn't enjoy doing and to ask questions he hated asking at a time like this.

11

The building was small. Jack looked up at the sign. It was a picture of a Red Hawk with the words, "Red Hawk Tel Com" underneath the tail feathers.

The place was drab, devoid of decorations, and smelled musty. Inside a small front office sat an old metal desk and behind that sat a young girl somewhere in her mid-twenties.

"May I help you?" Zero enthusiasm; she was apparently bored beyond bored.

"Yes, ma'am, I'm Detective West. This is Detective Luck. We're from the Houston Police Department. Is Sean Stegwig here?" He badged her.

Police detectives! That snapped her out of her stupor.

"Uh, he's in the back; I'll go get him." She jumped out of the dilapidated office chair and darted through the door behind her.

"We should inform the city health inspector. Tell them they need to do a thorough inspection. The place smells like something died in the walls or like raw sewage. You smell that? How can she stand working with that odor?"

"You can report it, Lucky. Right now that's not my biggest worry."

Sean Stegwig came through the door, followed by the young girl. Sean was about five foot eight, one hundred thirty pounds, with a peach-fuzz goatee, and he needed some Clearasil. Dressed in baggy jeans and a T-shirt with the name of some local metal band, he was stylishly unkempt, or a downright slob. His shirt had *Battle of the Unsigned Bands Contest 2011—Black Shadow Rises. Support your local Houston Boys*, written in orange, yellow, black, and red across the top and the bottom, touting this band contest.

He didn't portray an up-and-coming entrepreneur or the son of a wealthy couple. He reminded him of the nerds in school, those who had dark secrets. Dahmer came to mind. That was a scary thought. Those nerds and outcasts back in his day had been unassuming and invisible when he was a kid, and this is how he saw Sean Stegwig, one of those types.

"Sean Stegwig?"

"Yeah, Darla said you want to speak with me. What about?"

"Is there a private office where we can talk?" He glanced over at the young girl, who was latching onto every word.

"My office is back this way."

His office was stale-smelling and in a dirty mess. Papers askew, empty Diet Sprite cans, and disposable coffee cups littered his desk. Work files and papers were scattered on his desk and on the floor. Jack noted the trash cans were full and tamped down. He scanned the area and saw a pile in one corner. He noted a pair of tennis shoes, ragged jeans, and T-shirts, and a blanket with a pillow on top.

Sean pointed to a chair across from his old metal desk. "Give me a second, and I'll go get another chair."

"No, Mr. Stegwig," Dawson Luck said, "I'll stand."

"Mr. Stegwig, my name is Jack West, and this is Dawson Luck, and we're homicide detectives from the HPD." Jack unclipped his badge and showed it to him.

"What's this about?"

He studied his face. If a homicide detective came calling, most people would act upset. Not this boy.

"It is about your parents, Mr. Stegwig. I am sorry to inform you they were both found dead, and we are deeply sorry for your loss."

He watched him to get a real handle on this boy's reaction to such horrible news.

"My mother and father are d-d-dead?" He slouched in his chair, not acting hysterical like most kids would've reacted to such horrific news. He lowered his eyes as if he was giving respect to the dead—that act would not win him any Oscars.

Neither Jack nor Lucky spoke. Uncomfortable silence most often triggered someone to speak. Sean Stegwig broke the awkward silence. "I-I-I can't believe this, my parents, d-d-dead, d-d-dead." His stutter not convincing. Again, this was no Oscar-rated performance.

"We realize this is a bad time for you, but we have a few questions, then I am sure you'll want to call your sister in Dallas. Best coming from you, don't you think?" He kept a close eye on his reactions.

"Uh, yeah, I hafta to call Shayla and arrange the funerals. They both wanted to be cremated, I think. I'll ask my sister. Should I call my attorney about the will and any insurance benefits?"

"Mr. Stegwig, there's a bunch of red tape before we can give you the go-ahead to have their bodies released to a funeral home. We have some questions first."

His inquiry about calling the attorney and already talking about insurance benefits put Jack on high alert. Second, Sean had not asked how his parents' demise had come about. Had they been in an automobile accident, were they murdered, did they get it from a drive by—no damn questions at all, and this wasn't a good sign.

Sean Stegwig nodded still unemotional. "Fine, what can I answer for you?" The young twat's voice was tight.

"Detective Luck, will you please take notes?"

He looked at Jack, his mouth dropped open, then he shut it, and he pressed his lips in a flat line, nodding.

"Sean, when was the last time you saw your mother or father?"

"Let me think, that would have been I believe, let's see, today is Monday, I saw them last on Thursday of last week."

"How often do you see them, every day, every other day?"

"Not every day. They have, or rather *had,* their lives, and I had mine. I'm independent of my parents." The young kid half-pouted, showing little to no grief.

Jack noted the dingy office walls and a single picture. A red-tailed hawk hanging crookedly in a cheap frame behind Sean's desk. "But you live on their property in a converted pool house."

He turned back to see the boy.

"I'm not on a curfew or have to answer to them. I'm on my own." He acted indignant that someone would think he was under his parents' domain and rule at his age. Sean sweated, although the room was relatively cool, and his body language became twitchy.

"Okay, so you lived your own life, rent free, no house expenses, bill free, huh?" Jack prodded into his personal life.

"Just because I've had it better than most people my age doesn't mean shit. So, Detective, what are you getting at?" He leaned back and through hooded eyelids looked at Jack.

"Trying to figure out why, if you lived on the premises, you never saw your folks."

"I saw them, but not every single day. We tried to eat a meal together on the weekends but—" He stopped.

"You didn't see them this weekend? Why not?" If he admitted to seeing them, he knew they were dead.

"I went—I was not home, and I needed to get away. Is that a crime?" he ground out.

Jack ignored his question.

"When did you leave and where did you go?"

"You're asking for my alibi? My parents are dead. You waltz in here and spring that on me, then what, you give me the third degree. Am I a suspect or what?" His face got red and his eyes popped. Anger washed over him.

"We have to investigate. This is what we do. We ask questions, hard ones, intrusive ones, but we do it, we ask questions. We're going to stop for now, Sean. You need to call your sister, and in a couple of days we'll be contacting you again."

"I'm sorry, but this is j-j-just too much to take all at once. I hafta go call Shayla and I—need to go." His voice was back to normal.

"We can show ourselves out. Here's my card. Call me if you think of anything that might help us. And just like the T.V. cops tell everyone, don't leave town." Jack stuck his hand out and Sean reciprocated.

"Again, we are very sorry for your loss, Sean."

Sean mumbled his thanks, preoccupied with his own thoughts.

Jack doubted the boy was thinking about his dead parents.

Once they were out of earshot and in the truck, Lucky griped. "What gives, now I'm your stenographer?"

"Teach you a lesson about dealing with people. How was I to know the sexual orientation of this kid, or how you'd react?"

"You're an ass, a Jack *ass*, West."

"This jackass knows the boy is lying through his teeth. Get a search warrant for his office and the pool house. No one searched the pool house, did they?"

"No, the pool house wasn't searched, and I admit, he didn't act broken up about his parents. Whatcha got up your sleeve, Tall Drink?"

Jack rolled his eyes. "Lucky, if you don't want a punch in your big honker," Jack warned him.

"All right already, I'll stop with the tall drink thingy. What did you get in there, a premonition, gut instinct, or what?"

"His office is a huge disaster. He needs a housekeeper like Mrs., uh, what was her name?"

"Beatrice Gonzales."

"She'd have that place spotless. He must not have a cleaning crew unless he has Darla taking out the trash, cleaning the toilets, and doing the janitorial job. She's an airhead, the kind that doesn't break a fingernail, not even at her own desk. What I saw in the far corner behind where I was sitting was a pile of clothes, a blanket, and a pillow. He was lying, he slept at his office, and that, my friend, was his 'getaway.' He was hot to trot on calling about their wills and the life insurance policies. Plus, he never answered my question about where he went to get away. Check your notes, Miss Macgillicuddy."

"Yeah, he never answered the question, did he?"

"Lucky, drive around the corner, then go park by the pharmacy. We're going to see if he takes any trash to the dumpster."

"Why?"

"If he tosses anything into the dumpster, we're going to confiscate it. He dumps it, it's free pickings."

"You think he's tossing incriminating trash?"

"It ain't gonna hurt to check. If there's nothing, there's nothing, but if there's something, there's something."

"You're a loon, Jack, a real loon."

In the parking lot, on the corner across the street, they watched the building. Sean Stegwig came around from the back carrying three overlarge trash bags twenty minutes later. He tossed them into the dumpster next to the building, headed toward his motorcycle, and they watched him leave.

"Going for a dumpster run, so put some latex gloves on. We'll catch the captain up and then we'll be digging in this trash."

In the captain's office, Jack updated him on the case while Lucky started the warrant paperwork.

"What are you thinking, Jack? You thinking the son did them?" Captain Yao sat back, tilting his chair.

"Not sure, but he's lying about not knowing something. I think he found them and he took the gun, but why didn't he call it in? That has me doing a head scratch."

"Your gut is telling you something?"

"My gut tells me a lot, Davis, like when to eat. However you want to spin it though, my gut, or my intuition, tells me something's not right."

"Listen, I know the Stegwig name, Jack. Marta Stegwig is, rather was, loaded; not sure how much her net worth was. She kept a low profile, but word on the street was she had it to burn. From what you're telling me, it doesn't sound like it was a robbery gone sideways. We still have all the other reasons people commit murder to look into though, you know, revenge, jealousy, or greed."

"Yeah, I know all too well, Davis."

"Keep me posted on your progress, Jack."

"Will do, Cap."

Back at his desk, Jack picked up his messages.

The first one was from a woman named Daphne Walden. The message said to please call her; something about a person named Celeste Mason. His brows shot up. A call about the cold case—that was unexpected. The new case took priority; the cold case was on hold. He stuck the message in his pocket. He would call her back in a few days, he hoped.

The second message was from a woman named Gretchen. "Fetchin' Gretchen," as Jack called her, and she bartended at the Lone Star Saloon. The bar sat at the corner of St. Joseph and Travis Street. He enjoyed going there for a beer when he closed an investigation. He felt comfortable there, sitting on the end corner of the bar, nursing a beer and people-watching. The first night he had stepped foot in the bar was when the Griffin murder investigation was closed. After that, it became his regular place to sit and have a beer. Jack never went in as Detective West, he just wanted to wear the regular drinking man's shoes, drink, and ponder life.

Besides, he wasn't going there to meet a girl or for a hookup until Gretchen came to work there. She made him smile. He did not go there just to unwind any longer, now he went hoping to see her. He had let it slip that he was a cop one night, and she was easy to talk to;

and, as the saying goes, your bartender is your therapist, just like your barber.

He opened up to her about the case of the murdered fifteen-year-old. Gretchen gave him her full attention that night. He had given her his card and told her to call him anytime. The message simply said, *Jack, when you can stop by the Lone Star, I'll buy you a beer; miss seeing you, Gretchen.* Jack slipped that message into his wallet. He did not have time for her right now, but damn, he needed to make the time. Deep down he was sure she would be worth it. Jack promised himself he would call her no matter what case he was knee deep into working. Or should call her before he cracked the case; women did not wait forever. The cold case, sure he wanted to get back on it, but he needed a life.

Jack woke from his daydreaming of I need to get a life *and* thoughts of Gretchen when his phone rang. He glanced at the blinking numbers in the corner of his monitor. It was almost 7:40; who was working this late?

"Jack West, Homicide, Bennie, got a report, some good news for me?"

"You think it's too late to swing by the morgue? I've got some interesting stuff I wanna show you." His voice had a certain giddy lilt.

"If you've got something interesting to show us, it's never too late. Be there in twenty, you're still going to be there?"

"If I ask you to come by, Jack, it means I'll be here, you dumbass. Use the rear entrance. The place is dead right now." Laughing at his joke, he hung up.

Jack thought Bennie was a hair wacky.

"Lucky, you got the warrant written up yet?" Jack walked around the desk, hovering over Luck's shoulder.

"Yep, all that's missing is a signature."

"Come on, we've been summoned by Bennie. He has something for us, and he sounds giddy. When we're done there, we'll come back and go through the trash that we fished out of Stegwig's dumpster."

"Well, yippee, Jack, I can hardly contain my happiness."

"Quit being a sad sack, and before we leave, let's fax the warrants over to the criminal courts building. On the cover page, tell 'em we'll pick them up first thing in the morning."

"Yeah, yeah, I'm gonna call the wife on the way, tell her I'll be getting home even later." It had been a damn long day and he, for one, was ready to quit and start over in the morning.

"Let's go see what Bennie has." Jack was excited anytime Bennie wanted to show them something—it meant something was going to happen.

"Lord, Jack, when the morgue is closed and this quiet it always creeps me out." Lucky scanned his I.D. card over the laser eye to the rear door to gain access.

"Not a place I'd want to be alone in at night either."

They'd both seen enough dead bodies at crime scenes and in the morgue. But it was nothing like being alone in a funeral home with dead bodies. The eerie sense you got like you weren't alone, and someone was watching you from *beyond*.

Bennie stood in the autopsy room with a ham and cheese sandwich in one hand and a Diet Coke in the other. On the stainless steel table the corpse of Marcus Stegwig. The dead man's upper body exposed his chest and sewn up in the obligatory Y, with a white sheet covering his lower half. Mrs. Stegwig lay chilling in the cadaver lockers in the back.

"You guys want to split a sandwich? I have another ham and cheese on rye in the fridge." He chomped again, taking another bite, following it up with a sip of his Coke.

The look on Dawson's face made Jack laugh. "Man, he doesn't keep his lunch in the cadaver freezer. He keeps them in the fridge next to it."

"I'll have to pass, Bennie, I don't like the dinner company altogether." Dawson glanced at Marcus Stegwig on the autopsy table.

Food and cadavers, these were never a great combo. Lucky still had a weak stomach. He was better than he used to be. At least now he no longer turned green and headed for the nearest toilet.

"Nah, Ben, we'll grab a bite on our way out. There's a James Coney Island on our way back, and I've been craving a chili cheese coney, but thanks all the same. Whatcha got for us?"

Bennie walked over to the LED x-ray view box and motioned for them to follow, his mouth full of ham and cheese. "Commere," he garbled.

Flipping on the light, an x-ray of a skull with a hole in the right temple emerged.

"Picture of our boy here on the table's skull?" Jack leaned in toward the x-ray.

"Yep, sure is. See this,"—he pointed out—"what do you imagine that is?" He stood back grinning.

"A bullet...well, I'll be Jack Sprat."

"No, you'd be Jack West, and that would be bullet number two."

"Didn't Loren take a bullet out of the wall? I thought they only found the one shell casing by the body."

Dawson took his turn looking at the x-ray and then turned his head to the dead body that lay on the steel table. "He was shot twice, is that it?"

"So it would seem, Lucky, so it would seem. The bullet," Bennie began, "or the first one I should say, went in then exited out. CSU found it lodged into the second layer of the wood in the doorjamb. The second time, whoever shot the gun held it at a different angle against the same entry point. The bullet went in, but it lodged in his skull, which means no second exit wound. Up close and personal, the first bullet was a through and through. The guy's brain mass was damaged from the first shot.

A .22 caliber does most of the damage by bouncing around. That's why they're lethal. The second bullet bounced off already messed-up brain matter, and it lodged in the parietal bone. I would venture to say it tumbled around then, hitting the bone, it stopped bouncing. The shooter left two things—one shell casing and the second bullet in the skull, but no second shell casing. I'm betting your shooter searched for the second bullet, not knowing it had lodged in a wall. When he couldn't find it, he got frustrated, so he quit looking. If your shooter had any idea, it was in the head, I doubt whoever this person was, would not dig in the dead man's skull to retrieve it."

"We can clearly rule out a murder/suicide, right?"

"You know, the Mr. could've been the wife's doer, then someone else came in and *he* got it. That doesn't even sound plausible now that I've said it aloud. The mister got it twice. I just don't see it. Did he shoot himself first and then someone came in and shot him again? What had the second shot been for, good measure?"

The three of them stood staring at the x-ray. Jack continued his thoughts aloud.

"Could someone have walked in, saw that the husband killed the wife, got mad, then shot him and made it look like a suicide? Did the mister get off a first shot? Then it wasn't enough to do the job, and he could pull off the second shot? After that, what, he got up and disposed of the gun? That's all pretty inconceivable."

"No, the first shot was clearly the kill shot. It hit the gray matter. He may not have died instantly, but he wasn't going anywhere, and he wasn't capable of taking a second shot. The first bullet's trajectory hit the parietal lobe taking out his eye-hand coordination. He wouldn't have been able to take the gun in his hand and reshoot. He had no coordination to do that, and it nicked his motor sensory. But there's more."

They waited as he took the last bite of his sandwich, smacking his lips. "Ah. That hit the spot until I get home. Come here, let me show you." Bennie walked over to another long countertop where microscopes, glass slides, petri dishes, and glass tubes set in nice neat rows in holders with a plethora of chemicals.

"In my examination of the clothing for any trace evidence, I found three hairs on the man's slacks. They appeared to be the same color as the victim's. I took a hair sample from our boy over there and then got a hair from the misses, and it wasn't her hair nor was it his. I'm thinking it was our suspect's, but I have nothing to match it to."

"The housekeeper has medium to dark brown hair. It could have been transferred somehow, hypothetically, that is." Lucky scratched his head.

"Could be," Bennie said, finishing his soda and tossing the can in the wastebasket. "Get a sample and I can check."

"The son has brown hair too." Jack's heart kicked up a notch. He was itching to get to dig in the trash bags. "What about her?" Jack thumbed toward the cadaver lockers. "Whatdaya get on her?"

"She was hit in the throat, would have bled out, but there was so much blood in her lungs she aspirated in seconds. Other than that, she was in excellent health for a woman of her age. She had bruises in other areas, old and new bruising like her old man may have smacked her around. When I opened her up, her right ribs were broken and splintered. Someone kicked her damn hard, but she didn't feel a thing. She was kicked postmortem. Whoever killed her had pent-up rage."

"That would account for the blood smear. It had to be the killer's shoe. At least she didn't feel the kick to the ribs." It disgusted Lucky that the killer had already killed and then inflicted more violence on the victim.

"I guess I'll never understand it. To be murdered is an awful thing. Then someone kicks your lifeless body viciously. That's just monstrous. That's pure hatred of the worst kind. You guys know I understand the medical aspects. I have to say the psychological issues will always be a mystery to me." Bennie never wanted to be in the head or mind of a psychopathic killer. Everyone knew that was a scary place to be.

"You get anything off the shoes?" Jack got back to business.

"We didn't find any blood on her husband's shoes, not a speck, just dirt, and nothing usable. He could have hit her, but no item in the room had any blood on it. The killer was someone else, which to me is the obvious conclusion, but you fellas will have to confirm that. I did tox screens but won't have 'em back for a few days. As soon as the reports are in, I'll call you."

Bennie had been a wealth of information. It was all fishy, the way Sean had reacted, and Jack got a gut feeling. They needed to search the pool house. Two bullets—yeah, they needed to get into that pool house. Tonight they would both be digging in the trash, hoping to find any kind of clue.

"Got your booties and gloves, Jack? Here's a mask. We don't want to inhale trash odor. No telling what's in these bags."

"You take a bag, and I'll take a bag. Cripes, the boy has both of them stuffed, no telling what we'll find."

"Let's dump, I'm not digging." Lucky had no desire to stick half his body into these large, nasty trash bags.

"Sounds like a plan. There's a broom in the corner. Whatever is left we'll bag and take it to the dumpster."

The bags were the large contractor bags stuffed full. Papers from his company, along with gross items Dawson Luck pointed out from the bathroom—"ladies trash" he called it.

Jack sifted through gross trash. Under the piles of paper trash, he found a pair of men's white sneakers. The kind you wore on a boat, the kind that slipped on your feet with no laces. They were tatty and worn, and they were wet. He held one up, and he sniffed it. Bleach, he smelled bleach.

"Here, what do you smell, Lucky?" He held one up under his partner's nose. Dawson sniffed.

"Smells like a cover-up or an attempt. I smell bleach, Jack-Oh." Man, he was Jack Rabbit, Jack in the Beanstalk, Jack-o-Lantern, and Jumping Jack Flash, and all of this was okay. He was not a Tall Drink of Water. That was where he drew the line.

"Hand me an evidence bag, gonna bag 'em for Bennie. Keep digging, we don't quit till we sort this out."

"Lookie here, Jack, a pair of ragtag jeans rolled up with large rubber bands."

He slipped off the rubber bands and found a wet orange t-shirt rolled up inside the jeans. "He must've dumped these in last. They were underneath a pile of wet papers, and other shit I won't mention."

Jack reached over and took the wet t-shirt. "It seems he tried to rinse them out. I hate to say it, but that looks like blood."

"Here, I'll bag the shirt and the jeans and you pack the shoes, Jack."

"That boy is looking more and more like our suspect. He could claim he found them dead. He got upset getting blood on him, and he was nervous, so he left. That was how he got his clothes tainted. He could play that angle. We need a motive, and we hafta find the gun." Jack took stock of all the trash scattered on the floor.

"So, we keep digging through the rest of this pigsty." Lucky continued sifting through papers. Ten minutes later he whistled, and Jack looked up.

"You find a written confession?"

"No, it's a trust form, the kind you fill out and have signed to withdraw money. It isn't signed, it's just filled out. Take a gander at the amount in the far right column."

"Now there are, I would venture to say, three million motives for murder, you agree, pard?"

Lucky turned his lips downward. "Uh-huh, and I've seen murder done for twenty bucks, stinks, huh?"

"Like this putrid trash. Keep looking, the more we find, the more we have and the more solid of a case, if that pans out."

They had shoes that smelled like bleach, wet jeans and T-shirt, with possible blood, and the form for the early extraction of funds. What was missing was a gun or witnesses that put Sean at the scene. He lived in the house, too. That would explain his prints or other

DNA. Other than the trust fund monies, no other motive jumped out. But three million was more than enough motive for any cop to investigate.

"I think we've dug enough. Let's get this garbage bagged back up and go get a beer. You game?" Jack got the broom and pushed the trash into a pile that they could bag up and dump.

"Sure, why not? Got a place in mind? I'll call the wife and let her know."

"It's too early to go to the Fifth Amendment. They don't open until ten o'clock. How about Proof's Rooftop Lounge or Frank's Backyard? Both have decent food. We can have a beer, or I know you like Jack and Coke and both are close, so won't have far to drive. You choose, Luck, I'm fine with wherever we go."

"Frank's, I like the burgers. One Coney didn't fill this boy up, and a burger and beer would hit the spot. I'll call the wife."

They sat at Frank's Backyard up to 11:30 drinking a few beers and eating.

Jack was replete when he dropped into bed. He needed to hit the department's gym soon. Not that he worried about staying in shape, but age was a factor and he would not end up like the paunchy front desk Sargent, Cal Wickers. The man had been on the force for nearly twenty-five years, and he could not outrun one of the ocean's manatees known as the sea cow. Wickers rather looked like the manatees with his huge paunch and a slick bald head, and he had a nice word for everyone he met.

At six one and two hundred ten pounds, Jack was a clean-shaven man with dark eyes and a boyish grin that gave a hint to small dimples on both cheeks. The reason there was no woman in his life was no mystery. It was the job and the complications his job instigated. He had a few ongoing relationships in the past, but the job was a stumbling block because he was driven. Most women would not take a backseat to his occupation. This wasn't a huge worry though. One day the right woman for him would come along, he hoped, before he was fifty. Somewhere in the recess of his mind, he had figured the right woman might be in law enforcement or in the legal trade, or an attorney; she would understand him much better than the regular female did. Gretchen popped into his head. A detective and a gorgeous bartender—well somewhere there was a joke, but he couldn't think of one.

12

J ack was getting out of his truck when Lucky pulled in and parked beside him.

"Morning, Dawson, how are ya?"

His voice in sleep mode, he yawned. "Dang tired, wife wanted to hear all about it, and then, you know." He blushed.

Jack knew all right, he knew Dawson Luck was a blessed man, and he hoped one day to be as blessed. From his mouth to God's ear, he thought.

"Let's go up. I'll get the reports to the captain and grab a cup of jo before we strike out, okay?" Dawson stifled a yawn.

"Yup, coffee is necessary today."

They hit the break room first, headed to the pot of coffee that was blackest and smelled burned, brewed by the night shift; it would be strong.

Reports in a nice neat stack on Captain Davis Yao's desk, they headed to the courthouse to get the warrants.

"Been a while since I've seen ya, Detective West, you fine hunk of a man."

Jack blushed. Mava always had that effect on him even though the woman was nearing sixty, but you would not know it unless she told you. She was tall and lithe, with a massive mane of hair and a sparkle in her eyes that had not died, fortunately for her husband. Mava would have chased him, had she been twenty-five years younger and single.

One day she'd let that slip out, embarrassing him to death.

"Hey, Mava, how are you?"

"Since I've seen you, I am wonderful. Hey, Detective Luck, very nice to see you too. How are y'all?"

Pleasantries over with, Dawson Luck got down to business.

"Mava, I faxed over some warrants last night. Did you get them?"

"Yes, I did, and Judge Wolff has them. He's in chambers. You want to see if he is accepting visitors?" She winked at Jack.

"Uh, yes, ma'am, if you would, that would be mighty fine." Jack winked back and gave her his best dazzling smile. It was Mava's turn to blush and giggle.

Ten minutes later, they were in Judge Wolff's chambers discussing warrants, and Jack briefed the judge on the situation.

Wolff had been a judge in Houston for over twenty years. Most considered him a fair man. He had been a bang-up lawyer in his day, and his private practice flourished back in the late sixties until the late nineties. Then he ran for placement as a judge and won, and remained steadfast, winning each judicial election consecutively.

Jack and Judge Wolff did not always see eye to eye. As a beat cop, there were rumors about the judge being unfaithful to his wife and being corrupt. Overall, since Jack had been a detective, he had no problems with Judge Wolff, and scoffed at the rumors, taking them as being rumors and nothing more.

"You think this Sean Stegwig looks good for the murders, Jack?" Judge Wolff read over the search warrant.

"Judge, this kid, Sean Stegwig, has about three million motives for being the doer. I dropped off the tennis shoes, wet T-shirt, and jeans we found in his trash at the forensic lab. I'm telling you, he's going to find blood on them and not the kid's blood either. The kid didn't even ask what happened, how they died, nothing, not a damn question, not one. He faked his emotions. I've seen this before. The first thing he asked us was should he contact the attorney about the will and life insurance policies and a red flag popped up."

"No gun, no prints, no witnesses. Jack, you know how hard cases like that are. I understand that there were two shots to the man. It very well could've been an intruder. Before I sign the warrants, what's your probable cause?"

Jack's nose flared, his patience wearing thin.

"Three million reasons, Judge, is that enough PC? The dead woman was kicked in her ribs, hard. Whoever did this was furious, so this was personal, not a random intruder. I would stake my badge on it."

Judge Wolff looked up. Lucky knew not to get in the middle. He had been there before. It was not an enjoyable place to be standing between Jack and any judge when Jack was in full swing and excited.

"I'm sorry, Judge."

"Jack, I know you. Known you for over fifteen years, and when you get excited, you're passionate. I also know, ninety percent of the time you get it right with the occasional hiccup here and there. I realize there are two bullets, but the gun is missing. Find the gun, Jack, that's imperative. My job is to make sure *we* are all doing our jobs and in a legal manner. I do not have to tell you the consequences of getting it wrong, now do I?"

"No, I understand."

"With that being stated, I am going to sign this search warrant and there better be good news afterward. Get with forensics to rush those shoes, jeans, and T-shirt, find her blood, Jack, and that gives it all a whole new spin. You got me?"

"Thanks, Judge, and yes, I'll call the lab on the way out, get them to put a rush on it. I'm telling you, I feel it here,"—he pointed to his gut, then he pointed to his heart.

"Yeah, when I feel things there, it means I am hungry or I have heartburn. Now get out of my chambers, I have work to do." The judge had his own problems to deal with.

Back in the truck in less than three minutes, without a word Dawson Luck picked up his own cell and punched in the medical examiner's number. "Hey, Bennie, this is Dawson, yeah, we're both good. Listen, I am calling to see if you can put a rush on the tennis shoes, jeans, and T-shirt. Yeah, call us, either of us, thanks, man."

"So?" Jack asked, as he focused on the road.

"He's on it, soon as he finishes up on a victim brought in from last night. 7-11 caught a new case. A store manager at Quickie Mart got popped, going to ask 'em about it later."

Jack punched in Cassandra Sparrow's cell.

"Hey, Cass, it's West, is the crime scene over in Glen Cove still taped off? Yeah? Sure, thanks."

"What did Cass say?"

"The daughter, Shayla Stegwig Burdett, is at the house. She got here from Dallas yesterday afternoon. She called the department, she wanted to remove the crime scene tape, it was upsetting her. Cass got the call from her. She had left her card with the housekeeper who showed up at the house. Nice lady, that Beatrice Gonzales, she had her husband drive her over to help the son but was happy to see the daughter there instead."

It was 10:15. "You ready to get this one solved, cuz I have that feeling?"

"Yeppers, partner, let's get this done."

ONCE A NEIGHBORHOOD WAS MARRED with a heinous crime such as this, it never felt the same. People were fearful, somber, and overall distrusting of everyone. Jack felt the ambiance as he drove into the neighborhood. It was a ghost town. No one was active, and not even a dog yipped. Dawson Luck felt it too.

"Sad that such an affluent community had to go through this type of criminality, isn't it?"

"Sad *any* neighborhood has to go through it, but I suppose you're right, they don't get this type of issue often, not like the people in lower-income families do. Hell, these people have a chance—on the other side of the tracks, many lives are doomed, being poor can cost you your life. Gangs, drugs, and some people have no blessed chance to escape the hood."

His mind went to the victim of his cold case. She had been poor and alone, and she had ended up dead.

Knocking on the door, a woman answered, her eyes red and swollen, and her face blotchy from crying.

"Mrs. Burdett, Shayla Burdett?"

"I-I-I'm sorry, I'm not interested in buying anything, and I have no comment for you if you are a reporter."

Well, shit and shinola, this was the second time he had been mistaken for a salesman, now a reporter. What was it, should he get a different haircut? Crap, most of the time he got made.

"No, ma'am, I'm Detective Jack West, this is Detective Dawson Luck, and we're from the Hou—"

The woman rushed her words not letting him finish. "Yes, yes, please come in." Sniffing she opened the door to let them pass and then peering out, she looked left and right, then shut the door, and locked it. Jack watched as her hands trembled.

"I—I'm sorry it has been very frightful here, and I'm—" She raised her palms, knowing that both detectives needed no further explanation.

Leading them into the front sitting area, she took a seat, motioning for them to do the same. "Please, have a seat, won't you?"

"Ma'am, first—" Jack began. "We're very sorry for your loss, and we know how hard it is for you right now." He held up the search warrant. "This is a search warrant for the pool house. After we've looked inside, we would like to talk to you."

"I'm not sure I understand. Weren't the police already here once when they found m-m-my parents? Didn't you get everything you n-n-needed then?"

She broke out with fresh tears.

"Ma'am, we apologize. Yes, we were here."

She blew her nose and wiped her eyes. "Where is your brother, Sean?"

"At his skanky office and on a day I need him here. You'd think he'd put his damn work on hold at least until we bury them. I don't understand him one iota."

Her disapproval was obvious, and her tears were replaced with anger, anger that she was alone when she needed her brother. "He hasn't lifted a finger to call anyone to make any arrangements. I'm doing it all alone." She wiped away a straggler tear.

"Did he say when he would be home?" Lucky threw in.

"When he got 'damn well ready to be here,' his words exactly, I quote." Her hostility shot out, her nostrils flared. She was furious. Sean laid it at her feet, to shoulder the burden alone.

"Mrs. Burdett, tell us about your mother and father, their relationship with each other, with Sean," Jack said, "and with you."

"Why? Why do our relationships with each other matter?"

"Trying to get some facts straight, Mrs. Burdett. If we know everything, even things you think wouldn't matter, we can see a bigger picture of what may have occurred."

"Sure, but please call me Shayla. Mrs. Burdett is my mother-in-law." A hint of bitterness slipped into her voice.

"Okay, Shayla. Can you tell us about your parents and their relationship?"

"I'm sure they were great together, in the beginning, you know, young love. Then they started a family, my father began his investment career and did well, more often than not, he made money. My mother came from old money, but he resented her for that later on in their lives."

She hesitated for a minute. "I guess it doesn't matter now that they are both gone. My father drank, oh, at first not that bad, but it developed into a nasty situation over the years."

She sat pensively for a few moments, a wry smile on her face.

"Ahem." Lucky cleared his throat to get her attention.

"I am sorry. Ten months ago, my mother had confided in me that my father had been slapping her around. It was infrequent at first and he was sorely apologetic the next day, saying it was the alcohol. You know the story I am sure. When his drinking binges came over three times a week, she got to where she would stay clear of him altogether. I think it was about four months ago, he lost on a large investment and got very depressed, the drinking got worse. If my father killed her then himself, I understand why. I wished she had tried to leave him sooner."

Shayla stopped crying and all the emotions the surviving goes through—sadness and sorrow, anger and hatred—afterward the guilt overwhelmed you because you lived and they didn't. Emotions were waging a war inside of her. Jack wasn't sure which end of the spectrum Shayla was at, but he felt she had all feelings rattling inside that were trying to escape one right after the other. It had been that way with Cole; he understood.

"There's more, isn't there?"

"My mother had her own money, but she wouldn't give my father or Sean another dime. She told me that my father was angrier than ever and got even meaner. Dad gave Sean start-up money for that stupid telecommunications business. His motto is that he is the eye of the hawk for his customers." Her laugh was involuntary. "He was always a goober. His business is in the red, the building is about shot, and he has other money problems my mom told me about."

Tears she didn't know she had left filled her eyes. It was apparent to see that she and her mother had been close.

"Sean owed a great deal of money for gambling, and on a get-rich-quick scheme. He wanted her to sign over his trust to him early."

Jack gave Lucky a sideways glance.

"She didn't want to do it?" Lucky pressed her to go on with her story.

"My mother *is*, sorry, she *was*,"—she exhaled—"a very staunch believer on a few things. If you wanted something, you had to work hard to get it. Any dream you felt was worthy of your hard work, then it was worth it. If you had to wait because getting to your dream took longer and you had to work harder, you learned patience. Sean knew nothing about hard work or waiting. He wanted things to fall neatly into his lap. Patience was not a virtue he exhibited. Our mom thought thirty was the right age to have the responsibility of a large amount of cash. I'm six years older than Sean is, and I received my full trust four years ago. He doesn't know how much. It was substantially more than she was leaving him because the money he received for his business start-up came from his trust."

A fresh set of tears escaped her, and she took a few more Kleenex, wiped her eyes and blew her nose, then continued.

"My mother thought that was fair since I wasn't given any extra money for a start-up business. Instead of the five million, he would receive three million. He took two million to start his business, saying that would tide him over until it was up, running, and profitable. Sean's mistake had been to out and out purchase that ratty building and the empty corner lot, in case his business grew exponentially. Land in Houston is high, and that area is growing. He paid a very hefty price, and then his cash flow dried up. Now with our mother gone, I'm the trustee of his trust, and I'm like she was, hard as a rock. She made me promise to uphold her wishes if she were to die, and I intend to do just that." She drew her lips together in a tight scowl and crossed her arms to solidify her statement.

Shayla Burdett's life was going to change and not all the changes would be pleasing, even after this horrendous part of her life was behind her.

"Your father, did he have any pull for your brother with your mother? I mean, I heard your father and Sean were close and that he was a daddy's boy."

Shayla's laugh was a true belly laugh. It was a nice sound to hear coming from a woman who had the shroud of gloom descend on her life.

"No, not a daddy's boy at all, he was 'the son'." She used air quotes. "Sean loved to pretend they were close to get what he wanted. My father wanted to be a success, and he tried. But when it came crashing on top of his head, he gave up. He thought my mother should care for it all and that wasn't her way. My mom and dad turned into oil and water and weren't ever going to mix again. I'll tell you something else she told me—she had a lawyer and was filing for divorce next month."

Jack figured Marta had been seeing a lawyer.

"What about the relationship Sean had with your mother, how was that?"

"He hated her and told everyone she was never on his side. Sean would always say our mother wanted him to fail, and he whined constantly. But Mom had helped him all she could. She wanted him to grow a pair of balls. Oh!" Shayla let out a groan, then blushed. "I'm sorry, that was not very ladylike at all."

"Ma'am, this business we do is not for the ladylike. Don't worry about it, please go on." Jack liked this lady; she was a decent person all the way around.

"They had what I would call a hate-hate relationship. She loved him because he was her son, but she didn't have to like him, and in fact, she didn't like him at all, and he knew it. He always thought she should give him everything he asked for, but that wasn't her way."

Rich kids. Jack scowled. They expected the parents to dig into their wallets whenever they asked.

"About the divorce, did your father have any idea?" Lucky wondered how much Marcus Stegwig had figured out.

Jack was eager to get inside of the Stegwig's pool house.

"He had his suspicions. I'm sure he knew that if she left him, she would be giving him a settlement. That's what I find peculiar. Why he would kill her and then commit suicide—the prenup was set up when they got married."

"She had to give him money?" Jack's forehead lifted a smidge.

"Yes, a divorce started by either party, my mother would be forking over two million dollars to him. My father would take the money, but then he would be poor and living below his common standards." The disdain showed in her eyes.

She looked around at the room they sat in. "This house is very nice, nice furnishings, and we always had very nice clothes, ate in the nicest restaurants. As a family we had wonderful vacations. Some I have very fond memories of, but Detectives, my mother was never one to squander money. Just opening the windows and letting it fly, it wasn't who she was, and it's not how she accumulated her own fortune."

The case was fresh, and they hadn't pulled financials, but Captain Yao said she was worth a mint.

"What was your mother's net worth, Shayla?"

"Around $13.5 million, she didn't brag about how much money she—" Shayla didn't finish her statement, the look on her face changed in a split second. The revelation had just hit. All of this was now hers. This thought hadn't crossed her mind, and her life was about to change.

Jack and Lucky saw every emotion from A to Z cross this young woman's face.

"Will you please tell me something? And I would appreciate your brutal honesty."

"Yes, ma'am, if I can, I will."

"Did my father kill my mother and then himself? Or is this a murder?"

"Shayla, I can't give you a definitive answer, but hope to soon."

Jack couldn't express his thoughts. Even though he had his hypothesis, he kept it to himself.

"Then let me show you out back."

As they followed her, Jack noted her losing her mother affected her more than anything else did. He didn't miss the remark about her mother-in-law and saw something behind her eyes. Shayla Burdett was getting out of a situation he presumed not so unlike her mother. Often with close family members like this daughter and her now-deceased mother, the apple just never left the tree.

13

The pool house was in a paramount mess, not unlike Sean's filthy office. Clothes and shoes strewn all over and in a far corner sat a metal shelf with an array of pool chemicals and pool cleaning apparatuses. Evidently, the upgrade to the pool shed had been to add in some shoddy furniture and an oversized rope rug. There was a full-sized bed in the center. On one wall a large chest of drawers. Next to it a long dresser with a seventy-inch television, cable equipment, and the latest video gaming system available on the market with fifty game boxes. Jack noted there were all kinds of military games to play. In the back corner closer to the head of the bed sat a single-door fridge and a small microwave stand with a microwave on top littered with empty dinner boxes. Apparently, Sean ate in his room all the time. So much junk, it looked a bit like hoarder's garage, with a bed slap dab in the center.

"Do either of you mind if I go back inside the main house to put on a pot of strong coffee? Driving straight in from Dallas, I need a jolt. Would you care for a cup?"

"No, ma'am, you go right ahead. I'm sure you're exhausted and not just physically either. When we're done, we'll knock on the back door."

Shayla Stegwig Burdett looked at them, her eyes sad. "You do your job, Detectives. I want this all sorted out so I can get to the business of burying my parents. And my kids need me back in Dallas."

Latex gloves and booties on, they went to work, again sifting through crap piled everywhere.

"Find anything yet, Jack?"

"Not yet. This place is a pigsty. I venture to say that Beatrice Gonzales does not step foot in here, not because she couldn't handle it, but because he doesn't allow her in. Man, there is dried-up food on his bedcovers, the trash smells like dead fish. I think it's—let's see—" Jack leaned in to sniff. "Yep, what I thought, there is a half-eaten can of sardines molding in this wastebasket."

"Well, shit, I thought for sure we'd find a gun. Keep looking. This pigsty could hide all his dark, dirty secrets." The neat freak in Lucky wanted to take a fire hose to the room.

Jack picked up a heap of clothes. As he had just shaken them apart something hard fell to the floor at his feet. He whistled.

"Look what we've got here, partner."

Lucky walked over and looked at what lay at Jack's feet. A large Ziploc bag and inside a .22 caliber semi-automatic, and a folded piece of paper from a yellow legal pad, and it looked damp.

As Jack bent over to retrieve the oversized Ziploc baggie, a voice sounded behind him.

"What in the hell are you doing in my room? You have no right to be in here, none."

Sean Stegwig stood at the doorway, his face red, his hands balled up in fists at his side. The boy was furious, and he hadn't heard his sister walk up behind him.

"Sean, they have every right to be here." She held up the search warrant. "This is the search warrant, this isn't your house, and they have my permission, not that they needed it with this warrant."

Sean jumped, startled, and then he stepped through the pool house doorway. "No, *big sister*." His voice dripped with contempt. "It's not all right with me."

"Ma'am, we've got this." Dawson Luck flipped his strap to unholster his gun.

"Mr. Stegwig, it is in your best interest to take a step back and stay calm."

"Please, Mrs. Burdett, go back into the house." Jack looked at the boy. "You move over here and take a seat on that chair now."

"Detective Luck, please keep Mr. Stegwig there, by whatever means necessary."

Jack retrieved the Ziploc baggie from the floor. He sat it on the bed, and then picked up more clothing, shaking it out, talking.

"Is this your gun, Sean?"

"No, I don't own a gun, that's my father's." He smirked; not a becoming countenance for the kid, and Jack wanted to slap the smirk off his face.

"Why are you hiding it then? There's a note. I have yet to read the note. Any talking we do, we'll be doing at the station. Do I make myself clear?" Tough cop Jack emerged.

Sean said nothing while his face turned three shades of red. If smoke existed out one's ears from anger, the place would have looked as if it were on fire. But the boy just couldn't keep his mouth shut.

"You're freaking joking. You're going to arrest me for taking the suicide note and my father's gun? I wanted to avoid the disgrace of having a father who murdered my mom and then offed himself as part of my family story. It's a lot to live with at my age."

Sean got off the chair, raising his voice. He looked sideways at Dawson Luck who had taken his gun out of his holster, recognizing a caged tiger when he saw one, and this kid fit the bill.

Sean sat back down, his eyes on the gun, and he clamped his teeth together so tightly that had his tongue been between his teeth, he would've bitten it off.

"No, but you keep yelling and don't stay seated, I will just for fun, so shut up. Are you going to go peacefully or do you need to be cuffed? It's in your best interest to come with us to the station so we can sort this mess out."

That false assurance he wasn't under arrest, reassured Sean. The detective had said they wanted to talk and sort this mess out. He would explain what happened, and he felt positive if he explained it, he could clear it all up.

"Yes, sir," not a trace of anger in his voice, "I'll be glad to go with you to get this mess sorted out."

Dawson Luck holstered his Glock but left it unstrapped.

Sean watched as Jack finished the search. Had Jack been looking at the boy when he put his gloved hand into a wastebasket full of papers, he would have seen the sweat trickle down his temple.

Jack took out the crumpled pages to what looked like trust paperwork, the same paperwork found in Sean's trash from his office dumpster. The second of two pages with his mother's signature on both of them, written two different ways.

Without saying a word, he took an evidence bag out of his pocket and placed both of the crumpled forms in the bag.

"Okay, Mr. Stegwig, you ready to take a ride?" He turned and looked at the kid. Jack's eyes were hard, hazel-colored marbles.

Sean jiggled his nerdy head, and Dawson Luck took him by the arm and led him out.

"Mrs. Burdett." Jack rapped on the door.

"Yes, Detective West, are you through with your search?" Her eyes bore into her brother's face, and in an instant, Jack saw the hatred and disapproval she felt for him. Shayla was making her own deductions. He had already come to his conclusions, now he just needed to put the pieces together.

"Yes, ma'am, for now, we are. Sean's going with us. He has some things to explain. We feel it's better if he does it down at the station. And please, don't let anyone touch his room while we are gone."

Shayla Burdett looked at Sean then back at Jack. "Do what needs to be done, Detective West." She stepped back a few steps, crossed her arms, and glared at her baby brother.

"Stand right there, Sean, I want a word with Detective Luck."

Jack watched the boy from the corner of his eye. Sean Stegwig was not acting like such a badass now, nor did he act like the poor little rich boy whom the world owed. If Jack didn't know better, he'd guess the boy needed a clean change of shorts from when Lucky unholstered his Glock and aimed it at him. He had no pity at all for Sean, and if it turned out the boy didn't do it, he didn't care; he didn't like the boy.

"We're going to the station, and I'm going to put him in a room. You're going to take the bagged evidence, the gun, and the forms, drop it off at the forensic lab. See about prints on the gun ASAP."

"Whatdaya want me to do if this goes to the back burner, Jack? I mean, the lab's been busy."

"Have someone call the captain. This woman was high profile, and I'm surprised the High Profile Division detectives didn't bump us off of it. Get the wheels moving, then come back to the station, text me, let me know you're back."

"I'm on it once I drop you and him off at the station." Then he stepped away and toward Sean.

"Sean, go with Detective Luck. I'll be there momentarily."

Without a fuss, he walked out in front of Detective Luck, knowing that he needed to keep his cool. Dawson Luck had no problem taking his gun out and shooting him, no sense in tempting him.

"Do I need to get him an attorney?" Her voice betrayed her; she didn't care a fig about that boy. "Look, Detective West, you may think I am being cold. Sean and I are six years apart, and we've never been close. If he is why I've lost my mother, I'll do what I have to do, perhaps even less."

Jack knew what was fixing to happen. In her heart, she knew too. Evidence was circumstantial now, and one thing he knew, forensics told the truth, and he knew there was a story to put together. He would wait until he had the proof in his hands. Right now all it was, was conjecture.

"Ma'am, what I need right now is a copy of any paperwork signed by your mother. A letter or any document, anything we can use for a handwriting analysis."

"I have a letter here in my purse she wrote to me about a month ago."

A sad expression crossed her face. "I know, silly, huh? I mean, we can talk free on our cell phones anytime. My mom, she loved sending me things to surprise me, and her letters always brightened my days. Now I'll never get another letter, another phone call, nothing. I never thought that would happen, not until she was too old to write or call."

Jack took the letter, assuring her it would be returned to her as soon as possible. He made a mental note to himself to call his mother and father; one never knew what the future had in store for the days you had left that God had given you.

14

Lucky headed over to the Houston crime lab, dropped off the gun for fingerprints, and then asked them to send the gun to ballistics. He took the suicide note, with the trust form documents, along with the documents Shayla Burdett had supplied for analysis to the handwriting analysis department. He had a slew of departments, all jumping into action when he told them it was a high-profile case with a possible double murder. No one wanted Dawson Luck to call the captain, who would then get the chief of police, Darren Pratt, involved.

Back at the station, Jack had not yet read him his rights and Sean was cooperating. He had no doubts Sean was the doer. He expected the jeans, T-shirt, and tennis shoes would yield the forensic evidence and the fact that his father had not one, but two bullets put through his head. But, he wanted to hear the kid's lame story. If he was fortunate enough, the kid would confess. He wasn't sure how much strain the boy could take.

"Sean, let's go in here so we can talk." He led him to an interview room, and the boy took a seat. Just by his expression, it was plain to see how confident the kid was.

"You want some water or a soda? I'm going to grab some coffee before we start."

Sean thought for a minute. "Sure, I'll take a Diet Sprite if you have one."

"I can round that up; be back in a minute."

Closing the door to the interview room, he wondered if Sean understood he was here of his own choice and free to go anytime. He would remind him again.

"Here you go, one Diet Sprite." He set the plastic bottle on the table and then a tape recorder and legal pad at his side.

Taking the Sprite bottle and unscrewing the cap, Sean eyed the tape recorder.

"You're gonna tape our conversation, why?" His voice was steady, but his face said otherwise.

"This way I can't twist your words. You know, in case you say something and I took it out of context, this tape backs you up, understand? If you need to leave, we can do this a different way."

"I don't want anyone to mess up what I say, and we need to straighten out this misunderstanding. So, yeah, I'm glad we're recording it."

The kid knew he could justify his reasons for covering up the incident. He had planned it perfectly. It was smooth sailing at least in his small mind, but it was overconfidence to the nth power. He sat up straighter; he could handle this.

"Okay, tell me, Sean, what happened last Thursday night."

"Nothing, I worked late. I didn't feel up to going home, so, I, uh, slept at my office."

"Were you home Friday night?"

Sean shook his head—no verbal answer—and he didn't say where, so he had to ask.

"Where were you Friday then?"

"Uh, at my office again. I had work to do, and it got late. I spent the night there."

"Can anyone verify this, Sean? Is there anyone who can corroborate your story?"

"No, I was alone, my secretary doesn't sleep there, and I stayed in the building all night."

He got indignant and raised his voice a half degree, but Jack gave him a stare.

"Did you go home Saturday?"

"No, man, I didn't. I told you before I didn't want to be home, I needed to get away."

"But you said you have your own place, the pool house, you have a nice bed and food there, why not just go home?"

"You don't get it, do you? It might be my *room*," he used air quotes, "but I don't like it because it is my parents' place and they freaking drive me nuts, okay."

"What about friends, don't you have any friends who'd let you crash at their place?"

"Huh, friends, fair-weathered they are. I mean, when I have money, they're around, and when I'm broke, they're invisible. It's been that way my entire life. Christ, I had friends because of the money I tossed around to impress them or buy them. Dude, look at me, I'm a washout, not tall, not handsome, and to top that off, I am a freaking geek."

The kid played the Pitiful Polly routine and Jack wasn't buying it. Sean wanted him to see the poor lonely rich boy, a boy without friends unless he was tossing about money—that was bunk. Jack didn't feel sorry for him. The kid should've tried to work on his personality, there was no money involved to do that. He saw a crybaby, wet blanket, and a coward.

"Tell me what drives you crazy about your parents. I have parents and stuff so tell me."

Jack relaxed, taking on the persona of a man talking bullshit about parents. He wanted Sean to think he understood how parents drove you bonkers. He wanted to work up to the real reason he had brought him in. But he needed to bide his time. Jack needed to show Sean it was over once Lucky handed him the evidence.

"I don't know, my dad's always coming out there to talk to get out from under my mom, and he likes to drink with me. My dad thought he was a cool dad. You know, he tried to be my best friend. What a joke. And my mom, no worries there. She doesn't come out to my place, ever, and I'm glad." Hatred permeated the air when he spoke about his mother. He had never met a kid that hated his mother as Sean hated his.

He tried to hide his own disgust pretending to agree, with a nod. "Parents can be a drag when you're an adult and you feel like they are holding you back."

His laid-back attitude, maybe Sean would believe was a friendly move. Perhaps the stupid kid would relax and get chattier. Sean nodded, content, thinking Jack understood him.

"You stated you didn't want the stigma your father's murder/suicide would bring, so when did you find the bodies?"

Sean took a long drink of Sprite, and Jack noted the boy had sweat on his brow. The room was too cool to cause a sweat. Jack was getting to the boy.

"I, uh, found them, uh, Saturday night. It was late. I didn't get home until around midnight."

"Tell me what happened, Sean."

He looked first at Jack then the tape recorder, and he paused.

"How should I know, I wasn't there, I found them that way. My m-m-mom," he tried hard to conjure tears. "She was on the floor, blood all over her, and coming out of her mouth and nose. She wasn't breathing. I called out for my d-d-dad, and he didn't answer then I went into his bathroom, and that's where I found him sitting by the tub. He'd shot himself in the head." His fake tears never appeared, and that pissed him off.

"Had to be an awful scene to see, I mean, that would upset anyone. So you panicked. Is that what happened?"

Sean bobbed his head like a bobble doll, and then reclined in his chair, a posture of—who cares.

Jack noted his posture. "Then what happened?"

Sean gulped and took in a large breath of air. He began his act of a grief-stricken son. But Jack wasn't buying it, although he put on a face that said, "I am so sorry," to pretend he was empathizing with him.

"When I saw the gun I was upset."

"Where was the gun before you removed it?"

"It was, uh, in his lap, his hand was lying on top of it. Blood was oozing from his head, his mouth, and nose; it was a-a-awful."

He feigned his despair again, but not convincingly.

"I am sure it was a horrifying sight to see. Where was the note when you found it?"

"It was—he left it on the countertop. I didn't see it at first. It upset me. Why would he do this to me? I mean, I have my own problems. Why couldn't he have talked to me before doing such a terrible thing? I mean, why did he have to kill her too?"

He let out a wail that was so phony even he didn't believe himself. It was too late to back down, so he laid his head down, and his shoulders lifted, as he pretended to cry.

"Pull yourself together." Jack did an eye-roll. This was ridiculous, and his acting was piss poor. Good thing it wasn't his life's calling; he would have starved to death long ago.

The boy banged his head, not very hard, on the table, trying to make a show if it. He raised his head and covered his face with his hands to pretend to wipe nonexistent tears from his face. Oh, he had wetness on his face, and he knew he was perspiring. He was wiping his salty sweat into his eyes hoping the salt would cause them to tear up.

"That was about when on Saturday night?"

"Uh, it was, I think about one in the morning."

"What did you do next?"

"I—" Sean stopped talking when Jack's cell phone beeped. It was a text from Lucky. He was back.

"Sean, wait here. Let me go see what this is about. I hate to be interrupted, but, this happens in my line of work. Makes me darn mad to be interviewing someone and get pulled away by my boss."

Sean looked at Jack with a self-confident grin. "Messes you up, I can understand. I'll be here when you get back, and, uh, you think I can get another drink, Detective?"

No remorse, the boy was callous.

"I can get you another. Here, let me take that empty bottle. Them buggers don't even put trash cans in here."

He took the plastic bottle by the bottom and scooped it up.

Sean believed he was making a new friend. Jack wanted the young man to relax; this way he'd slip up.

Lucky was in the hallway. "Interviewing the titbag?"

"Yep, got it started. How'd it go over at the crime lab? Are they rushing?"

Lucky let out a short bark of laughter. "Yep, looked like a beehive swarming when I left. What, have you gone to drinking Diet Sprite? I thought you might be a Diet DP man." He pointed to the empty bottle.

"Nah, got Sean a soda, gonna get him another. I pretended to complain that we don't have trash cans in the room. I'm taking him another soda but wanted this bottle because now I have his fingerprints and DNA. Get someone from CSU to pull prints."

"Way to go, bud. How about I come in with you and stare at him, make him nervous?" Lucky smiled and patted his gun, who he named Greta—Greta Glock.

"No, call Bennie. Get the time of death from him, and get a copy of Marcus Stegwig's skull showing the second bullet. Get the pictures from where CSU removed the bullet from the doorjamb and a picture of the bullet. Then get a copy of the report stating that there was just the one shell casing found at the scene in the bathroom. Get pictures of Marta Stegwig's broken ribs and get me the prints off that bottle."

"Do you need me to get you a sandwich and the winning Lotto numbers while I am running all your errands?"

The stare he gave his partner would have disintegrated anyone else but not Dawson Luck.

"Hey, ease up, Jack, we got this. That boy ain't going anywhere, you and I both know that, and even if he saunters out of here thinking he has pulled one over, we know the truth. Once we get all the forensic results, we'll have everything we need, so stop fretting and stressing."

"We've already got him here, and I'd hate to worry about trying to find him later. I'm going to let him stew for a few minutes. I am running out of reasons to keep leaving him alone. The sooner we get this stuff, the faster we can take this boy to Booking."

"Then I am wasting valuable time standing here jawing with you."

With that, he darted out to do everything Jack had asked of him or at least get all he could.

"Text me when you got it."

Dawson gave him the thumbs-up.

Jack went to the room where he'd left Sean. He was sure the foolish, self-confident brat thought he was in no trouble at all. He hoped to keep him at ease, talk himself into a corner. After he was trapped, the kid would shed real tears. The waterworks not meant for his dead mother or dead father. His tears would be for the life he would no longer have. What a change in his lifestyle—a six by six room, with a cot and a hole to pee in—to be rich, Sean was just the lucky boy.

"My apologies, Sean, here's a Diet Sprite and a package of crackers. My captain has me working on a call. I'll be right back. Will you be okay until I get back?"

Jack needed to buy Lucky some time. After this he would be placing Sean under arrest.

"You bet, and thanks for the crackers. I didn't eat today; my stomach was growling a bit." Sean's voice quavered, but only slightly. The kid had an appetite, but not a sense of right and wrong. If a person was under strain or stress because of guilt, their stomach knotted up, and eating or drinking was the furthest thing from their minds. Sean was, right now, cool and overly confident.

"You know, Sean, you can leave whenever you want to."

Jack needed Sean to understand he was here of his own volition. "Oh, no, sir, I want to get things cleared up, so I'll stay." Sean opened the crackers.

Jack left him alone to eat his crackers and drink his soda and hoped the kid choked on the crackers.

Lucky had been gone for over forty minutes. He couldn't keep stalling, or Sean was going to get suspicious and lawyer up or leave. Jack had to keep this controlled and rolling *his* way.

He'd wait for five more minutes before going back into the interview room to do what he needed to do. Lucky would show up, he just wished he would hurry.

Five minutes passed in what felt like a blink. As Jack headed back to the interview room, a text sounded on his phone. *In the hall headed to you right now,* was all the text said.

He stopped, relieved that Lucky was back, and he geared himself up. He was ready for what was to occur.

"Sorry," Lucky said out of breath. "I ran up the stairs. Bennie had it all ready for me, and since traffic stalled, I put on the *Kojak* lights cuz I knew you were waiting."

The volatile behavior Sean exhibited in the pool house was a concern, and this new evidence could put the boy over the top. Jack decided they would need to cuff the boy, just to keep him in check.

"Lucky, I think he is more scared of you than cuffs."

"Yep, I'd say he's a change your shorts kinda scared of me now."

"Come on, bud, let's go nail this guy's nerdy ass to the wall."

Sean sat up straight when he saw Detective Luck. He didn't care for him much; the crazy cop held him at gunpoint.

Jack set the folders on the table and looked at Sean, and then Dawson Luck walked behind the chair the boy was sitting in.

"Stand up, Sean; you're under arrest for the double murder of your parents, Marcus and Marta Stegwig. Sean Stegwig, you have the right to remain silent, anything you say can and will be used against you in a court of law—"

Sean stood dumbfounded.

While he read him his rights, Dawson Luck cuffed the boy's hands behind his back.

"Hey, wait, I thought we were just talking. I agreed to talk to you. Why am I under arrest? I told you what happened." He talked over Jack, but Jack ignored him.

"With these rights in mind, Sean Stegwig, are you willing to continue talking to me?"

"Yeah, let's clear this up before it gets any worse. Being cuffed and having him,"—he gestured with his head to Detective Luck —"Quick Draw McGraw, next to me, dude, that's as bad as it gets."

Jack had him sit with his cuffed hands behind him. He hadn't lawyered up and the tape recorder had been rolling—now he would make his play.

Dawson Luck stood against the wall, his eyes boring into the boy. Sean started sweating, and Lucky's glare was penetrating into his deepest fears.

"It's time to tell me the truth, Sean, because it's your last chance."

"I have told you the truth, I mean, what else can I do, make up a different story?"

"There are some facts you aren't being honest about. Isn't that right? Let me fill you in. First, a witness puts you at the house on Thursday night, Friday night, Saturday night, and Monday morning. You say you were at your office sleeping, but you have no witnesses and no way to corroborate your story. That means you don't have a solid alibi. Second, the time of death noted was within a 72-hour window. Your parents were both dead by last Thursday night to very early Friday morning. Add in they haven't been seen, either of them, since Thursday night. Third, I've got a few pictures to show you."

He slipped out the pictures he'd had Lucky get from the medical examiner's office.

Sean sat quietly, his face paled as the sweat broke out on his forehead.

"Now look at this photo."

Sean stared, his eyes fixated on the wall across from him. He snapped his fingers. "Sean."

"I-I thought you wanted to hear," he droned, and then his voice gained some force, "my story about what happened, Detective, is that out the window or what?"

Sean tried to regain his control over the situation, but Jack was not about to give him the upper hand.

"It's my turn right now. I've listened to your story, and it doesn't fly. Look at this picture—now." Jack's forefinger was tapping the first picture on the stack of photos he'd set on the table.

Sean Stegwig looked at his finger jabbing at his dead mother. There was an obvious hole in her throat, her half-naked body on a stainless steel table, flayed open, and her rib cage exposed. The picture showed broken ribs and heavy postmortem bruising. Sean didn't flinch, his eyes like button eyes on a stuffed animal, non-seeing, without emotions.

"It is my dead mother. I don't hafta see pictures, I know she is dead." His voice was deadpan, no sadness, no remorse.

"Now look closely. Do you see her ribs and the bruising? That happened after she was already dead or while she was dying."

The kick to her ribs had been postmortem, but Sean didn't know this unless he'd leaned over her, checking to see if she was alive. The fact was he hadn't cared if she'd died, or not, he despised her.

"Someone hated her, hated her enough to bash in her ribs, breaking damn near every one of them on her right side. This is what we call a personal act of violence, Sean. The killer knew his victim. He loathed the victim so much, even after they were dead, he wanted to inflict pain. It's a known fact that you detested your mother."

"Just because she and I weren't close, doesn't mean that I would do that." The boy's attitude became defensive.

"Sean, go to this picture."

"I—" he began, but Jack stopped him.

"Look at the next picture. Tell me, what do you see?"

It was an enhanced picture of Marcus Stegwig's skull, x-ray viewable without the help of an LED light. Sean looked at the photo.

"A skull, so what, what's that to me?" He licked his lips then slouched away from the pictures.

"This is your father's skull. I want you look at this, Sean. It's a bullet lodged into his skull. To be exact, his parietal bone, see?"

He leaned in and looked closer shrugging. "What have I got to do with that? I mean, he shot himself. If the bullet didn't exit what does it matter to me? I only removed the gun and made sure not to get my prints on it. Detective West, that's not a crime, now, is it?"

"Yes, it is, it's called tampering with evidence, and it is a criminal offense. You can be charged with a felony, so by all rights we have you on that account."

"Maybe I do a few months and get out since it would be my first offense. Odds are I get probation for a year. That would be a cakewalk. I'm used to a pool house as my living quarters, hell, it's my personal jail, and I have no real friends." He was very blasé about the situation.

"If you go to prison on a misdemeanor, you might just do a six-month stint. But, son, federal prison is up to twenty years and a fine, not that the fine means much to anyone doing twenty now, does it?"

"I'm telling you I moved the gun and the note. That was all I did. Go arrest my father for killing my mother, because I am sure you can legally kill yourself. Besides, if he had attempted and failed, you guys would have him for murder *and* in the nuthouse," Sean spouted out.

Jack squared his shoulders and pulled out another photo of the bathroom doorjamb, and the bullet that CSU had dug out. He needed to break this kid's confidence; he needed him to confess to the murders.

"Suicide *is* against the law, but it's difficult to prosecute a dead person. You're right; your dad may have gone to the nuthouse. Now, let's add to the charge of tampering with evidence. There is another fact as well. You forged your mother's signature on the trust forms, and we know why. When we get the results back from the handwriting analysis, we'll have you on forgery. We're going to examine the suicide note, and I'm betting that's not your father's handwriting either."

"I think the note was too messed up to read. He killed her and was nervous so his hands were sweating; it smeared."

"Technology has come a long way, you should know that." Dawson Luck stared at the boy.

"Okay, now back to the bullet in the x-ray. You're telling me your father shot himself *twice* in the head. Because here is the other bullet we found, and it matches ballistics on the gun we found in the pool house where you live."

"It was a small caliber, maybe he had to shoot himself twice. I've heard there have been people who've had to shoot twice to get the job done. They say you have just enough left in you if you missed the first time. I read it somewhere. Or he had a practice shot, you know, to get his nerve up. Man, this is horse shit, how would I know?" He screamed each word louder than the first.

Jack hitched his brow and stared at him.

Sean continued his rant. "Were my prints found on the fucking gun? Is that what this is about? I can assure you, my prints are nowhere on that damn gun. So what do you have, speculation, that's damn well all you have," he shrieked in Jack's face.

Sean's hands were cuffed behind him. His chair facing the table, the boy popped up out of his seat and shoved the table with his midsection, trying to knock Jack off his chair.

Lucky took a step in and got into Sean's face, so close that he felt the detective's hot breath.

"If I were you, Mr. Stegwig, I would sit back and lower your voice. And don't try shoving this table again because if you continue to do so, I'll call and have someone bring me some leg irons and a white jacket with buckles. Have I made myself clear?"

He looked up at Dawson's face not even an inch from his own, and the detective's eyes were cold as steel. The boy did not doubt Detective Luck would go through with his threats. The boy sat down, and a sudden change in his angry demeanor occurred. Sean relaxed, sat back in his chair, and slouched giving an air of impudence. The boy thought he would be untouchable. They'd never be able to pin this on him. They had no real proof; just circumstantial evidence, nothing more.

"Sean, you're right, your fingerprints weren't found on the gun. So here's what we have." Jack gave a dramatic pause and then looked at his partner.

"Detective Luck, will you go get a fingerprint clerk, so we can get Mr. Stegwig's prints? Wait, I have them on the first bottle of Sprite you drank, isn't that right? He freely let me take that bottle. I'm betting we can get his DNA to match up to the hair Bennie found since it wasn't a match to his father, mother, or the housekeeper. You know what else? I am betting we'll pull prints from the Diet Sprite bottle and they'll match the prints found on the gun clip, from a gun which is the same gun that killed your mother, and your father."

Jack narrowed his eyes. "All the gun clips were empty in the house. This made me think. If they were empty, then so was the gun used for your father's suicide. It was a gun registered to him. Funny thing is, for a man who supposedly killed his wife then turned the gun on himself, it was odd. I had figured his prints would have been on the gun clip, but somehow he must have killed his wife and then wiped them off, after he shot himself—twice. Is that what you think happened, Detective Luck?"

At that moment all the blood drained from Sean's face and all the air went out of his pompous attitude. He was beaten, and he never asked for an attorney, he thought he had it all covered.

"Let me offer you this. You're facing the needle here, a double murder in Texas, that's a capital offense and punishable by death. You walked in with the gun, which showed intent to kill or harm. I mean, what happened, you argued, and then you got angry. You didn't storm out, you lashed out, with a gun you had with you, prepared to kill your parents. You have two first degree murders to answer to, Sean, and you *will* have to answer for them."

The kid had all but passed out as Jack spoke these words.

"Or you confess. Write your confession, sign it, and I'll put a word in for you at the D.A.'s office, and you may get life with no possible parole, but you'll be alive. What's it going to be?"

They had him. His fingerprints, his DNA, the forms he tried to forge his mother's name on, and the suicide note he wrote and signed his father's name on. The detectives had it all, and he was in no position to talk his way out of it; it was impossible. Crap, he didn't want to die, even if he had to go to prison for life, at least he would be alive.

If she had given him that trust money, he would not be in this position. God, he hated his mother, that stingy bitch. Sean wrote out his confession. The stupid kid owed large amounts of money to several people. People who wanted to break both his legs and worse. In prison he could avoid them. It never crossed his mind they had hands doing their bidding in prison—Sean was in for some major life lessons. Jack walked the handcuffed boy to Booking. Booked, and fingerprinted, Sean got his obligatory phone call. Jack figured he would call his sister. Once she found out all the facts, he highly doubted she would do much to help him, except get him an attorney. Then let him fry.

15

J ack sat in Captain Yao's office waiting for him to finish a call—
story of his life. His captain was constantly on the phone.
   "Yes, okay then. I'll talk to you later. What? Milk and cereal,
got it. Yep, me too." He put the phone down with a sigh. "Sorry, Jack,
talking to Patricia, one of my many daily calls. I gotta go to the store
on the way home. She's stuck at home with a puny kid today."
   "Nothing serious I hope?"
   "Nah, youngest has a cold, no fever, just not up to par. Speaking
about kids, tell me about Sean Stegwig. What was the story?"
   "Dave, this kid might be looking at the needle. His old man had
talked the wife into giving their son an advance on his trust for a cool
two million. Sean used it to buy the building and adjacent land to get
what he needed to start his stupid company. He gambled the rest
away, and got into debt, a debt he couldn't payback. So he thought
he'd be smart and took a loan out on the building. Then he sold the
empty lot. You can see where this is going, I'm sure. He lost his ass
and went to loan sharks."
   "Leg breakers or worse, too bad he was such a fuck-up." Davis
would never understand this type of behavior.

"Yeah, and he was in waist-deep and sinking, so he asked his mom for help. He begged her for money from his trust to get him out of trouble, and she wasn't about to give him another dime."

"What about his company? Was it making any money?"

"Enough to pay his one employee a minimum wage and his utilities. The kid wasn't even paying his loan back and was in foreclosure."

"He didn't ask his old man for help? Didn't he have money too?"

"Marcus Stegwig lost on a huge investment and was trying to get the wife to bail him out. From what the daughter told us, she was a tough cookie. She would not help either of them. The kid figured he would do them and make it look like a murder/suicide. Then he could draw on his trust. Since he was also a beneficiary on the four million dollar life insurance policy, he thought he'd get that too."

"Greed and gambling. How many lives does that ruin?"

"We got him by his wimpy nuts, Dave. His prints are all over the clip in the gun and the ballistics match. The hair found on the father was a DNA match to Sean. I called Bennie an hour ago. He found tiny spots of blood on the white boat tennis shoes we got out of the kid's trash. The blood on the jeans and the T-shirt was a match to both Marta and Marcus Stegwig. Captain, the kid, kicked his mother postmortem, breaking her ribs. He blamed her for his issues. When his father walked in, he held him at gunpoint. He panicked, made him go into his bathroom to do him. In the end, he figured a double indemnity payout on the life insurance policies would increase his cash intake, not to mention getting his trust fund upon their death. Sean Stegwig was trying to double down, and he went bust on both hands."

"Doubling down is right. He'll get double all right, consecutive life sentences or the needle."

"He wrote out and signed his confession, Cap. I told him I'd put a word in with the D.A. to take the death penalty off the table. I can suggest it, but it ain't my final call."

"Good work. You and Luck did a bang-up job."

"Thanks, and I'll tell Lucky you said so."

"Where is he? I thought he'd be in here to get his own pat on the back?"

"Typing the reports, and I'm sure he's cussing me for not doing some of the paperwork."

"Are you and Luck getting back to the old cases you were working?" The captain shuffled some files on his desk, looking for something.

"That's the plan until the next fresh one comes in. You know, this case has me a little stumped, because I can't find a plausible motive. Davis, you know me, I'll dig in and hunt to find the pieces to see the entire picture, but," he paused.

"What, Jack?" Yao looked up from his paper shuffling.

He placed his hand on his chin and stroked it, and he felt the stubble.

"This girl was a poor nobody for all intents and purposes. Reports state there was no sexual assault. But no one ever dug into the case. The work done was piss poor, no follow-ups, nothing. I think the dicks working the case let it fall by the wayside."

"Jack, you know Houston; it is a big place, lots of crime, like Dallas, Los Angeles, hell, New York. These places all have one thing in common—they're a breeding ground for criminals. Unfortunately, Houston is a member of this elite group. You know how it is. Sometimes you have to let a case go, and you move onto the next one when you have zilch or all your leads dry up. We weren't here back then. Who can say why this case amongst many got sent to the dark recesses of the unsolved and archived cases, huh?"

The captain was right. But it didn't make him feel any better. Unsolved cases where any perp roamed free was not right, leads or no leads, forensics or nor forensics. He felt justice should be, no, *must* be served, and it never mattered how many days or years slipped by.

"Jack, if you weren't a cop I think you would've made one heck of a prosecutor."

"No, Davis, not me. I'd want all those killing assholes to get the needle. Taxpayers would've loved me, prisons would've been smaller, and our tax dollars put to better use. Regardless, I have always loved being a homicide detective. It's who I am."

Jack was mentally exhausted. It had been a very long day, and it was almost seven. He was famished. Besides, he needed to keep the overtime down, but some days you did what you had to do. Neither crime nor reports had a time clock; they started and stopped on their own time.

"We can wrap it up and tie loose ends up in the morning. Whatdaya say we go get a burger and a beer?"

"Thanks, but I'm going to head home to see the wife and eat leftovers. Besides, all these late nights, we haven't seen each other very much."

Jack turned his lips downward. "Gotcha, partner, I understand the wife and all."

Lucky waved at him as he headed toward the back stairwell.

"See ya in the morning." Then he was out the door headed home to his beautiful wife and leftovers.

Jack groaned. He hadn't been to the grocery store in a few weeks. What waited at home for him was a can of chili, a half sleeve of saltine crackers, and one lone beer that sat in his fridge. Lordy, what a dismal picture this painted, but it was his life. Reaching into his pocket for his keys, his head shot up, and a name popped into his mind—Gretchen. Fetchin' Gretchen, she was an enchanting woman, and he needed a woman in his life. Not a wife, not yet, but he needed someone. Everyone did.

With a grin on his face, he decided a beer at the Lone Star Saloon was what he needed to complete his day. In fact, they served pizza. He was starving.

Jack had extra clothes in his locker and he headed to change and dressed casual. With fresh clothes on, he looked at himself in the mirror. It was a good look on him, or so he thought, with his well-worn Wranglers, a pullover shirt with a collar, and his black Justin Ropers. He needed a shave but didn't have shaving gear with him.

His eyes looked tired, but at least he didn't have the usual bags most homicide detectives touted.

Running his fingers over his head, he thought he had nice hair but needed a haircut. The ends were touching the collar of his shirt. Next, he assessed his physique—his left side, right side, and his frontal appearance—not too bad. He had his hair, and his teeth and an okay face he figured. Next, he looked at his posterior. What a dumb thing to do. Not overweight, a love handle was forming; too many James Coney Island chili dogs, too much fast food.

Jack smiled, and here he was off to eat pizza and drink beer—because of her, because of Gretchen. Then a sad thought settled within. He wondered how she saw him. Did she see a worn-out cop, a man with too many ghosts? He'd seen some horrid things and met some bad people in his years on the force. He took dangerous chances every day on the job, but this thing with women, it was more dangerous. If it didn't work out, it was like a homicide, a homicide to your heart.

It was almost nine. The Lone Star Saloon wasn't as busy as normal, and the crowd was not overly boisterous, either. There were five customers at the bar top; the other barstools were empty. A smattering of patrons sat at tables or played pool, but not many. It stood to reason. It was a weeknight, but the place had plenty of people on weekends, some of them even cops he knew.

Jack hoped to not run into anyone he knew tonight, though. He didn't want an audience when he asked Gretchen to go on a date. The constant ribbing he would get if anyone found out she shot him down. He wanted to avoid this as well. Perhaps he should have worn his Kevlar to keep from getting a direct shot in the heart, if she was unavailable and sorry Jack, or flat-out not at all interested in this cowboy cop.

He inhaled deeply, popped his neck from side to side, and decided she was worth the chance.

"Hey there, can a guy get a beer, tallboy, draft Miller Light?" Jack called out as he sat at his spot on the corner.

Her eyes lit up, and she smiled. "Hey there, Cowboy, they got you in the trenches at the HPD? My, you look very dashing tonight, Jack, my goodness." She wiggled her brows up and winked.

He blushed. "Uh, thanks."

She drew a frosty tallboy, carried it over with her bright as the sun smile. "It's nice to see you, Jack. I all but thought you'd left the State."

"What! Me? Leave Texas? Uh-uh, no way, darlin'."

He took a healthy swig of his frosty cold beer. "The kitchen still serving pizza? I didn't eat lunch today and I'm starved."

"Double hamburger pizza with thin crust, the usual?"

"You know me pretty well, thanks, Gretchen."

He watched her saunter off, and he took another long drink of his beer, thinking how beautiful she was.

She brought him another cold beer and waited on the few customers at the pool tables, then headed to the kitchen to check on his pizza. Jack watched her work, admiring everything about her—her look, her smile, her walk, her way with the customers. She had cheeriness about her and the customers loved her. Gretchen took their joking good-naturedly and joked back, making each of them feel special.

"Here's your pizza. Enjoy," Gretchen said.

He thought about his cold case, and he contemplated telling her about it, but not tonight. Tonight he was a regular man, not a detective on the beat.

"Not too crowded tonight." Jack dug into his pizza.

"Oh, there's some to-do over at one of the other local bars, a new band or something. I heard some customers talking about it last night and figured some of my usual cronies are at a mini concert."

"Chat with me while I eat my pizza."

"Sure, I'd love to chat until someone wants another cold beer. Jack, how long have you been on the force?"

"It's coming on close to fifteen years now."

"It must be interesting, full of drama and some grossness, all at the same time I bet."

Gretchen leaned into the counter setting her elbows on the bar and propping her head in her hands as she studied him. He grabbed another piece of pizza trying not to eat like a ravenous dog.

"Look at me." She sounded like a sergeant.

His head popped up to meet her blue eyes. Eyes so blue they all but hypnotized him. Taking him to a place he'd never been, near euphoria, and it felt good—and Lord, this was just her eyes.

"Yep, uh-huh, I see it, the mind and soul of a man who has seen a lot of horrible things. But inside, I see a glimmer of goodness. It shows through a tad. I'd venture to say, with the right coercion, that bit of glimmer would sparkle brighter. There's plenty of goodness left in you, Jack. Never lose that spark of good."

"I am glad to hear you can see a little glimmer." He looked deeply into her blue eyes. "You know, your eyes and the window of your soul kind of thing. How about you, Gretchen? What's your story? You got a fella, a husband, your likes and dislikes—that sort of stuff?"

She rolled her eyes upward and giggled. It was a sexy sound, and then she impishly grinned. "Now, Jack, are you asking me if I am available?"

"Um, well, er, uh yes, I am." The words a little muffled because he had a mouth full of pizza, and he was trying not to be a complete buffoon.

He had no qualms about facing the most hardened criminal, or blasting a man who was a threat to an innocent person without a second thought. Even looking at dead bodies at a crime scene or an autopsy table didn't bother him. But this woman unnerved him. He could almost feel himself sweat as he waited for her to say something. A blush colored his cheeks again.

"Wellll." She drew the word out. "No, I am not attached to anyone, haven't been for, let's see, well, too long to say."

She pulled away from the counter, stood up straight, took a bar towel, and wiped off a clean countertop. He noticed now she was nervous as she kept wiping the same spot.

"Hmm, so you are not attached. And I'm a free agent. Say, how about we pool our resources and have dinner one night?"

It was not the suavest or most romantic way to ask a woman out on a date. Crap, he had been out of touch, and it was better than not asking at all.

Gretchen grinned mischievously. "With an offer like that, I can't refuse. That's a first for me—*pooling our resources together* for a date."

"Hell, let me try again. Gretchen, would you like to have dinner with me?"

"Detective West, I would love to have dinner with you. I thought you would never ask. You've been coming in here for months now, and I've been waiting for you to make a move. Gee, I figured you would have known that by now, you being a detective and all, didn't you see the clues?"

"I detect criminals, Gretchen, not beautiful women like you. Now that I think back to the attention you gave me, I assumed you were just being nice to the man in blue. You know, when I let it slip that I was a detective. It's not something I advertise, but you, darlin' are an extraordinary listener, not barraging me with questions."

"A dinner date, huh? When would you like to go? I mean, I can arrange any night but you, you are the one who protects our city, and I can work around your schedule."

Gretchen knew what his job was, knew how much he loved it from all the conversations they had. She'd understand if plans were changed or interrupted, at least for a while, until she had to take second place to the job, and then he'd see what would happen. Right now, this very moment, he wanted to have her in his life in some fashion, starting with dinner.

"So, uh, how about a week from this coming Friday? Are you free, then?"

"It sounds perfect."

"Uh, what's your address?"

"You mean you haven't already looked me up, checked my background and stuff?"

He looked at her in surprise and saw she was teasing. Her address and cell number written on a napkin, Jack took it folded it, and stuck it in his pocket.

He finished his pizza and a couple of tallboys and was drinking water. The Miller High Life Beer clock on the back wall said midnight. Heavens, the time had flown. Jack hated leaving such wonderful company, but it was late and time to head to the house.

Jack paid his tab and left a nice tip, then turned to look at her. "See you next week or sooner if I stop by and you're working. One more thing, uh, Gretchen, what's your last name? You forgot to write it on the napkin."

"Ah, so you detected, didn't you? It's Benson, Gretchen Benson."

Jack left with a wide smile. He was ready to face whatever he had to face—he had *her* to look forward to.

16

"You're chipper this morning. You win a scratch-off ticket or something?"

"What, can't a guy just be in a good mood? Maybe it's cuz we solved the case in less than seventy-two hours, making the Houston Homicide Department look good, as well as the captain and the chief of police?"

"Huh, that's not it. I know you, and your chipper stages, and this has woman written all over it. I'd stake my next meal on it." Lucky gave him the eye.

"You just think you know what you don't know, ya know?"

Dawson Luck rolled his eyes up toward his bushy caterpillar brows. "I've seen it once, before, about a year and a half ago. You met that lady, the one with the jet back hair and amber-colored bedroom eyes. We were at the Fifth Amendment for a birthday shindig. She was a bartender. If I recall correctly, you said she was *saucy*. You took her on one date, remember?"

He'd forgotten about her, Tina. After one date, they had decided the chemistry wasn't there. Recalling this, he realized Lucky was closer to the truth than he had known. Here was the other thing. Did he have a penchant for women bartenders?

"Okay, let's go to work, and you stop trying to analyze my chipper mood. Besides, we might not have enough time to get more footwork done on these cold cases. This is Houston, and like Dallas, New York and L.A., crime doesn't sleep for long."

He took his seat, grabbed his notes and his messages. The first one he read and smiled. It was the message from Gretchen, and he thought about her for a fleeting second. Excited about their date, he berated himself. Why had he picked a Friday night? It was a busy night at the Lone Star. He'd call her when he was out of earshot of his partner and move it to Thursday night. Even better, one day sooner.

The next message was from Daphne Walden. Who was she and how did she know he was working on the Mason investigation? He had talked to two people exactly, the no-tell-motel owner Tully Cranston, and Jenna Berrie. His bet was on the woman. A better question: what did Mrs. Walden have to do with his cold case? Jack picked up his landline and dialed her number.

"Walden residence."

"This is Detective Jack West from the Houston Police Department. I'm looking for Daphne Walden."

"What's this regarding?" the man asked, rudeness dripping from his tone.

"I am returning her call. Is she there or not?"

Jack would not play games with this man. Either she was there or she wasn't. He wasn't about to waste his time. She had called him about a cold case, a case she couldn't have known he had reopened.

He heard the silence as he hung on and he wondered if the man was contemplating whether he would let him speak to Daphne Walden or not.

"Sir, tell me please, is she there or not? That's a simple question. If this is a prank, I'm not finding it humorous, so—" He stopped when the man's heavy sigh blew into the phone.

"It will take me several minutes to get her up. Can you wait, or can she call you back later?" The tone of his voice sounded sharp, as if this were a huge imposition on him.

Not being able to see through the phone, Jack had no idea what the man meant.

"Sure, I'll hold."

He sat with his phone pressed to his face, wondering what was taking so long. Jack was just about to hang up when he heard a weak voice come on the line. She sounded very ill.

"Detective West, this is Daphne Walden. Thank you for calling me back." Her voice sounded breathless.

"Ma'am, if this isn't a good time, I can either call back later or perhaps come by in a few days."

Her breathing was shallow, and it was all he heard—her attempting to breathe.

"Mrs. Walden?"

"Later won't be good. Come by this afternoon. I need to see you, and the sooner, the better."

"Do you mind giving me an idea of what this is about before I make a trip? I'm a bit confused. Just how did you come to find out I was working the Celeste Mason cold case? What does this have to do with you?"

Jack had not seen this woman's name anywhere in the case files, and he did not want to waste his time. He sure as shit had no time for crank calls.

"Detective West, I worked for her some thirty-odd years ago."

She rasped, inhaling, and Jack heard the struggle she had to take in air, let alone to talk, but he wasn't about to hang up on her.

"You worked with her at Bella's Boutique?"

He knew this was possible, but why hadn't the detectives interviewed her back then?

A laugh sounded, which turned into a major coughing spell. Jack could hear the man telling her she needed to hang up and go lay down. Her voice was stronger and very clear. "Not until I get to talk to this detective, Harvey. I mean it."

"Ma'am—Mrs. Walden," he spoke louder.

"Detective, I'm not deaf. I am sick, but I'm damn well not deaf. I'm going to tell you something and then I expect a visit from you. Talking in person is easier for me for several reasons, and no, I didn't work at that ratty Boutique. I was in one of her *stables* back in the day."

Stables. Was she joking? That was an old Vice phrase. It was a phrase a homicide detective rarely heard when working a case. Was his victim a madam or did she own horses?

"Detective, are you there?" She suppressed a cough.

"Uh, yes, ma'am, I am. You took me by surprise and I'd like to clear up one thing before I get your address."

"Uh-huh, what is it?" Her voice was hoarse.

"Mrs. Walden, are you talking about stables where they keep horses, and you worked in the equestrian business, or, uh, a human stable?"

The woman on the other end of the phone burst out with a laugh and was lucky no coughing fit ensued this time.

"Yep, I was in a human stable. I know when you meet me you're gonna wonder how that happened, but Detective West, forty years ago—hell thirty years ago, I was a stunning woman."

He got her address and thanked her. As she was hanging up the phone, he heard the man in the background.

"I don't know why you have to do this. It can't bring the dead back, Daphne."

Jack got a feeling in his gut—this was a good thing.

Daphne Walden's address was near Katy, Texas. Another out-in-the-middle-of-nowhere address, just off FM 529, more white dirt roads and not much of anything else. Jack should call his investigation the Farm-to-Market Road Case or the Country Road Case. He'd be kicking up dirt as he drove—again.

Taking a minute to stretch his legs, he stood up and worked out the kinks, then walked around to Lucky's side of the desk and looked over his shoulder. Head in his hands, he was reading a case report, and he had a picture of his missing person laid out to the side.

"That your girl, the missing call girl, uh, Princess, who ya who it?"

"Yeah, and it's Princess *Lay-Ya.*"

"You think she was a big *Star Wars* fan?"

"Maybe she played out the gold bikini bit with her johns. Who the hell knows what these girls do now or then?"

"She wasn't a bad-looking gal, and made up in her finery she probably turned a few heads." He looked over Lucky's shoulder at the picture. Lucky studied the picture. She had been a pretty girl, however, her lifestyle made her unattractive. For the man Dawson Luck figured himself to be—a *ladies' man*—he had no desire for that type of woman. He preferred women who had self-respect. Hookers didn't respect themselves, and this was a disgrace to all females.

Jack considered telling Lucky about Daphne Walden and her admission to being a hooker like his missing girl. But he'd keep it to himself because he didn't even know how the woman connected to his case.

"You headed somewhere?" Lucky flipped a few pages back in the file.

"Another lead and it's funny. So far, all my leads have literally taken me down a dirt path." Laughing, he explained his trek on the Farm-to-Market to Waller.

"So, you're gone for the day after your dirt road trip?"

"Yup, headed out, gonna grab a sub at Antone's. Should make it there, depending on traffic, in about an hour, then a long drive home."

"Sure, catch ya in the morning, then." Lucky, preoccupied, lifted his hand, but not his head, as he waved.

———

WITH AN ANTONE's sub and a drink, he headed out for the long drive. Damn, it was only a mere forty miles, but on those kinds of roads you felt as if you'd drive forever. Turning the radio up, a song came on, and he thought of Gretchen. A Johnny Lee song played. *Looking for Love.* The music was on the sound track for *Urban Cowboy,* and he smiled. It all fit. He was an urban cowboy, looking for love. Was he looking in all the wrong places, as the song implied?

Taking out the napkin with her phone number, he made his call. "Hey, it's Jack."

"Jack, this is a surprise, a call before the date? You aren't canceling, are you?"

"Uh, no way. I wanted to know if Thursday night next week would work for you."

"Sure. Why?"

"I figured Friday night is a busy night, and I thought—" He faltered.

"Jack, believe it or not, they let me have a life."

"I don't want to cause you any problems with your job."

"It's fine. I arranged my schedule next week to have Thursday and Friday off. So Friday is perfect, or both days are perfect."

"Okay, see you Friday night; pick you up at seven."

"Uh, Jack, how should I dress?" She did not know what the plans were for the date.

Silence. He hadn't even thought about that yet. "Jack?"

"Gretchen, I never made definite plans."

"How about casual for the first date, no pomp and circumstance, I'm not a pomp kinda gal, no fancy food, or high-rise place? How about we play it by ear once you come pick me up?"

Jack liked that idea. He thought it was fantastic.

SURPRISED HE HADN'T DRIVEN on as many white gravel roads as he had on his drive to Waller, Jack had reached his destination.

A small light-colored brick house with a two-car garage. Surrounded by a chain-link fence, the house sat back off the road three hundred yards. His car rolled onto the gravel driveway. To his left, he saw a quarter-acre garden in desperate need of weeding. It was a shame, all that work to have a productive garden was going to waste. Weedy and dry, it could also use a heavy watering.

Parking in the drive, he took his coat jacket, smoothed out a few wrinkles, and put it on to hide the shoulder holster and gun. He had already made sure his recorder had a full cassette.

Once again, he was out in the country where dogs roamed freely, but no barking dog appeared. He unlatched the gate and walked into the yard, and then he heard the howl of a basset hound. They had a pooch, and it was inside; good for them. It was too hot out for any animal today.

The front door opened before he reached the last steps up the wooden porch and a rather tall, large man stood waiting.

"Boomer, settle it." The guy used his foot to push the mongrel back into the house.

"Howdy, I'm Detective Jack West, are you Mr. Walden? Nice dog you've got there."

"Yep, we're expecting you. Come in." He unlatched the torn screen door, the work of the dog from where the rips were located. Jack walked in, noting the house smelled like death. Not a dead body smell, but as in dying.

The man didn't proffer his hand, walking in ahead of Jack, expecting him to follow as he spoke.

"I'm Harvey Walden, Daphne's husband. She's in the back."

Jack followed him in, taking in the house's disarray. Dirty dishes were everywhere. Empty beer cans lined up on a sideboard in the dining room. The kitchen a disaster and that was saying it nicely. A plethora of pill bottles lined up on the same sideboard, and he knew then Mrs. Walden was gravely ill.

His suspicions had been right. Jack walked into a bedroom where a hospital bed sat. Daphne lay hooked up to oxygen. Her skin pale and her body wasted away. She couldn't weigh over 90 pounds. Her short black hair was stringy and streaked with gray. Patches of missing hair allowed her white skull to be seen. The woman's cheeks hollow, and her face skeletal, with dark circles under her closed sunken eyes.

"Is it okay to wake her?"

"I am not asleep, Detective West. I'm resting my eyes. Harve, get him a chair. He can sit by me," she said weakly and began coughing.

Harvey raised her upright a bit more, and the coughing subsided. Mr. Walden got Jack a chair from the kitchen.

Jack sat and waited for her to open her eyes.

"I realize I look a fright." She cut her eyes to her husband.

"Honey, bring me my photo album."

Her husband scuttled away to do her bidding, then she turned and looked pointedly at Jack.

"You know, I called you four days ago. What took you so long to return my call? I mean, I could've kicked the bucket in my situation, and you would've never been able to hear my story." Even in her frail condition, she sounded miffed.

"My apologies, but I was working a fresh case. So I had to set this cold case aside, and I obviously was not aware of your state of health."

He didn't want to piss her off, but hell, he didn't have a crystal ball, and if he did, he would solve all of his cases.

"Mrs. Walden," Jack started, but she raised a boney finger.

"Please call me D or Daphne. I'd prefer to drop the formalities if you would."

"Okay, Daphne it is then. I'm sorry to find you ill."

He wasn't just being nice because it truly saddened him to see anyone in this shape. How impolite would it be, and cold hearted to burst out with, *"What are you dying from?"*

"Lung cancer." She'd read his mind. It was easy to do. "Stage four. Not sure how much longer I have."

He had no words to give her, encouragement would be an insult to her, and so he decided silence was his best option.

"Now, let's get to why I asked you here. As you can see, my situation is dire. That's why I wanted to meet with you face-to-face.

Harve, put the photo album right here." She lightly tapped the sheet next to her hand.

"Daphne,"—he pulled out his tape recorder—"I'm going to record our interview as long as you are okay with it. It's easier than taking notes."

"Good idea. I tire easily, and repeating stuff doesn't help with my breathing. Fire your recording thingamajig up and we can begin."

He pushed record. "This is Detective Jack West of the Houston Police Department." He logged the date, time, and his badge number. "I'm speaking with Mrs. Daphne Walden." He documented her address and date of birth. "We're here to go over information Mrs. Walden has on the cold case for Celeste Mason, file number 081286. Okay, Daphne, it's all yours."

"Detective West—" Her voice was wispy, and it was hard for her to take in breaths because her lungs had been weakened by the disease.

"How about you call me Jack? It will be easier for you."

"Jack, open this album up please, and turn it three or four pages over."

He complied and was staring at an eight-by-ten headshot of a gorgeous woman. She wore no heavy makeup. The woman's once long jet-black hair, nicely coiffed. Thick dark hair piled atop her head with tendrils falling about her fresh face. Her smile dazzling, showing off nice straight white teeth between full red lips, sexy amber-hued eyes with a come-hither look. The picture on the opposite side showed her dressed in a stunning red dress. It sparkled off the page. It was a low V-cut neckline, her bosoms popping as the dress hit all the right curves, hugging her slender hips.

Daphne smiled when she saw the admiration in Jack's eyes as he looked over her photos.

"I told you on the phone I had been stunning, didn't I?"

"Yes, you did, and you sure were," he responded as he gawked at her picture.

"I was working at the Blue Marble, as a dancer at first. I didn't have skills for a proper job, mind you, but it didn't mean I had no skills. What I had was that body and face going for me back then. When I applied I knew it was a skin show, and I needed work. The money wasn't much, not at first. I could've just waitressed, but I jumped right into dancing."

She stared at her own picture, recalling those days when she was vibrant and healthy. Daphne cleared her phlegmy throat and continued.

"After one girl told me if I got nasty and naked, I'd make more money than I could imagine. I wanted more cash like everyone else, but I was timid about showing off all my *goods,* so she took me under her wing. This woman had been doing it for a few years. When she let me know how much she was making, I couldn't believe it. Once I agreed, she helped me overcome my inhibitions about being—well, nastier, and more naked." Daphne stopped to inhale oxygen, and Jack sat silent.

"I began using Quaaludes, and you can say fortunate or unfortunate for me, I began a very lucrative career. Before you think I became a drug user per se, I stopped using the Quaaludes a few months later. They made me feel weird. Even without them, I could perform nicely. I was very good, just me in my stilettos. Then the naked lap dances started, and I got fists full of money. Hell, I even had cash stuffed into my high heels, and it was amazing."

She stopped talking again and tried to inhale as her breathing was shallow, and Jack waited. Harvey leaned over her and turned up the regulator, giving her more oxygen.

Daphne shut her eyes briefly, letting the canned air take its course through her nose, and she exhaled in relief.

"Now, where was I? Oh yes, I was in high demand. A year later, a girl came to me and asked if I wanted to make big bucks. I was pulling in about forty grand or more a year and this was a lot for a girl with no schooling back then. Shit, more sounded great because I liked the high life. Fuck, all us not so smart girls like more cash, and living it up. And yep, I curse too."

"I do too, more than I should, I'm sure. What kind of deal were you offered?"

"A deal which had me back on Quaaludes for a little while. The owner of the clubs, three of them—the Blue Marble, the Crystal Barrel and the Silver Moon—were running what I prefer to call an escort service. Hell, I knew what it was, out-and-out prostitution. I hadn't finished high school, and I had no schooling to get me up the ladder of success. But let me tell you, Jack, I was pulling in over sixty grand a year. More money than a college graduate did. It wasn't an honorable job, but I didn't care. I had money, and I was happy. The girl who started me, Jenna, she—"

"Would this woman be Jenna Berrie, by any chance?"

"Yes. Now, back to what I was telling you." There was a bit more feistiness in her voice. He decided interrupting her was not good. He'd hold his questions until she finished.

"Jenna had been doing it for a while, and she was making plenty of money. She was the one who recruited me. At first, it was a bit like pandering. You know, the bartenders would arrange the meet and greets, and the girls would hand in receipts and cash. The customers were bar patrons. We didn't venture out of the club, ever. Of course, word of mouth created more and more business for the girls, and the clubs were getting packed. Some girls got greedy and decided they would work outside of the protected bar business and go out on their own. You'd be right if you guessed it didn't go well. Some gals got pinched and booked for solicitation."

She stopped for a minute to take a deep breath, filling her diseased lungs with fresh oxygen, and then began again.

"Several years later, the owner of the bar died of a heart attack, and a new person was running the show. We all thought it was the sleazebag attorney, but it wasn't Roger. If it had been, he would've been a bigger asshole. We all knew it wasn't the dead owner's son either, because the place would have imploded. He was an idiot. All he did was work at the Crystal Barrel. Every so often he drove the girls to where the johns wanted to go, and then he would wait for us."

Stopping again, she took several deep breaths. Jack waited with controlled patience.

"At first, we didn't have any idea who was calling the shots, but we were happier. Some girls had to deal with our A-hole attorney. He had to bail them out of jail. It was bad for the girls who got tossed in jail because the asshole was charging a fee and extorting sex. I never got busted, I kept it in the clubs, and the cops on the payroll protected me."

She stopped again, closing her eyes, and it looked like she was falling asleep. Jack cleared his throat. Daphne's eyes reopened, and she looked at him. What Jack saw was her determination. She would get her story out, no matter what.

"Sorry, Jack, this is very draining, if you understand, not just physically, but emotionally too."

"Look, Daphne, there's no need to apologize."

Jack saw a small amount of sweat forming on her brow. Harvey saw it too.

"You need to rest for a minute, and I hafta get your pills. Take a break for a while, please, Daphne." Harvey looked over at Jack and gave him a please-help-me look.

"Sounds like a terrific idea. I'll step out, stretch my legs, and write a few notes."

"You can't leave until I finish my story, Jack, because I've waited thirty-four years to tell this story to the proper person, and I mean to do it before I die."

Jack was staying. You couldn't pry him away. This woman was telling a tale, and it sounded like a made-for-TV movie.

17

Harvey let Boomer out for a short walk around the yard inside the chain-link fence. The poor dog was overweight; with short legs and ears so long they dragged the ground. Jack bent over and scratched him behind the ears, and then the old dog left to find a place to pee. Pacing, Jack was going over his notes when he heard the screen door squeak and open.

"Detective, Daphne's ready to go again." Harvey's demeanor seemed more hospitable, although Jack felt the undertones of *I wish you'd get the hell off my property* seeping out.

"Uh, Mr. Walden," Jack began. He wanted to apologize because this was taking strength from his wife, but Harvey Walden cut him off.

"You can call me Harvey. Detective, I wasn't for all this tell it all business. I mean, the past is the past, and you can't change it. Daphne insisted on talking to you, and I promised her. It was her last request, and I felt I should oblige. I wanted her to let sleeping dogs lie, but it's *her* story. It's not mine."

This one sentence made Jack wonder if Harvey Walden had a story. Why would he want to let sleeping dogs lie? Was he hiding something? Jack's gut stirred. The man could have postponed this visit. His poor wife is at the threshold of death's door, and if she died, there would be no story. But he was here, and she was still alive, so he dismissed the thought.

"I understand, Mr. Walden, uh, Harvey."

"Detective West, I will not make any excuses or explain our past, or apologize for our life either."

Jack looked at Harvey, not understanding what he meant exactly. The fellow was hurting at the thought of his wife's looming death, and he was right about one thing; Jack was there to get her story, not his.

"Harvey, you can call me Jack."

"Okay, Jack, let's go back in."

Back in the makeshift hospital room, Jack took his chair. He noted Harvey had changed out the top sheet for a fresh one and had moved her oxygen tank, enabling him to regulate it without having to reach over the poor woman. Harvey had sat a bottle of water next to Jack's chair. He took a drink of the cold water.

Jack raised the water bottle. "Thank you, Harvey." The other man nodded his you're welcome.

"You ready to continue, Daphne?"

Her chest heaved, and she began. "It wasn't just the pandering. Other things were going on in the clubs. Gaming and gambling in the back rooms, and I knew it was illegal to gamble in a place that sold alcohol. This money was big business, primarily the bookie business and gaming. These people weren't pitching pennies. We're talking about some major betting going on. I didn't realize you could bet on everything. I mean, you could even bet on your bet. They were running a numbers game too, just like the Mafia did it."

"Numbers running is dirty business. People don't just get legs broke, they get worse. I'm not a gambling man myself, but I've heard of people making bets on the strangest things."

"This brought in some ruthless people, Jack. The shot-caller had cops, lawyers, TABC agents and judges, to name some of the more prominent types, on their payroll. I was nobody important, and I minded my business. Besides, I didn't feel threatened."

She paused again, inhaling more oxygen, and Jack knew this was a struggle for her, but he exhibited patience.

"There were a ton of people you could have arrested back then. From low-lifes to important somebodies, but cops got paid to ignore it. New muscle, if that's what you want to call it, moved here from Chicago, and that's when things started going sideways."

Daphne stopped talking, but she wasn't coughing, nor trying to fill her diseased lungs with more oxygen. She was thinking. Jack saw it in her face; she was deliberating something, a war raging in her head to what she wanted to say and whom she wanted to, for lack of a better phrase, rat out.

"It's not revenge I'm after. Shit, I'm dying, so revenge is a moot point. And I'm not trying to ruin anyone's life. Someone needs to hear the truth and I want to set the record straight. Another thing, Jack, this is not a confession either, because I did nothing wrong. In my past profession, well, hell, everyone was consenting, get what I mean?"

"Okay, just so we are clear, Daphne, if you give me names and events, I will do my job. I have to. If you feel you need to stop this interview and take your story, uh, with you, uh, just tell me now."

He almost said *take the story to your grave*, however, he felt it was a heartless statement.

"I understand, Jack, no problem. Okay, back to the girls. As I told you, I got requested more than my fair share. Powerful men who paid big bucks asked for me specifically. Some men didn't even want sex, they wanted companionship. Hard to wrap your head around that, but it was true. I was a high paid escort, without having to work on my back or my knees." Daphne sputtered out a laugh, and Jack blushed.

"The new boss kept the jobs within the bars and ran a tight ship. None of the girls were unhappy. Hell, over time, the business got more upscale and the men who worked the pandering drew in the local bar yokel to the more high-class clientele. I was with lawyers, city officials, corporate executives, cops, a mayor and a few councilmen. The girls weren't the only attraction because gambling drew in high rollers. There were plenty of men who had money to burn and add in the scummy cowboys. Dirt bag cheap ass laborers who wanted to gamble and get fucked. So they did. The gamers fucked them and then the girls got the rest of their money, so they got fucked twice, losing all the money they had. Stupid bastards kept coming back too. It was a never-ending cycle until you were so deep into a bookie you either left town, by running away and trying to hide, or they disappeared you outta town Chicago style." Daphne coughed and spittle mixed with nasty phlegm spewed out of her mouth. With the corner of her bedsheet she wiped off her lips and chin.

Jack looked away as she cleaned it off, not wanting to embarrass her.

She began again. "After a while I felt it go sideways, and then it became a dangerous career."

"I have a question, Daphne. Was it Celeste Mason who took over the girls? Because you haven't mentioned her, and she is the sole reason I am here."

"Yeah, it was her. She worked it from 1981 until 1986. I'd heard she was getting multiple death threats. Someone wanted her to either sell out or disappear permanently. When that attorney got popped, I figured it would stop because I thought it was him, but the threats kept coming, or so I heard through the grapevine."

"This attorney, what happened?"

"In late 1985, I think it was August, or early September, at three or four in the morning, someone shot Roger Stockard, in the head. The man was at his office and no one knew why he was there in the wee hours of daybreak. His buddy Archie Bowers was with him. Bowers got shot, and he died too. It made page five in the newspapers, not even big news, even though it was big news to all of us. Someone paid to have it covered up. It wasn't random, it was a hit. What I'd thought was the attorney was the target, but I come to find out this Bowers guy was also a target."

She shifted in her bed, cleared the phlegm from her throat, and spit it into a Kleenex.

"How could you know that?"

"Because, Jack, I slept with men, important men, powerful men, and some of them talked when they'd been drinking or after some fantastic sex. Pillow talk can be about all kinds of stuff and, hon, men loved to talk to me about everything, much to my dismay."

Pillow talk with prostitutes—not something he would have ever imagined existed.

"Then Jo went missing, and I haven't seen her in thirty years. One bartender had a mysterious accident. Then those four boys found Celeste in her car, dead. A new boss came onboard and things changed. The girls weren't happy, not like they had been with her."

"What changed?"

"Drugs were being brought in and sold and this business was growing. They continued to run girls and bookmaking, but meaner people were infiltrating the system. Some girls ended up strung-out on drugs. All they were working for was a fix, and all the money went to the new boss. Some of the other girls went M.I.A. If they ran away, nobody knows where and no one has heard from them since."

"Someone was murdering hookers?" This was a dreadful thought.

"No, I think they ran off, but not Jo. Jo would never leave. I knew her better than anyone else did. She was the most popular hooker the stable had, and she was bringing in the big bucks. I was second in demand, but we were like night and day. Jo went missing. She hadn't left. I'd swear on a stack of Bibles, she'd never up and leave. Someone reported it, but the police never looked into it. Hell, no one cares when a whore is missing, Jack. It's one less vile person on the streets. The cops on the take let it go, looked the other way."

"You're right, dirty cops would've ignored it."

"I didn't have to explain this to you at all, but it's my story. Jenna called me giving me a heads-up, telling me that the police had reopened Celeste's murder investigation. Look here, I'm dying, and not afraid to die. Back then, I worried about getting whacked knowing what I did."

"You said a bartender had a mysterious accident. What do you know about this? Take your time, I'm not going anywhere," he assured her as she sucked in air, laboring a bit.

Inhaling the oxygen, she relaxed when her lungs filled.

"The bartender was a cop's son who was a screw-up. Randy made some idle threats, and he hated Celeste. His job was pandering for the Silver Moon. Randy was found dead after a one-car accident. He hit a tree, broke his neck. But I never believed it was an accident."

"Why not, Daphne, what was suspicious?"

"They said he was drunk, and we all knew Randy didn't drink. He talked too much and was a general pain in the butt, but he didn't smoke, drink, or do drugs. This accident happened after Jo went missing. Randy caused a big stink about her being gone, because they were tight, and he was digging where he shouldn't be digging. Then Jenna up and quit hooking and dancing. Sarge took her off to live in that little town, Waller, and she's been there ever since. Sarge stayed on at the clubs; but he was always loyal to Celeste. Even if she was out of the picture, Sarge needed his job."

"Which cop was Randy's father, Daphne?"

"Ian Simpson."

Jack sat up straight. Ian Simpson and Pete Bullard—they had worked the case, more like *had not* worked the case.

"How can you be sure it wasn't an accident?"

"For God's sake, like I told you before, Jack, pillow talk. One night I got the story from a client. Randy got whacked."

"Who?" Jack leaned in. "Who did it, Daphne?"

"That doesn't matter any longer, Jack, that person is dead too."

"It may not matter to you, but it does to me, so tell me. For Christ's sake, Daphne, it was a cop's son."

Daphne saw Jack would not let it go, and even if he knew who it was, it wouldn't change a damn thing.

"Bullard, Pete Bullard."

Jack's jaw dropped open in shock. Ian Simpson's own partner killed Simpson's only son. This was crazy.

"Ian Simpson knew?" Jack was in shock. An officer of the law committed a murder; to him this was inconceivable.

"Yes, he did. He had no other choice. Randy was threatening to blow the whole organization up, take it all to the law. He was mad because Jo was nowhere to be found. Pete didn't want it to go down, and neither did Ian. They threatened to kill Ian too if he didn't get his son to shut up. What I heard is he tried to calm his kid, but Randy wouldn't leave town, nor shut up. People have sold out their own grandmother if it means life or death to them." Daphne inhaled, and then hacked until her face had a tinge of color. Jack's insides were rolling into a fire ball.

"How, Daphne? I mean, I'm not sure what to do with this." He raked his hands through his hair.

"Let it be, Jack. You can't charge a dead man with murder, and you can't bring Randy back. We heard Pete Bullard died, so just let it go. Now, Jack, the girls, please."

"Sure, Daphne, I guess I'm shell shocked right now."

His head was spinning. He should report this but would it matter if he did? Bullard was already dead, his wife was too, and they had no children. Daphne might be right; this part of the story could stay buried since Bullard was dead, however, this really was not his call to make.

Daphne understood and didn't blame him, but she hoped he would let it stay buried. Harvey turned up the oxygen a bit more, and she closed her eyes for a moment before resuming her story.

"In the old days, with Celeste, there was no need to worry about cops. Like I said, we kept it in the club and she paid cops to watch our ass. New person in charge meant new rules. All at once us girls were 'streetwalkers' and upscale was dying out. Johnny Law pinched quite a lot of us and I think Jenna was smart for getting out when she did. It was a catch-22. The new boss wanted us to work outside the clubs on the streets, but we didn't have enough cop protection, and he was getting pissed."

"No one walked—just tried to leave? It doesn't sound like pimping, not the way I know it," Jack threw in. Daphne never implied that anyone forced her to be a hooker.

"No, you could leave whenever you wanted. Most of them were strung-out on drugs so they couldn't leave. Top dollar stuff wasn't what it used to be. I blended into the shadows and kept a low profile. Girls and drugs were big money; even the bookies were losing business and pulling out. The boss got his illegal deals swept under the rug. He should've been in jail, but he got out of all of it. Even his goons got away with crap. All they ever got was a tiny slap on the wrist. It pissed me off."

She opened her eyes. Her voice was louder and stronger than it had been before. With the vehemence used to spit out those last four words, a coughing fit ensued.

"Sorry, Jack. That happens when I get excited and pissed."

He could ask her not to get excited, but he did not think it would do much good. She was bossy, even if she was a dying woman.

"I don't understand how he could get away with all of this."

"The boss had an attorney from hell, and I mean he was the Devil. At first, all he did was offer free legal counsel—represented them in court and kept them out of lockup. It's like he knew someone and had it all worked out. Most of us were fortunate not to have to sit in a jail cell. When he became more influential, the cost of staying out of jail was steeper."

"He charged them a fee? Why didn't the boss pay the fees? They were his employees, weren't they?"

"The bastard took the price out in flesh, Jack, he extorted sex, that was his deal, and that's how the girls paid him. The damn attorney was mean, and he liked it rough. Sadomasochism and bondage. Hurting his partner was his sexual pleasure. Before he became the boss man's attorney, he was just another john. He always paid top dollar and repeatedly asked for Jo. She wasn't always available when he wanted *some*. I got him once before he was working for the new boss full-time. He enjoyed hurting, inflicting pain, and he just about choked the life out of me with scarves. When he got finished, I wanted to kill him."

Jack's eyes narrowed. He would never understand this kind of perverted thinking. He considered himself a very passionate and gentle, giving lover. What made a man like that?

"This is all an interesting story, but what does this have to do with the death of Celeste Mason?"

"It's my story, Jack, you want to hear it or not?" Her eyes burrowed into his.

"Of course I do, Daphne." He was expecting to find out why someone had murdered Celeste Mason—his sole purpose there.

18

"As I was saying, things changed for the worse. There were crooked cops, corrupt attorneys and judges who were lining their own pockets with ill-gotten gains. But that wasn't anything I cared about. All I was concerned about was where Jo was. No one had seen her in over six months. I looked for her and called her family up in Ohio. Her family had written her off, so they were of no help."

Closing her eyes to think, not struggling to breathe, she was quiet. Jack felt like pulling his hair out—what did this have to do with his case? This woman was dying, so he told himself to relax.

"It was common knowledge that Jo was a weirdo, and she went in for that kind of sex, the S & M stuff. She made buckets of money for doing kinky, scary crap. If the money was right, she would do some crazy, filthy sex. The more dangerous the sex was, the more she liked it, and the more the johns paid. She told me about some of the stupid stuff she allowed, from hard spanking, whipping, bondage, and even choking sex. In fact, the cop's son and a few of the cops got off on a kinky weird sort of sex, and she was giving it to Randy for free. My guess it's why he was so adamant on knowing where she was. Nasty business. I tried to tell her one day it would go too far." Daphne's tears cascaded down her sunken cheeks.

"Is this too difficult for you? Do we need to stop, Daphne?" It concerned him this conversation was becoming too much for her and maybe they should stop.

"No, give me a minute." She took a second to compose herself.

"I liked Jo. The woman was sassy, confident, and ballsy. The other girls tolerated her, and she hated Celeste because she had Jed. Jo wanted Jed for herself. Randy told me he thought she did this stuff to get Jed out of her system, but she let it go too far."

"Logan? Jed Logan." Jenna had mentioned him. A light bulb flashed over his head.

"Yes,—Logan. One night I heard a story," she began but stopped when she saw his expression.

It smacked him in the face. Missing whores—Lucky's girl was a prostitute, and her name was JoAnn—could this Jo be the same person? What were the odds?

"Detective, what is it?"

"Did you girls have call names or street names you went by?"

"Some of us did. The fellas all called me Dee-Dee for Desirable Daphne. Why?"

"Was Jo one of the girls with a street name?" A far-fetched idea ran through his head.

A croaky laugh spewed out of her tired body. "At first, she was calling herself Juicy Jo way before the movie *Star Wars* came out in the late seventies. The girl loved that movie. She saw the damn thing four times. When the second one released in the mid-eighties, she was first in line. Jo saw the bit about the gold bikini and she changed her name to Princess Lay-Ya, in honor of her hero."

Jesus Christ, his case, and Lucky's case could be, no, not could be, *were,* connected. This was absurd and more than unexpected. What were the odds in this happening? Holy shit! Jack's adrenaline was pumping.

"Jo went missing, they found Celeste dead and Jed Logan

stopped working the clubs. I was at the Barrel one night and the bartender, Skip, was closing up. He was a sweet moron. My last john dropped me off, and I was there having one last drink for the night, watching him close up. Not sure why, but I made a comment. I said I missed the old days and Celeste. Skip responded, not conscious what he was saying and told me he'd mention it to her when he saw her. I don't think he even knew he said it. His voice had been so low I almost didn't catch it."

In Jack's peripheral vision, he saw a slight change in Harvey's posture; he sat up, tilted his head, and clenched his jaw.

"Did he say anything else?"

"Not right away. I excused myself, said I'd be right back, and I went to the ladies room to think. I could manipulate men. Hell, I was a prostitute. I'd sell you a shitty blow job for a hundred bucks or more, making you believe you just went to heaven, and it only took me about six minutes. In my profession, I figured I could get Skip talking without him even knowing he was talking."

"So?"

"I wasn't ready to call it a night. Watching him, I got relaxed and told him I never had time to talk to nice men. He told me he wasn't very nice, and he wouldn't look at me while he was talking. The guy was immature for a near thirty-year-old, and had fewer marbles in his bag than most, but he didn't have a mean bone in his body. We talked and drank. I have to tell you alcohol and Skip combined made it easy to get information."

She sounded breathless, so Harvey turned up the oxygen. He had a hostile look again. Jack figured it was because Daphne was wearing out and he was ready for him to get out of his house and out of their lives.

"Daphne, if you need to stop you should." Harvey looked at her. "This is the most you've talked in six months. It's wearing you out."

Her eyes said no, as she let oxygen fill her nostrils and her lungs, and then she took up where she had left off.

"Skip said the new boss was okay, but he was intimidating, and he was a little scared of him. He let me in on an enormous secret, mouthing to me like a drunk tells a secret, but I couldn't mention it to anyone. He was shushing me, and he leaned into my ear and whispered that Celeste was in hiding, but I couldn't tell anyone. I tried hard not to come unglued, and then I thought about Jo and where she was and if this was true, what else did Skip know?"

"Did he tell you anything that will help me, Daphne? Your story is interesting—"

"Detective West, keep your pants on. This is my story, and damn it, I'm telling it." She coughed until Jack thought she would vomit, and Harvey gave Jack the evil eye. When her coughing spell subsided, she inhaled more oxygen and began again.

"Skip started crying, with the tears of a drunk who had a burden to release. That was when I found out what had happened to Jo. He killed her, but he hadn't meant to."

"Skip killed her, he killed JoAnn?"

"No, I'm getting to it." She felt spent, but she wasn't about to stop her story.

"Skip told me what happened and made me promise not to tell a soul. Just like that, he sobered up. He had worked at the club for several years when it just a regular club, and not a front for hookers and gambling. He knew too much, and he had to keep his mouth shut. They had threatened him with his life."

"If he was worried about threats, then why tell you?"

"Jack, please," she wheezed, "you saw what I used to look like, and he was drunk, and he needed someone to tell."

"What did he talk about?"

"One night, a man told him he had heard a john had killed a hooker. Skip wouldn't tell me who told him because it was too dangerous. He said he did some asking around. Really, no one ever thought Skip was smart enough to figure out two and two are four, not eight. People talk to their bartender same as they do with their hairdresser. He found out who the john was who was in the room when the hooker got killed. He said it was a sexual misfortunate incident. Like that makes it all right, shit."

"Did he say who?" Jack would not leave here without a name.

"I asked him who was such a big shot that a murder needed to be covered up, accident or not. Skip told me it was a guy they called Big Bad Wolff. He was some young badass lawyer."

She saw the look register in his eyes. It was more than shock. Jack's mouth opened, but he closed it, letting this new information sink in before he spoke. Holy Mother of God! Judge Troy Wolff was involved. This was preposterous. Jack had known Troy Wolff for years, and never had he ever imagined he was like that, not even back then. The judge has always been a refined and distinguished citizen of Houston.

"I can't go accusing him. For God's sake, he's a respected judge in our city."

"You said you wanted justice, and I thought you meant it." Her breathing more labored the sweat on her brow heavier. This had upset her.

"Okay, I do, I do, Daphne, but this is—I would need proof."

"Let me finish this because I am getting tired, Jack, tired of everything. That's when I realized it, when Skip said he would be sure to tell her. I knew."

"What, you knew what?"

"That Bullard and Simpson covered up a load of crap. No one ever found Jo. Now here you sit, looking into a cold case that got buried and forgotten, but Skip said she wasn't dead. Celeste hadn't gotten out, and Jo was her body double."

This was ludicrous.

"Why would she fake her death?"

"There was major pillow talk, I mean, every john after Skip's news I got to talking. I sex-talked them out of any information they'd tell me. Word was somebody put a contract on Celeste's life, she had to get out, sell out, or die."

"Why not leave town, or leave the country?"

"I can't answer that. But they needed proof that she was dead."

"Who, Daphne? Tell me who and stop beating around the bush." Jack was literally sitting on the edge of his chair.

"I heard it was the Buccella family, mob family from Chicago."

"The mob wants you killed, Daphne. You're dead."

"Scottie may have been a Buccella, Jack, but I know something not many others do."

"What?" Jack's head was spinning with the story. Was it true or not?

"He had a thing for Celeste back then. He no more wanted her dead than he wanted his own mother dead. I was his hooker one night, Jack—men talk, and Scottie talked. He told me that if something ever happened to Jed, he would make a move on her."

"Why didn't he have Jed whacked then, I mean, if he had mob affiliations?"

Daphne scarcely moved her bony shoulders in an upward motion. "Love is an odd thing because I asked myself that same question and never came up with an answer."

"So, where is Scottie Buccella now?" Jack was thinking he needed to talk to him.

"He's dead, been dead now for at least fifteen years."

"How'd he die?"

"Contract murder. They said it was someone from Chicago, that's all I heard. I wasn't sure what to believe. I always thought it was a local hit. Will you look into this or not? Are you gonna arrest Judge Wolff?"

"On the word of a moronic bartender, as you call him. And, pardon me, an ex-prostitute. I will do no such thing unless can you elaborate a bit more. I cannot point fingers at an official figure, Daphne, and I damn well am not going to either until I have concrete proof, Jesus!" Now *he* was sweating and worried.

"Set me more upright, will you, Harve?"

Harvey hit the button, and the hospital bed brought her into a full sitting position, so she was more eye to eye with Jack.

"They claimed it was an accident, Jack, but I didn't believe that. JoAnn was a crazy whore in the sack, but she told me she was safe. She didn't wish to die. I always warned her she was taking too many risks. Her style of sex got her killed, and I believe it was all a conspiracy. Wolff had an upstanding wife and his father-in-law had big bucks. The wife's father was supposedly backing him in a political sense. Wolff had aspirations on being a supreme court justice. It was his dream to have a lifelong term in the court system. Funny though, isn't it?"

"What do you find funny, Daphne, because I'm in no laughing mood right now?" Jack's jaw flexed as he began grinding his teeth.

"No, it's not ha-ha, laughing funny; it's a weird sort of laughable, a contradiction kind of funny." Her voice was getting weaker. "He was all for law and order, but his sexual pleasures got in the way. The man was no better than the people he wanted to bring judgement down on. This slime ball was cut from the same despicable cloth."

"What about Jenna, what more does she know? If Sarge stayed on and they live together, I'm sure they had their own pillow talk. I need to go back to Waller and grill the both of them. I have half a mind to charge her with obstruction of an investigation."

She had lied to him, and he was damn well pissed.

"I can't stop you, so I'll just tell you. One night Jenna came up to the Crystal Barrel. Sarge was working there, and she came to pick him up. She and I had a few drinks and waited for them to get all the receipts in order. It had been over six months since Jo went missing and Celeste ended up dead. Jo liked Jenna, even though Jenna didn't care for Jo, so I wondered if she had heard from her."

"Had she heard from Jo?"

"No, Jenna said she thought Jo left town for good. I out-and-out cracked up. I said the only thing that would keep Jo out of Houston and this line of work was if she was dead. When I said it, Jenna's face went pale. She fumbled her words, and right then Sarge walked up. He looked at her, then at me."

"What did he say to you?"

"That I needed to mind my business like Jenna was told to do, and there wouldn't be any trouble."

"Why, what trouble? What did he have to do with it?"

"I think he helped move the body, and he was in too deep. It bugged Jenna out, always looking over her shoulder kind of behavior. About a week later, I called her. I wanted her to know I was going to the police about Jo because I thought someone had killed her. She started crying. I asked her what was wrong, and if she didn't tell me I'd come out to Waller, and beat the living shit out of her."

More excitement, more coughing, took a few minutes for her to talk again. Jack waited.

"Jenna begged me not to get the police involved. She knew Jo wasn't coming back. Then she told me Sarge had her sneaking round, stealing Celeste's car. There were some of her clothes in the car, and she took them to Sarge. She didn't go in, but she got a tiny glimpse into the room."

"What did she see?"

Daphne puckered her forehead. "A naked woman's feet on the bed, and not much more because Sarge was blocking her view. He's a big man. All she claimed to have seen were feet. She only guessed it was Jo, but she really didn't know."

"What motel was this?"

Jack knew which motel but he wanted to hear her say the name.

"Off Southwest Freeway, All Occasions, and it's still there, or so I've heard. So that's it, Jack. I feel bad all these years for not coming forward, but with crooked cops and people who were just plain mean, my worry was about my ass. And, because I didn't know who to trust back then, I buried it all, but I didn't forget about it. This is my deathbed confession and I feel I owe it to Jo, to get justice for her."

"Thank you for having the guts to get this out, Daphne, I

appreciate your candor. It's an amazing story, and I promise you I'll try to get all the physical proof I can to back your story up. But I cannot guarantee it will happen. You understand, right?"

She nodded weakly, worn out from everything, not just physically, but mentally exhausted as well.

"Yes, Jack, I understand. I am going to trust you to go the distance and get these bastards, and vindicate Jo's death. She might have been a lowly prostitute to most people, and I don't give a damn about those higher-than-mighty, my-shit-don't-stink kinds of people. JoAnn was my friend. Someone needs to pay for her murder. Now, I'm exhausted and want to sleep."

With a sincere, I'll do my best, Jack walked out of her room and Harvey followed him.

"Daphne doesn't have long. Hospice is coming. They are taking her off of her meds because she wants it to be over. She told you her story. Other than that she can't just free herself of cancer, or hang on just for me. My wife says she's ready to die." Harvey was back to formalities. "Detective West, I got a few more days with her because you didn't return her call right away. Daphne told me she couldn't die without telling someone on the police force her story. Your delay gave me about an extra week or two. Thank you for that."

"Good luck, Harvey. You'll be happy when she is no longer in pain, but losing her will be heartbreaking."

Harvey Walden offered Jack his hand, and Jack thanked him for letting him into their home.

Sitting in his truck, he felt a sense of sorrow for Harvey Walden and admiration for Daphne, for coming forward. Her story was bizarre, as bizarre as the make-believe stories written by writers with outlandish imaginations.

He'd been there for three hours, and had taped the entire conversation, even turning the tape over. This was an amazing story. How would he verify her story? And physical proof, where would he find it?

He wanted to call Lucky, but he didn't. Not everything was a sure thing, and he had to get all his notes in order before he shared Daphne's story. A missing whore and a dead madame, who was not dead, and Troy Wolff's name linked to the case. That had to be the worst part of her story. Jack did not want the proverbial shit to hit the fan, not yet. What he had to make sure of was it was not his shit hitting the fan and him losing his career.

19

S till awake at three A.M., Jack's mind was in a whirl. All he could think about was Daphne's story, the most enlightening interview ever. It was a confession, sort of, but she was not guilty of anything except keeping secrets. No use in tossing and turning in bed, he figured he might as well go into the station and start transcribing the notes from his tape, get a jump start on his paper work.

Jack was in the break room, pouring himself a fourth cup of coffee, when one of the night-shift officers still on duty came in for one last cup of jo.

"Here kind of early, aren't you, Jack?"

"Yep, Dutch, got a lot to do today, so I figured I'd get an early start." Jack yawned.

Dutch poured himself a cup, draining the pot.

"This sludge ought to open your eyes. I get off in an hour and it'll keep *me* awake until I get home." Dutch stifled a yawn.

"So, did the graveyard shift have anything exciting happen last night?" Jack leaned against the counter, sipping his hot coffee.

"Nope, it was sort of quiet for a change. We got a few domestic and drunk calls, none for homicide. No one got popped last night in our sector for a damn change."

That was not normal news—no fresh case coming in—but it was better than a new murder. It would cost Jack his job if people stopped killing one another. If murders stopped occurring altogether, it might mean the world had ended. It was a macabre way of having job security.

At 8:00, with most of the tape transcribed and his body wired after six cups of coffee, Jack was starving. Luck walked in as he was walking out.

"Whatdaya do, Jack, sleep here?"

"Why, do I look like something the cat dragged in or what?"

"Your eyes are bloodshot, and you have a coffee stain on your shirt, and your hair is a mess."

Jack had no sleep, too much coffee, spilling some on his shirt, and had run his fingers through his hair, going over Daphne's statement. Even if he looked like hell, he had energy. Jack would crash and burn later, but at present he was all keyed-up.

"Wonderful detective work, man, I almost slept here, been here since about four."

"Why so early, partner? Something came in, and you didn't call me? What gives?" Luck took his seat.

"Grab your missing girl case, because when the captain gets in we all need to talk."

JACK FINISHED RECOUNTING Daphne Walden's story. Captain Yao and Dawson Luck sat there, mouths opened, stunned into silence.

"This is more than—I mean, we can't, look I—" Davis Yao ran his hands over the back of his neck. "This is the craziest story I've ever heard."

"Judge Wolff possibly involved in this mess, that's crazy, man, just ca'rayzzy." Lucky whistled.

"Look, no one, no detectives worked this case thirty-four years ago, and we have to check it *all* out. I've heard stories and always dismissed them as gossip. Shouldn't we get to the truth?" Jack sat up and leaned in, watching Davis Yao's face, waiting.

"I will not let you go question Judge Wolff, not yet. For now, he is off limits. You have another plan in mind?" Davis Yao was getting a new ulcer; he felt his stomach burn.

"My best and only idea is to get Jenna Berrie and Max Renner in here. Better yet, we go to Waller. Give them a surprise visit and catch them off guard before they can concoct a story between them."

"That's a good place to start. Keep me posted. Boys, we have to get some damn concrete evidence before we even think about speaking with the judge, or this could go sideways. If this blows up in our faces, I want to be as far away from the judge as a person can get."

Davis Yao sat pensive for a moment, his brow wrinkled. Jack knew the captain's impromptu speech wasn't over.

Yao stood up, placing both hands flat on his desk, leaning in.

"If you find any proof that Wolff had a hand in any of this stuff, nail his hide to the floor, Jack, I mean it. People like him disgust me, going up the ladder with more skeletons in their closet than a graveyard, and hiding behind their black robes. How people climb to the top by covering stuff up pisses me off. It's always about money and power, those that don't have it end up faceless with cut-off fingertips in a car, left to rot."

"Captain, we'll do what we can, I promise."

Davis Yao rubbed his temples. A new ulcer gurgled, and a headache began building.

"I want to sort this out, but keep this on the down low. We don't want any type of gossip to start. Second, report to me and no one else. Fellas, we have to have all of our ducks in a damn straight row on this one."

At the small mom-and-pop diner, they took the back booth furthest away from the door.

"This is ludicrous, Jack. This Walden woman is an ex-prostitute. You think she's just out for revenge?"

"Listen, I was thinking about something that's bothered me about my case. It's what they found in her purse. The witnesses all said the same thing about my victim. This Mason chick was very timid and wasn't dating anyone. If she faked her death, why did the purse in her car have a roll of unopened condoms, and why were there zero pictures in her wallet? Everyone carried pictures with them back then."

"Let me recap to get this straight. My missing Princess Lay-Ya could be your girl, because your dead girl isn't dead. If this Mason person faked her death, she would need a body double. I read the reports. Your vic had no finger tips for printing, or a face since she had the back of her skull blown off. Now factor in my missing gal was a streetwalker, and ten to one she used condoms, so it stands to reason those condoms were hers."

"If this all turns out to be true, then it's premeditated, and they planned for your missing hooker to die that night. Here's what we have. A whore goes missing. They find a dead Celeste Mason, who, if Daphne is telling the truth, is not dead at all. Pete Bullard and Ian Simpson were both crooked cops, and Bullard whacks Randy Simpson. Scottie Buccella is the new *boss*. Daphne Walden thinks Judge Wolff knows what happened to the missing prostitute. Skip, a man with no last name yet, spills his guts one night because he's drunk."

"It's a complicated story, Jack, that's for sure. This Walden woman said this Mason woman was getting threats. Did she say who or what the threats were about?"

"No, all she told me was she thought it was mob related. Let's look up this Scottie Buccella. See what pops."

"The cops paid for the hookers too. You think Simpson was the cop?"

"Who knows? He's in an old folk's home. Apparently, he has dementia. But, we need to question him—"

Lucky cut him off. "There's a big chance he won't remember what happened."

"Listen, the mind is a strange thing and some stuff, bad stuff you can't forget, wish you could, but you can't. Look, no one worked this murder investigation. Daphne's story points that out clearly. Cranston, said Simpson and Bullard never came back to question him. Her body was behind his place. You'd think they would have grilled him more, wouldn't ya?" Jack paused, and Lucky jumped into his thought pattern.

"It's a conspiracy then?"

"I think someone knew or hoped someone was going to die that night, and Judge Wolff's in so deep he can't get out. That's what I think, and what we have to prove."

Jack's main thought was how to locate Celeste Mason. People changed their names and had plastic surgery—besides, if someone wanted to hide, it wasn't hard to do. Houston was a big, crowded place to hide.

"Here it is, Jack, a Scott Buccella, found dead in '93, shot once in the head, and the case is unsolved."

"Don't tell me it was Bullard and Simpson."

"How did ya know?" Sarcasm dripped off Lucky's lips.

"What else does the report say?" Jack rested back, his hands behind his head, propping a boot on his desk.

"They found his body on Southwest Freeway in an abandoned drive-in theater. Some kids went out there to drink. He'd been out there for eight days. The body severely decomposed because of the heat. They got his prints from the steering wheel and dental records, which confirmed his identity."

"They had his prints on file?"

"Yeah, he had an arrest jacket. His first arrest here in Houston was for a DUI." Lucky scrolled through the screen. "The dude has some stuff from up Chicago way, too. Ha. He got picked up for pandering, twice, illegal gaming, and running numbers and got off with a hefty fine and community service of all things. The creepo was also hauled in twice for the sale of illegal drugs, and did six months in county up in Cook County Jail, Illinois. Then the bastard got into a bar fight and was taken into custody for assault and battery with use of a lethal weapon."

"No kidding. What lethal weapon did he use?" Jack sat back upright and typed into his computer while listening to Lucky.

"He used a broken beer bottle."

"Do any time for any of it?" Jack listened as he typed and clicked on his computer.

"Sentenced to three years for the bar fight and got out in one. They issued Buccella a Texas driver's license in '82. He got the DUI in '83 in Texas."

"Okay, Luck, listen to what I found. The Buccella family has connections to mob syndications in Chicago. Says here this family was big back in the seventies up to the early nineties. Scottie was the nephew of Arturo Buccella. There was, let's see, Arturo, Savio and Mattia. These dudes were the main brothers of the Buccella Family. Their rival family, the Zumpanos, killed the oldest brother, Arturo, and that started a war between the families. They forced the Buccellas out."

"Then what happened? Did Scott Buccella's family ship him here to save his ass and then he starts his own funny business here in Texas? Jack, Italian families are close-knit. You think one of the Zumpanos whacked him for revenge?"

"Could be, but the case was never solved."

They sat in silence for a few minutes, absorbing this information wanting something to click, making sense.

"Okay, Jack, what's next?"

"We go talk to Ian Simpson."

A FENCED ENCIRCLED the property which sat back off the road. The main gates were shut, and there was a guard shack out front. The lawns well-manicured and cared for, the building not by any means large, with a wraparound porch that was the home to at least a dozen old-fashioned rocking chairs. They filled the flowerbeds with tiny gravel and there were large pots filled with marigolds, zinnias, daisies, and daffodils. Rose bushes sat nearer the building beside the front doors. Crepe myrtles lined a walkway at the front of the building. To the side of the main building sat a small cabana. A few tables and chairs were lined up. It looked like a nice place for the older folks to take in some fresh air and sit in the sun on a nice spring day.

"A private company owns this place, so it's not a State Home. They cater to dementia and Alzheimer patients only. Guess they fence the place in so patients don't wander off. Place looks costly—think a detective's pension was enough?" Lucky wondered who was footing the bill.

"Good question. I checked his files. Simpson had one son, and his wife died in a car accident when the boy was a teenager, about sixteen. No mother and the kid, Randy, was on his own. Not good for a sixteen-year-old, and he got into a lot of trouble. His records showed he worked part time at the Silver Moon as security. Then later he gets sucked in and can't get out."

"I can't understand how an upstanding cop could be so easy to corrupt. Being crooked is far from my thoughts and makes no sense to me. Corrupt people get caught."

"Money, Lucky, that's the reason. Simpson had one kid and no wife bringing in a second income. Let's go jog his memory."

The candy-striped volunteer greeted them at the front.

"Good afternoon, welcome to Wood Haven. Can I help you, gentlemen?" the cute, pert receptionist greeted them.

Jack badged her.

"We would like to visit with Ian Simpson. He was on the force years ago, and we want to discuss an old case he worked back in the day."

"You understand the patients here have dementia and can't remember their own names. What makes you think he'd remember the past?" Her tone of voice insulting, inferring he had to be stupid.

"I understand, but they can recall things every once in a while. We're going to take that chance." Jack's attitude stayed pleasant.

"Okay, suit yourself, but it'll be a waste of time. I'll go get the charge nurse from his section." Miss not-so-cute-and-perky left in a huff, her blonde hair swinging.

"What a snotty brat." Lucky, not a fan of smart-ass young people, scowled at her as she walked away.

A pleasant looking woman in nurse's attire approached them a few minutes later.

"May I help you?"

"Yes, you can, I'm Detective Jack West." He badged her. "We're here to speak with Ian Simpson. Once upon a time, he was a detective with the HPD. There's a case we'd like to discuss with him."

"My, my, this is a first. Ian never gets visitors, not a one. This might be the medicine he needs today. I'll bring him to the sunroom." She pointed to the room.

"Thank you, Nurse, uh..." Lucky looked at her name tag. "Nurse Theresa."

In fifteen minutes, Nurse Theresa wheeled in Ian Simpson. He looked old and frail, and Jack hoped this idea worked.

"Ian, this is Jack and Dawson. They're detectives like you used to be, you remember?" She spoke to him as one would speak to a child, squatting next to his wheelchair, patting his hand.

The old man looked at his nurse, then at Jack and Dawson. "I was a detective, you know that, boys?"

They nodded, and Nurse Theresa took charge again.

"They are here about your work on the force. You feel up to talking today, Ian?"

"Sure. Did you tell them I used to be a detective?"

She looked at Jack and gave a tiny smile. "He repeats himself a lot. I have other patients to assist, but if you need me, this is a call button; press it, and I'll come running." The nurse pointed out a cord with a button on it attached to Simpson's wheelchair.

"Thanks for the heads-up."

"My advice would be to take it slow, get him talking first and comfortable with you. There are days all he talks about is the job, and some days," she held her hands up, "he can't recall how to feed himself. He's had a few better days this week. I hope it continues for you today, and you get the information you need."

Nurse Theresa left them, and Jack began.

"May I call you Ian?"

"You betcha, I'd like that. Don't get many visitors anymore so it's nice that you fellas came to visit me." There was a sincere smile on his withered, old face. "Wife's dead. I got a worthless son. Yup, glad to have visitors."

"Your son, doesn't he come by to see you?" Jack wondered if he remembered Randy was dead.

"Hey, you fellas, I used to be on the police force. Boy, I loved my job."

Jack saw a spark in the old man's eyes. Ian missed his heydays. "So, your son, did he follow in your footsteps?" He fished again to see how his memory was.

"The boy was a pussy, and it didn't suit him, so I got him a job in a bar. Kid needed a job, but he mouthed off back then, got him in hot water. Randy's gone now, did I tell you that?"

"No, you didn't. Where did he go?" Jack kept his tone light and steady.

The old man cried, shaking his head. "It was bad. I should go to hell, I'm going to hell, and I don't wanna go to hell—please don't let them take me to hell."

"Okay, Ian, we won't let them take you anywhere, I promise. Can you tell me what happened?"

"He did it. Said he was sorry, but he had to do it. But he felt awful about it."

"Who did, Ian? Who did it?"

"Pete did. Do you fellas want to see pictures of me in uniform? I was a handsome guy once." His face became radiant, near animated.

"We can do that later, okay? What happened to Randy, do you remember?" Jack tried to keep the old detective focused.

"Was back in '57, or it was '59, I can't remember the exact year anymore, but they told me Randy was causing some problems, said they would have to shut him up." A pained look crossed his face.

"Who said Randy was a problem?" Jack was certain Ian's own partner hadn't wanted to kill Randy.

"The boss did. He was a mean bastard. And he had us—" He stopped and clamped his mouth shut.

"What did he have you do, Ian?" Jack understood these memories were painful, but this the only way.

"Well, he could kill me for this, but guess since you fellers are the police you guys can protect me, right?"

"Of course, it'll be our secret." Scottie was dead, too, but it was no use telling the old man.

"What happened to Randy?"

"It was him or me, that's what they said. Randy was running his mouth, causing trouble. Wanted me to do it, but I couldn't do it. Shit, I was his old man." He stopped, his face twisted up with anger.

"Pisses me off Randy left me, here and all alone. Ungrateful brat doesn't even come to visit."

"Yes, I can see how that would upset you. Can we talk about Pete Bullard, Ian? What kind of partner was he?" Jack hated manipulating the old guy, but if he gave them any clue, it was worth it.

"Pete was okay. I mean, he had to do what he had to do. We made it look like an accident, and I had to help. Randy was a football player, my son was. Did I tell you boys that?"

"What accident do you remember?"

Ian Simpson closed his eyes and a single tear fell.

"Uh-huh, it was in '58, just before New Year's Eve. Pete had already done it, broke his neck. It was real hard to keep from crying, but I had to man up, Pete told me, or I'd be the next one dead. We took the car, and we fixed things up, you know, like he had smashed head on into a tree, and he broke his neck in the accident. We made sure we got the callout, and that was that."

"Do you remember a man named Scottie Buccella?"

"You're Jack, ain'tcha?"

"That's right, I'm Jack."

"Well, Jack, that Italian son of a whore dog was an asshole. I never liked him. But, I did what he said to do because she told me I had to."

"Who told you, that you had to do what Scottie said to do?"

"Celeste did, who do ya think did? She was still the boss, even if that bastard wannabe Mafia boss thought he was."

Okay, that confirmed Daphne's story. She *was* still in the game. "What happened to Scottie, Ian?"

"Hell, Jack, *I* happened to that pasta eating bastard. When the order came down, I was happier'n shit to do the job. Like Dirty Harry said, that fucking made my day." Ian Simpson sounded forty years younger and pissed.

This shocked both Jack and Lucky; Ian Simpson had a fire in his belly. Before Jack found his tongue again, Lucky was already asking questions.

"What did you do, Ian?" Lucky leaned in, looking at the old man who now had a definite spark in his old faded blue eyes.

"One shot in the brain. I left him at the drive-in theater that was closed up and for sale. I wanted him to rot out there. Made it look like a mob hit. He was from a family of mobsters. I always figured it was a fitting way to do him. We had a boss, all he was, was a useless piece of chicken dung."

He got quiet, and the anger ebbed from his face, replaced with regret. While they were absorbing this new information, Ian looked at them both with a steady gaze.

"Back then, we had to do some bad stuff, but I was in too deep and they wouldn't let me out." He switched gears. "Listen, did you guys find Randy?"

Jack knew the death of his son more than bothered the old man—remorse haunted him.

"No, sir, I'm sorry, we haven't." Lucky tried not to let Ian hear the exasperation he was feeling.

"Alrighty, boys, what're we working on today; we got a fresh case or what?" Ian's eyes sparkled. He loved the job, even though he hadn't been on the force in over thirty-nine years.

"Uh, Ian, do you recall a case about a young woman found in her car? Her fingertips sliced off and her face gone. Someone shot her in the back of her head? It was a long time ago. If you don't recall it, that's okay." Lucky was back to letting Jack lead the interview.

The old man closed his eyes, concentrating.

"Let's see, back in what was it, '58 or '59, they found her on some land behind a motel, that case?"

"That's right."

"You boys heard I got some memory problems, right?"

"I do, but whatever you can remember might help us."

"Hmm, the Bull was with me back then. We were a great team once, ain't no more though. That girl, she was a looker, and had spirit," he cackled, "but then I used to, too. I was a detective once, did you know that?" he repeated himself.

"Uh-huh, we do, and I bet you were a great detective." Jack exhibited more patience than Lucky had.

"No, I wasn't. I didn't do my job like I should have." A single tear fell from his tired old eyes.

Jack scooted next to the wheelchair, and he put his hand on Ian's withered one.

"I hope you can help us with this case, Ian, make it right. Afterward we can say you did your job. You closed the case and helped the force out for old time's sake. That'll look good, your name on a closed file again. Whatdaya say?"

The old retired detective looked up at both of them. "I'd like that, but," he paused and looked around, "but you gotta keep it a secret, okay?"

"We're good at keeping secrets." Lucky angled his chair up closer to the old man.

"Do you remember a case, the one with the lady killed in a car? They discovered her body behind a motel?" Jack had his fingers crossed, figuratively. "What happened?"

"They said it looked like an accident. After it happened, things got nasty. Holy shit, those whores were something else. Some of 'em could make a man crazy. And by God, she was one gal who did it *all*." The old man's laughter filled with lewdness. "I was with her lots of times." He leaned in. "Don't tell my wife, keep that our secret."

"What happened to her, Ian?"

Ian Simpson sat quietly. He had that look on his face, he was thinking, remembering.

"That night they told us not to work the case hard, let it lie and go with what information we had left in the car. Bull and I did. We left it unfinished. We both got money to keep our mouths shut and for closing our eyes. I missed that whore. But you do what the boss wants, no matter what. Have you guys seen my son, Randy? He hasn't been around, and I sure would like to see him."

"No, sir, we haven't." Lucky felt sorry for the old man. "Who was the boss, Ian, when the whore got whacked?"

"She was. It was always her."

Jack nodded, understanding that he meant Celeste; she was the *her*, Ian was referring to.

"Ian, this prostitute, what made her special?" Lucky joined the conversation, knowing that the girl in question might be his missing girl.

"Hell, boys, she liked it every which way, including standing on her head. She was a mean one in bed, and she liked it when her fella was mean, too. Did I tell you I had a son? His name is Randy?"

"You did. Tell us about her. Can you do that?" Jack tried to keep him focused on the Cutter woman.

"Shit, Randy liked JoAnn, and the reason was cuz she gave it to him free, that skank. Made me pay for it, but heck, she never said no, she'd darn near let you do anything you wanted in the sack."

"JoAnn was a busy girl then, right?" Jack stayed with it.

"Oh, sure, we all wanted her. She did it all, and I mean she did it all. She liked the top dollar fellas more than us coppers. But you know, I know."

"No, I don't, what, what do you know, Ian?" Jack had some good information, but he needed more. He had an overabundance of dead people, and they sure weren't talking, and a high-ranking official he couldn't approach, at least not yet.

"That whore got carried away, was kinda scary. She told me once that she always made sure she was safe, never putting herself in any danger she couldn't manage. Lord have mercy, she was the best one of the lot. I think it was that young punk. I never liked him, but you can't like everybody I guess. He did it, I'm positive he did."

"Now who on earth would be so bad that you wouldn't like?" Jack searched the old man's face.

"Oh, them asshole attorney fellas; they thought they were better than us cops. We were just lowlifes to them. Boys, I am hungry. How about we drive into town and get a steak? I'd like that. You fellas want to eat?"

"Tell you what, soon as we get done here, how about I go get you a big juicy burger with some fries? Right now, let's talk about the case, okay?"

"Oh yeah, yeah, yeah, sure, sure, whatcha wanna know?"

"This woman, the one who did it all, did she have a street name?" To Jack's surprise, a hearty belly laugh emitted from the old man.

"Huh, I'll be damned, hell I hadn't thought about that in close to forty years, but she did, she did at that. Have I told you fellers I was on the force?"

Luck got up and looked at Jack with a *Heaven help us* expression. "Yes, and we heard you were top-notch back then."

"No, I wasn't. I used to be, but then I needed money. They sucked me in to the dark side. Just like the *Star Wars* dark side. I even had a Princess Lay-Ya. Bang-up super whore, but she was bad news for me. That's when it got worse." Spit particles shot from his lips, and his hands were shaking. Jack thought he'd be using the nurse call button, but Ian settled down as fast as he'd revved up.

"It's all right, Ian, everything will be fine, you hear me? We're on your side, brothers in blue all the way," he assured him.

Ian sat like a ghost in a gloomy state, and then his demeanor changed again. He was like flashing Christmas lights. You couldn't be sure what color would flash next.

"Is Randy ever coming back to see me before I die?"

"We'll check around for you, okay?"

Randy had been dead for a long time. Jack figured the old guy knew this deep down in his heart. It would be best for him now if he carried the hope that his son would show up someday. The old retired cop didn't want to recall that he'd taken part in covering up his own son's murder. His current state was enough punishment. He would answer to his maker one day, and it wasn't his call.

Jack got back to the girl. "What happened to Princess Lay-Ya, Ian?"

"Huh, that feller, the Big Bad Wolff, he happened to her, the damn fool. He was some hotshot, or he worked for some damn hotshot Asian lawyer. I hate attorneys. They think they're above the rest of us."

This matched up with Daphne's story—it involved Troy Wolff. Aggressive again, Ian scolded himself. "You dummy, you moron, you big fool." He started slapping at his knees. Drool slipped through his lips.

"What's the matter, Ian?" Jack was worried the man would have a stroke and his hand was reaching for the pull cord when Ian spoke.

"Damn it, I wish I was a better cop. Hope they never find out I ain't, because I gotta keep my job. My paycheck is all we got. Randy is on the football team, and he wants new cleats."

His face was angelic. "You guys want to come to the game next week?"

"Ian, I think we're all ready for that burger. I'm going to go get your nurse."

He wanted to make sure she would have the kitchen make him a big juicy burger, instead of them bringing one back. He didn't want the old guy disappointed.

"Did you get any useful information?"

Lucky nodded. "Yes, ma'am, we did, and you're right, he repeats himself a lot."

"Here's my card, and if he needs anything, call me. I'd like to visit him when I can—not as a fellow police officer, but as a man visiting another man."

"I think that's a fine idea, Detective West, a very fine idea indeed. Call me to arrange it. Oh, he'd love a ride into town for a day. Don't wait too long, because one never knows when your last ride is coming for you, understand?"

"Yes, I do." Cole popped into his thoughts. They waved goodbye to Ian at the door. Nurse Theresa backed up the wheelchair and took him back to his room. They both knew in time, after a brief time, Ian would have forgotten they were even there.

20

In the truck neither man spoke as they replayed what they'd heard. Lucky spoke up first.

"So, what we have is this. A dying hooker spills her guts, implicating Judge Wolff in the death of her prostitute friend. An old, retired detective who has dementia also says the big bad wolf, meaning Judge Wolff, had something to do with the alleged death of this hooker. And he tells us his partner, Pete Bullard, killed his son and he assisted in the cover up. Besides that, someone shoots two men in cold blood, execution style. The hooker, my missing girl, is the only witness and since she is dead, that case goes cold.

"Your dying hooker states the hit on Richmond Avenue was a planned hit, but on who's orders? This same hooker says the dead lady in the car is not who we think she is, because Celeste Mason was the boss, but she isn't dead because a sad, drunk, stupid bartender spills his guts one night. Add in our dementia-ridden retired detective, Ian Simpson, admitted he killed Scottie Buccella. After Buccella dies, there's a new person in charge, but there isn't a new guy because Celeste is still the boss. If what Ian says is true, she never stopped running the show. Jesus, Jack, this is like a bad crime novel, don't you think?"

"Yeah, it's a lot but, there are a couple of problems."

"My Lord, Jack, only a couple cuz I see half a dozen."

Jack ignored his partner's peeved tone of voice. "Ian Simpson is around seventy, seventy-five, and with his diagnosis of dementia, who's to say how much longer he has? The ex-hooker is dying of lung cancer. She was in terrible shape when I met her, and there is no miracle around the corner for her, so she's most likely already dead. Neither one of them will take the stand. We don't have a last name for this Skip, or if he's alive. This leaves us with zilch. I want to nail Judge Wolff. We have to think about what should happen to Simpson later. He's the least of our worries."

"Fine, Jack, then what's our next step?" His irritation gone, Lucky wanted to get to the truth. It was high time they solved these cases.

"We need to compare DNA. I want to see about exhuming the body to prove my dead girl is, in fact, your missing girl."

"One body? And just who do you have to compare it to, Jack?"

"Celeste Mason's mother, we'll have to exhume her body too."

Lucky's whistle was low and long and it turned into him just blowing out air, since he didn't whistle well.

"Who in the hell will pay for this, and who do you have in mind to sign off on this request? I don't think the captain will agree with this plan at all. And Jack, an exhumation, word gets out the judge might hear—"

Jack held up a hand to stop Lucky. "Yeah, yeah, I get it. I say we head back, and see what Yao says."

"Okay, what about finding a family member that will give you permission? Then Captain Yao's gonna tell you someone over at the courthouse has to sign off on the exhumation, then what?"

"I think we can bypass the family members, especially seeing how old this case is. As far as a judge, we'll deal with it, and try to keep Wolff out of it. I'm sure the captain has friends. All we need is someone in the court system that can be secretive and discreet."

"Uh-huh, good luck with all of that. Jack, are you hungry?" Lucky's stomach rumbled. "And no, I do not want a juicy burger like you promised Simpson."

"Ian Simpson is an amusing guy. His situation is sad, but he was comical. How about we stop for some chicken; you want takeout or dine-in?" Jack began scanning the area for a chicken place.

"Grab-and-go would be fine. We can't be fiddle-farting around."

Lucky was right, they needed to get the ball rolling, and exhumations would take forever. That was, if they got approval.

"You WANT to disinter that dead girl's body. Jack, are you out of your mind? Our budget is already taking a beating." Davis Yao was not happy at all about this suggestion.

"I know, I know. And it won't make you any happier, Captain, but it's not just one body we need to exhume."

"Christ Almighty, Jack, who else do we need to dig up?" His blood pressure rose to stroke level as sweat beaded on his brow, and Lucky was ready to dial 911.

"Celeste Mason's mother. She's buried next to whoever is really dead in the same cemetery. What I'd like to prove beyond any doubt is that the dead girl in the car was not Mason. We can use mitochondrial DNA. That's who, and why."

Davis Yao sat back. This burden was weighing on him. Exhumations were something you couldn't keep under your hat. He'd need permission from a family member, a warrant, and a judge to sign off on the disinterment. If word got out, it would spread, and he didn't want that to happen. It would take a lot of budget to do what Jack wanted done. Now with so many people in the mix too, this was not good. This was newsworthy. If it hit the papers, Judge Wolff would read it, and then he would find out they were onto him.

They sat wordlessly as they watched a range of emotions play across Captain Yao's face.

"Jack, tell you what," the captain began, "we won't go as far as exhumations—it has to be our absolute last resort. A huge concern I have is keeping this out of the papers. Hellfire, Jack, exhumations mean big news. No way can we keep that under wraps. I want to get this solved, but not this way."

Captain Yao looked at them, shaking his head. This was ludicrous. What would be next, tearing through Judge Wolff's house with a search warrant?

"First, see what else you can get from that Berrie woman and the fella she shacks up with. Before we have to dig up bones, Jack, I want some old-fashioned police work done. Talk to them, break one of them. If what the dying hooker says is true, then they both know more than they're telling you. If we have to exhume bodies, Chief Pratt will get involved. I'd like to keep him out of it, for now. There would be no need to dis-entomb bodies if we had everyone's DNA sample on file. That would be cheaper than an exhumation."

"I understand, Captain. I guess we need to head out to Waller right now."

"Why not call them to come into the station?"

"Lucky and I already discussed re-questioning them, but I want to go out there, surprise them. I don't want them to concoct a story before we get there."

"You're right, Jack. The element of surprise is a much better idea. Bring me back something, boys. You have my nuts in a vice, and if I get squeezed, you two can count on getting your nuts squeezed even harder and longer. Got it?"

Yeah, they got it all right. If it all went south, they could be in a regular squad car, wearing blues, and handing out traffic tickets to pimply-faced teenagers.

JACK'S TRUCK kicked up the dust as they drove on the county road to Jenna Berrie's house.

"Why do you think people want to live way out here? There's nothing, and I mean *nothing*, that could get me away from convenience and the city."

"Some folks like living out in the sticks, Lucky, but I have to agree, I ain't one of 'em."

Jack parked behind Max Renner's truck. Next to Renner's truck sat a beat-up, light-blue Toyota.

Stepping out of the truck, game faces on, they needed some answers.

He knocked with two sharp raps, and Jenna Berrie opened the door, and a look of surprise crossed her face.

"You, out here again, shit! I already told you everything the last time you were here." She crossed her arms and scrunched up her nose and eyes, annoyed that he had come back to their house.

"Ms. Berrie, this is my partner, Detective Dawson Luck. I've got some other information I would like to share with you. Then I intend to discuss all the information you gave me last time."

"Look, Detective, all I will tell you will be everything I already told you. How will that help you?"

"We can talk here, or downtown, your choice. You and Mr. Renner are both persons of interest in an unsolved homicide. If I have to, I'll see what legal action I can take to get you both to the police station. Do I make myself clear?"

She let out an exasperated sigh. "Fine, come in, but I don't want it to take all day."

Jack walked in behind her and looked around. "Is Mr. Renner here?"

"Yeah," she huffed out, "he's out back in the shed. I'll go get him." With that, she scuttled out of the room.

"The fear of God crept into her face when you said legal action, Jack." Dawson Luck scanned the front room in the small manufactured home.

The back door squeaked and Jenna came through the other room, Max behind her.

"Jenna tells me you detectives want to speak with us." He was wiping grease from his hands. "I got a motor repair I'm doing out back, gotta get it done today. You need to make this quick."

Dawson Luck took the big bald man in. A tall, barrel-chested man with a snake tattoo wrapped around his neck that looked like it was crawling upward and ready to strike at any moment.

"Mind if we sit?" Jack took a seat before Max responded.

"Since you already sat, I reckon that's fine by me. Now, what's this about?" He stuffed the greasy rag in his back pocket and folded his arms over his massive chest.

Jack pointed to the love seat across from where he sat. "Get comfortable, because the four of us are going to have a little chat."

Jenna gave Max a sideways glance that Jack didn't miss.

"Come on, Sarge."

Max sat by her, filling up the loveseat with his gigantic body. The large man crossed his arms and looked straight at Jack without blinking.

"So, we're sitting. You gonna tell us why you're here?"

Jack took a small tape recorder out of his breast pocket and sat it on the coffee table.

"I am sure Jenna told you about my last visit here. Is this correct, Mr. Renner?"

"She did, and I would prefer if you would call me Sarge. I don't go by Max unless it is official. Is this official, Detective West?"

"Yes, sir, it's an official call, Mr. Renner. I want you and Jenna to listen to the tape of an interview I had with Daphne Walden. I think it is very interesting and informative."

Jack looked at them. Jenna's face had turned ashen white. She fumbled in her back pocket for her cigarettes. Taking the pack, she tried to tap one out, and it broke.

"Oh, hell." She heaved a sigh.

Sarge took the pack, tapped one out, and then he helped her light it.

"I would ask you both if you minded if Jenna here smokes, but it's my house, and I say she can." He looked at Detective Luck.

"Open the front door if you don't mind. It'll keep the smoke from filling up the room."

Lucky obliged, opening the door, and remained standing. Once he'd got a look at Max Renner, he'd already unhooked the strap on his Glock. It wasn't often that he profiled, but his gut said to monitor this big tatted biker dude.

Jack took the tape and put it in the cassette player.

"After you've both heard the interview, we're going to talk, here or at the station. And like I told Ms. Berrie, that's up to the both of you."

"Okay by us, we have nothing to hide."

Jack doubted it, he doubted it very much as he hit play and the voice of Daphne Walden came alive in their living room.

———

THE CASSETTE PLAYER STOPPED, and Jack looked at Jenna.

"Okay, Ms. Berrie, let's start over. First off, you were one of the girls back then, and if what Daphne says is true, you were more than a casual acquaintance of Celeste Mason, is that correct?"

She took another drag of her third cigarette.

"Uh-huh." He scarcely caught her answer.

"You knew JoAnn. You, her, and Daphne were close friends, is that correct?"

"I was close to Daphne, not so much with Jo." Her voice trembled and she took a long drag on her cigarette.

"And what about Celeste Mason, she was more than just a gal you sort of knew? Why did you lie to me?"

"I didn't lie to you. Look, I knew her because she ran the girls, but I wasn't close to her. No one was. Can't you let her rest in peace?"

"Even if that were something we could do, what about JoAnn?

She was one of you girls. How about her, Jenna? No one has seen her for over thirty-four years. Are we just letting her rest in peace, too?"

A single tear slipped off her cheek, and Sarge took her hand.

"Look, she feels bad enough she lied to you. I wanted her to forget that part of her life. Now here you come and dredge all this shit up, she's a nervous wreck, look at her."

"And you, Max, you were an enforcer following orders, is that right? So, what orders did you get? Help kill off the whore and cover it up? Were you the one who shot those men on Richmond Avenue? I know you know, and I will find out." Jack stood up. His tone aggressive, his words delivered harshly. He was giving it a shot, trying to goad him into saying something.

"I had nothing to do with shooting, Scott—" Max stopped talking.

"Was it Scottie Buccella who shot that attorney, Stockard, and the man called Archie Bowers?" Luck jumped in.

"Even if it was, and you could prove it, what good would it do? I'm sure you know all about Scottie if you've been digging, and you found out he's dead." Max's anger smoldering, he was sick of this crap.

"Okay, Jenna, let's see what we have here. You lied about knowing Celeste as more than a mere acquaintance. I am betting you know more than you are telling me, so what else are you hiding? If I don't get some answers here, then we can all go downtown and discuss it, all night long, if that is what it takes." Jack slapped the coffee table, and Jenna jumped.

"I knew the woman because she was my boss, for crying out loud. I didn't have any idea about her life or stuff. It wasn't like we all hung out together. Most of the time back then, I was on my back making money for her. I don't do that anymore, I stopped when JoAnn—I just stopped."

"When JoAnn what, Jenna, when she disappeared off the face of the earth?" Dawson Luck stood more erect, looking first at her, then at Mr. Renner.

Renner ignored Detective Luck and focused on Jack.

"Look here, Detective West; if you want to arrest us, you better have a bloody reason to do so. I have a very smart lawyer, and I'm ready to make a call. Unless that's the case, I think you should leave now." Sarge was bluffing, he didn't have a lawyer.

"Take a seat, Mr. Renner, or we'll take a trip downtown and I am not joking, lawyer or not." He moved his attention back to Jenna. "Daphne wanted to make sure she told her story. She wanted this truth out, to clear up an old life, so how about you, Jenna?" Jack looked at the woman.

"I ain't dying, and my conscience is clean enough." Jenna tried to keep her voice from quivering.

"What about your conscience, Max?" Jack looked at him. "You wanna clear yours up? Do you have anything you want to get off your chest?"

"Like what?" The vein in Sarge's neck was visibly pulsating.

"As in what happened in the motel room, that's what. I'm telling you, if we can tie you to what happened, I will charge you both with capital murder. You might even face the needle." Jack's voice boomed louder with each word.

"Look, I'm gonna say this again. I wasn't involved with what happened in that room." Sarge stopped short, damn it the words in the air before he thought about what he was disclosing.

"If you say you had nothing to do with what happened, then you know what happened. So what the hell happened in that room?" They were pissing Lucky off with all the lying.

"How should I know? I've already told you I wasn't there."

Jack took a different approach. "Here's a question, Jenna—was Troy Wolff ever one of your johns? Because I am betting, if I figure this correctly, he tried all you girls, and he liked JoAnn the best. Is this right?"

"Yes, he was, once, but only once. The man was a lunatic, and every hooker was afraid of him, except Jo." Her hands no longer shook as she narrowed her eyes. She was sure Jack figured she'd hooked for the judge back before he was Judge Wolff. Even if he didn't, all he had to do was go ask Daphne. That was, if she hadn't kicked the bucket yet.

"What do you want from me, from us? It happened a dozen lifetimes ago. Just let the dead stay dead, because we can't bring them back. Nothing you do will change a damn thing." She stubbed out her cigarette, crushing it to pieces.

"Oh, I don't know, Jenna, a lot might change. People have gotten away with murder; and throughout this entire story, everyone keeps saying Celeste Mason is *not* dead. My job is to get justice for the dead. What I'd like to hear is what happened the night JoAnn disappeared. And damn it, where in the hell is Celeste, because she isn't dead!" Jack's anger was palpable.

Jenna sat up straight as a rod. She was shaking, not from fear, but from anger. Sarge felt her raging emotions. Jenna was at a breaking point.

"Don't, Jenna, you don't have to say anything else." A scowl crossed his face, and laid his hand on her to keep her quiet, but she flicked it off.

"No, Sarge." The corners of her mouth pulled into an ugly frown. "Look, I wasn't in the room. I can't tell you what I don't know. I thought it was JoAnn in the room, but all I saw were feet on the bed. A few days later, no one knew where she had high tailed it to, and a week later, Celeste's dead body turned up. Damn it, it might have been Celeste on the bed, because I'm telling you, again, for the fucking last time, I couldn't see who it was."

"You were there, weren't you, Max?"

Sarge was dead silent.

"Are you being blackmailed?"

"Sure, you can see we have buckets of money to pay a blackmailer. Look around at the pots of gold. So in answer to your effing question, no, no one is blackmailing us." Jenna's sarcasm was obvious. "Look, I wasn't as good as JoAnn and Daphne were in the *profession*, but I was a fantastic topless dancer. The other stuff I didn't care for as much. I supplied Quaaludes to the girls who needed to relax. They needed that edge to dance nude and get kinky. It was how they made the most money. And yeah, Daphne used to buy from me, but she wasn't a heavy user. After all of that other shit happened, we moved out here. I started selling drugs to make a little money for us, since I wasn't dancing or hooking anymore."

Sarge was stone-cold silent.

"Are you still in the drug trade?" Lucky spouted out accusingly, and she shot him a look of contempt.

She jumped up, her face turned red, and she stomped her foot.

"No, no, I am not. If I were and made riches, would I be living out here in Podunk Waller, Texas?"

If they hadn't been flat dab out in nowhere land, all of Harris County could have heard her. Lucky inched his hand toward his piece. If she were to go nuts, he would fire a shot and put a hole in their ceiling.

"You don't understand, do you? I left that life behind me, and I won't go back." Her arms were flying wildly; Jenna was royally pissed off.

"Calm down, Ms. Berrie," Jack warned her.

She plopped hard back onto the tatty love seat. Sarge got up off of the love seat.

"I think you need to leave now, unless we are under arrest. Are we?" The man's jaw clenched visibly.

"No. But this is not the end of this either, understand?" Jack stood and looked down at Jenna. "You and Max are both involved, and if I have to make it my life's mission, I'll find what I need to find to haul both of you in for covering up a murder and any other trumped-up charge I can think of."

Jack West didn't smile, flinch, or blink. Yet they both sat, wordlessly.

"Here, Jenna, take my card, again. I want to make sure you have my number."

"Ms. Berrie," Lucky spoke to her, and she twisted around to face him.

"What?"

"Do you know a fellow named Skip? He used to bar tend at the Crystal Barrel. Would either of you know his last name?"

"I don't know him."

Jack looked first at Jenna, then at Max, his best cop face on.

"I know you know Skip." He looked at Max. "Daphne stated in her story that you stayed on at the clubs. So keep lying Mr. Renner, because I will find out the truth."

He looked at Jenna.

"You." Jack pointed his finger at her. "You knew something happened, but you never said a word. From Daphne's story you told her JoAnn wasn't coming back. Max was still working for the boss back then. You just keep lying too, because I have no doubts that you know the truth too. I mean hell, you sleep together, I'm sure you share secrets."

"What we say in the bedroom ain't any of your goddamn business."

"Fine, keep lying, but we know the dead girl isn't Celeste. We've figured out how to get DNA to match to the dead girl, and when the reports come in, the truth will come out." He lied, knowing there were no reports coming, but they didn't know that.

"This was your chance to clear up a few things. But hey, it's your lives you're putting on the line. So keep telling me you know nothing. Because once the truth comes out, I swear to charge the both of you with as many charges as I can find." Someone was going to go to jail. Jack's determination to make this happen was his driving force.

Two unresponsive faces with narrowed angry eyes stared up into Jack's face.

"Detectives, I know you see the front door. Now you can use it and leave us alone," Max gritted out between clenched teeth.

Jack was mad at himself for not being able to break at least one of them to tell the actual story.

Lucky snapped the strap back on his Glock and put on his seat belt.

"We know they were there, Jack, and we know Jenna knows something. So does that big goon, Max. We got one thing out of this drive though."

"What's that?" Jack backed up, turned, and punched the gas, spraying white gravel behind him and kicking up white dust.

"A filthy truck. So, now what's the plan?"

Jack was silent; he was thinking.

"Jack, did you hear me? What's our next move?" The time on the dash said it was dinner-thirty.

"Tell you what. I'll drop you off so you can get home to your wife. I'll see you in the morning bright and early, say seven-ish?"

Again, Luck shook his head. What a freaking waste of an afternoon. Nothing significant had come of it, but he was keeping his mouth shut. He was glad to be quitting for the day.

"Okay by me. I'm starved, and I know the department would howl at the moon on more O.T. if it's not approved by the captain."

Jack agreed. Besides, this was way past the first forty-eight hours. Like 34 years past.

He dropped Lucky off on Travis Street and waved. Jack wanted nothing more than to see Gretchen, and then his day would be complete, case solved or not.

"I t's close to one, Jack, and I am starved. How 'bout I go grab us a bite?"

"Sounds like a super idea. Where're you going?"

"Antone's, you want your regular?"

"Two. Here's forty. It's on me today." Jack pulled out two twenties and gave Lucky the cash.

"Thanks, Jack, be back shortly."

Jack thought about everything, hoping two and two would somehow equal four, but he kept ending up with five.

What had perplexed him had been the condoms. No mystery now. The condoms belonged to the prostitute; the only safe thing she did. He gathered up the forensic report again. The medical examiner stated death was a gunshot to the head. There was no sign any sexual assault had occurred, so no rape kit was conducted. Jack thought about all of this, and Daphne's story. There would have been semen if this woman was sexually active with Wolff that night. Here she was found behind a motel, a place where crap like selling sex happens, so why had the medical examiner ignored it? Was someone paying him off, too?

He read the medical examiner's name: Layton Conch. Jack had heard of the guy. Conch had been an old fart, even back then. They'd found him dead in the morgue one day. The old man died during an autopsy. He'd had myocardial infarction, layman's terms: the man died of a heart attack. It had been the talk in the department back then. Was it bad luck or bad karma? Who could say? Shooting a woman in the head was not a sexual fetish. It was murder. The reports stated there wasn't much blood, just small bits of brain matter. Blood spatter would have been everywhere had she been shot in the car. It would have spattered on all of her clothes, too. Maybe she was naked. It would stand to reason in her profession. But why had they bothered to redress her then? And if they didn't shoot her in the car, where did they kill her? Cranston said none of his rooms were out of order that night. Had the killers done that good of a clean-up job?

Jack was also curious about Randy Simpson's car accident, so he did a file search on auto accidents around that same year. It took him a few minutes, but he found the accident report.

A one-car accident. The report stated his blood alcohol level was over the legal limit and his neck had been snapped when he hit a tree head-on. This had happened about three miles from the Silver Moon, and his car had been found at four in the morning by a passerby.

Scrolling through the reports, he searched for the responding officers. Well, whatdaya know. Pete Bullard and a patrol cop named Jacobs. Why would a homicide detective go to a car accident? He paged over to forensic report. Yep, there it was—Layton Conch's name. Seems he was the medical examiner called for every case Bullard and Simpson worked. The other medical examiner, Stan Harlow, Jack figured was a straight arrow.

"Two regular Antone's served up, with chips and a Diet DP, but no change. I dropped the two dollars and a few coins in their tip jar." Lucky handed Jack a sack with his subs and his drink.

"Okay, thanks for going." His voice trailed off as he took the wrapper off a po'boy and took a bite. His mind filled with a thousand questions and not one damn answer.

———————

THEY HAD BEEN at it for hours, and zilch was coming together—just more questions.

"You want something? I'm headed to the vending machines and for coffee?" Lucky stood and arched his back, stretching.

"Coffee, thanks."

Back with strong coffee, Lucky set a cup on Jack's desk, and then took his trove of chips and cookies, diving in.

"Get any ideas while I was gone?" Lucky had a mouth full of chips, and he crunched the words out.

"Yeah, just one. We need to locate this Skip dude, the one Daphne mentioned. I want to find out if anyone knows him."

Lucky chewed and then swallowed. "No one's given him a last name. What do you propose to do?"

"Take a drive over to the Crystal Barrel and ask around."

"Jack, man, it's been over thirty years. All you'd do is waste your time."

"Maybe, but if there were stories floating about back then, maybe someone has heard a legend about what might have happened. At least we can mark this off our lists of leads."

"You wanna go tonight?"

"Yes, tonight say about ten."

"Awe, man, you're kidding, right?"

"No, I'm not and I'll meet you here at the station at ten, and we can ride together. I'll drive."

"Okay, all right, I don't like it, but I'll do it." This little trip didn't excite him one inch.

Silence filled the room. They went back to work. Lucky cursing in his head because he had to drive back and Jack thinking about his dinner date with Gretchen tonight. He would have to cut the date short. Besides, he did not know how it would go, and this gave him the best excuse to leave early if he wanted to bug out.

It was almost four. Jack was frustrated, and so he packed it in for the day. He'd be right back at it later tonight, so leaving early was no big deal.

"See you tonight, here at the station, ten o'clock. I'm outta here."

"Okay, Jack, I'll be here."

It was 4:00. He wasn't Jack's boss. If he wanted to leave, he could. Hell, made no big difference; they were going to be right back here later. Lucky packed it up and left, too.

———————

JACK'S NERVES were jittery as he showered and shaved, combed his hair, and dabbed on cologne. He wore jeans and a nice button-down shirt. Dressed this way, he'd fit in at the club tonight. He would leave from her house and go right to the station.

Gretchen's neighborhood was nice, small houses, older, but nicely maintained. He pulled up in her driveway and took a deep breath. No bar, no barflies, no work, and his nerves were jumping like crazy.

Before he pressed the bell, the door opened. "Hey, Cowboy Cop, come in. I heard you drive up."

She was a breath of fresh air. Dressed in a pair of faded worn jeans, a nice blue pullover shirt, and barefooted. Her hair was hanging loose, her face makeup-free. He was secretly glad she didn't pack it on like some women did.

"Sorry I didn't dress up more, but like I told you, I am a no pomp and frills girl. Hope you don't mind."

"You look beautiful, and something smells mouthwatering."

"Hope you like pot roast and the fixings. I thought dinner in would be good. Can I get you a beer?"

"Dinner in is a wonderful idea, glad you thought of it, and yeah a beer would hit the spot right now."

Cold beers in hand, she offered to show him her homey place.

"It was my grandmother's house. I was her only granddaughter, and she left it to me when she died, which was about three years ago. This house holds memories for me, Jack. Some good and some not so good, but that's life for you."

"It's a nice house, Gretch, fits you."

Jack looked around. Gretchen's personality was all around her house. He felt it.

"If you're ready, let's eat." Taking him by the hand, she led him to the kitchen. Such a simple act, holding someone's hand, and his toes curled a bit—what was this woman doing to him?

"I haven't had a home-cooked meal like this since my mom and dad moved off to Florida."

"I have dessert too—homemade blackberry cobbler and vanilla ice cream. You let me know when you're ready for dessert." She winked at him. He wasn't sure what that meant, and she'd smiled at him with a devious, yet sweet smile. Jack blushed at what he was thinking.

"Come on, I'll clean up later."

She led him back to the living room. Taking a seat next to him, she curled one foot up under her leg and then angled toward him to see him as she talked.

"Tell me about Jack growing up."

Jack talked about his boyhood days and shared some of his memories, but he left Cole's story out. Right now, that was too personal. Besides, it was a demon in him, and he wanted zero gloom tonight. Gretchen entertained him with her grandma stories, and stories of growing up with a brother and male cousins.

"Jack, it's a wonder I act like a girl at all. Boys were all I had to pal around with. Even in school, my best friend was a boy."

His hand reached up and touched her cheek. "You're a fine woman, Gretchen, you're beautiful, smart, and—" He paused, and then he leaned in and kissed her, butterflies dive-bombing in his gut.

She responded, leaning closer to him. Pulling her foot out from under her leg, she put one hand on his shoulder and the other on his arm, and she deepened the kiss.

Gretchen pulled away a hair, their lips just touching, and she opened her eyes, locking hers onto his. "Wow, can we do that again?" She muffled a laugh as he took her lips again.

Kissing her, he felt like a sixteen-year-old boy. Jack hated to leave, but he had to. From her place, it would take him twenty minutes to get to the station.

"Gretchen, I've had a fantastic night, but I have to meet my partner at the station at ten. The food was wonderful, the cobbler was delicious, and you're a wonder of a woman." He took her hands in his. "I hope to do this again, sooner than later." He pulled her in, taking her lips, and she responded.

"Lord, woman, it makes it hard to leave with kisses like that."

"I've saved plenty of 'em for you, Cowboy Cop. Now, go save the world, and I'll see you soon."

She watched him back up, and as he drove off, he waved to her. Gretchen felt like a fourteen-year-old girl, giddy and fabulously happy.

LUCKY WAS ALREADY in the parking garage, a scowl on his face, when Jack arrived.

"You ready to go clubbing, Luck?"

"Not my kinda club, I'm sure, but let's get going."

The Crystal Barrel Night Club, what a nasty hole-in-the-wall. It was a complete dive. A large neon sign hung above the building and in large red letters *Crystal Barrel* flashed, and some bulbs were out. The letters were over a large barrel, which looked like a huge wooden keg. Outlined in tiny white lights, the keg sparkled, and it resembled crystals or diamonds, thus the name Crystal Barrel.

"They should have called it the *Old Crystal Keg*. Can't wait to see what this place looks like on the inside. What a dive, Jack."

"Come on, I'll buy you a glass of water."

"Hey, you're chipper again, you gonna tell me or what?"

"Nope, let's just work, and you stop worrying about my *chipper*."

Jack was in a super cheery mood. He felt that he and Gretchen had connected.

"Damn it, Jack, I love gossip. Fill me in."

"Nope. Let's see what we can find out in here, ya with me, Luck?" He was keeping Gretchen to himself. And it was fun driving his partner bonkers. Jack wasn't talking, but he would one day. Right now, they needed to be detectives, not gossiping old hens.

The place was just as Lucky had feared—rundown, drab, and filthy. White linoleum flooring, now yellowed, scuffed up, and in some places, torn. Mismatched seating and the stale odor of old cigarette smoke and beer filled the vents. The smell saturated the club. Lucky was sure anywhere in the place he sniffed, from the floor to the bottles on the shelf behind the bar, it would all reek of smoke.

"Don't want to have a drink here, Jack. Not even water. This place stinks, and I am sure it is not sanitary," Lucky grumbled out of the side of his mouth.

It was a Thursday night, not many customers. Those that were there looked tired and worn out. Regulars sat at one end of the bar grouped together—older barflies, men who reminisced about the old days and drank beer. A couple of road crew workers were at the pool tables. In the back corner, there were a few old women, worn looking, and rough around the edges. At a table in the middle, closer to the bar, a few bikers were drinking and laughing.

The bartender sauntered over; he wasn't in any hurry. "What can I get for you gents tonight—whiskey, beer?"

He was a hairy man in his mid to late fifties, stocky and gruff-sounding. The only place he was missing hair was right in the center of his head. Lucky didn't say it, but he thought the man should take some of the hair on his arms and neck and have it transplanted to his head.

"Nah, not drinking tonight. We're looking for some information." Jack laid his badge on the countertop for the man to see.

He stepped back, holding up his hands. "Look, I don't want any trouble here, okay?"

The man stepped back up to the bar. "I gotta serve ya something, looks odd if I don't, this crowd,"—he gestured toward the bikers—"can get uneasy when Johnny Law comes in."

"Sure, a short mug of beer, then." Lucky angled his head toward where the bikers sat. There were five bikers and two of them. No sense in tempting fate. One small mug of beer wouldn't hurt.

The hairy bartender drew them both into a mug. He wiped off the bar, and then leaned on one elbow, eyeing the crowd, not looking at either detective.

"Whatdaya want to know?"

"Your name for a start." Jack lifted his mug.

"Name's Ralph Delvecchio, what else you wanna know?"

"Delvecchio, that's an Italian name, huh?" Lucky picked up his mug of beer, raising it to his lips.

"So, what'da 'bout it? You got sumtin' against Italians, or what?" Ralph was easy to anger, and Jack saw his jaw tighten up.

"No, he doesn't and neither do I. Matter of fact, Houston's medical examiner is Italian. We love him to death." Jack took another drink of his beer, watching the burly bartender.

The stocky man folded his arms. "Is that all ya needed to know cuz I need ta—"

"No, wanted to know who you are first, like to know the man's name I am talking to. So, who owns this joint?"

"I do. Me and a silent partner."

"Who's the silent partner?"

"Silent, that's who, and they want to stay silent. It's in our legal agreement."

"You've owned this joint for a while then."

"Yeah, thirty-six long years now."

"Do you remember a guy named Skip? He used to bartend here."

"I know lots of people. There might have been a Skip here, maybe a long time ago." He was evasive.

"You recall a last name by any chance?" Jack wasn't letting him off the hook.

"Hell, it's been way too many years and way too many people have come and gone, so, no, I don't remember. Youse guys have some more questions?" Delvecchio plopped the bar towel on top of the cracked countertop and wiped off a clean spot. Jack didn't reply. The man was lying through his teeth.

Delvecchio rubbed his chin with his stubby thumb and index finger. "I have to run to the back, gotta change out two kegs. Any more answers you need, come back another night when I ain't so busy." He locked the cash register and disappeared to the back.

"He needs to change the kegs all right; this beer tastes like horse piss." Lucky pushed the near full mug away from him.

"I guess he is not charging us for the beer, either. He's lying, because the fat guys stiffened up when I asked him about Skip."

"Yeah, and I was watching the bikers. It's crazy. No matter what clothes we wear—suits, jeans, shorts, and a ball jersey—how do they *always* figure out that we are five-oh?" Lucky didn't understand it.

"Could it be our smell?"

"Jack, you're a dumb shit." Lucky said.

"No, I think the smell we're looking for is pig," he hooted. Jack deserved it—Dawson Luck flipped him off.

22

"Okay, last night we got zilch. What's the plan today?" Dawson Luck was a grump.

"I thought about going to old evidence lockup."

"What the hell for?"

"I want to go through the Mason evidence." He saw the look on Lucky's face. "I know, I know."

"Jack, just what do you think you know?" Luck folded his arms, bouncing his chair backward.

"You think we're just gonna spin our wheels looking because this stuff was processed back then, so what new stuff is there to find that wasn't found then, right? But the fact is, Bullard and Simpson didn't do a real investigation. According to Simpson, they got money to cover it up. They stuck all the evidence in storage, leaving it there to rot, and no one was the wiser."

"Damn, Jack, the entire department wasn't on the take. You think they had someone on the payroll who worked in CSU doing their bidding, too?"

"I don't know. You know how it goes, you get someone to do you a favor, turn a blind eye for me, here's a hundred bucks—that kind of deal. Unfortunately, I'm thinking Layton Conch, the past M.E., was on the take too, but he died, so we can't ask him."

"Ain't that funny, Jack? I mean, let's tick off all these dead people."

"Sure, Lucky, tick away."

"Dead people, let's see—Scottie Buccella offs Roger Stockard and Archie Bowers. Ian Simpson admits to putting a hole in Scottie Buccella, and Pete Bullard offs his partner's son, Randy Simpson. Pete Bullard dies of a heart attack. Troy Wolff allegedly killed the whore, JoAnn Cutter. The medical examiner, the one who did her autopsy, Layton Conch, is dead and may have covered up evidence. Celeste Mason was declared dead, what, thirty-some odd years ago, but might be alive. Not to mention Ian Simpson is pretty much dead for the life he has now."

"You're not spouting out information I'm not already aware of here, so what's your point?"

"Well, crud, Jack. Ain't very many living people in the mix any longer, so I guess, well, shit, what I'm saying is that all leads are just that—dead or dead ends."

Jack saw he was frustrated.

"Let's just focus on the ones that are alive, or we assume are alive."

"Sure, but how will it help us? We need some frigging physical evidence, not a retold story, because that's all it is, a freaky story."

"Let's just assume, mind you, Wolff is involved in the prostitute's death, and it was not Celeste Mason in the car, so she really isn't dead. Add we still aren't sure whose body was in the car. We are just assuming it was your missing hooker, JoAnn Cutter."

"I follow you so far; ain't hard." He was grumpy. "Two things I'm thinking about, equal DNA."

"Uh, Jack, that's one thing. What's the other?"

"It's all DNA. It wasn't tested back then like it is today. If they preserved the evidence, then Wolff's DNA will be on something, and think there will be no DNA for Celeste Mason on any of the evidence."

"Jack, I read some reports in her murder book. It was her car, and the clothes were said to have been her clothes. The possibility of finding her DNA is pretty damn high I would think."

"Lucky, she wasn't in the room, so any sexual items, if there were any, won't have her DNA—now will they?"

"Yup, I see your point there. Are we going to look for this Skip fella?"

"Damn skippy, we're looking for him. He's a major person of interest. We're going fishing tomorrow night."

"Tomorrow night?" Lucky had date night with his beautiful wife tomorrow night.

Jack knew the look on his partner's face, and as much as he could, he tried to suppress a grin. "Date night, huh?"

All Dawson Luck could do was nod with a sad look on his face, and Jack bust out laughing.

"It ain't funny, Jackson West. This has been happening more often."

"We aren't leaving until late. You'll have plenty of time for date night. By the way, don't call me by my full name again. You sound like my mom used to sound when I was in trouble."

"If I knew your middle name, I would've used it," Lucky sassed back.

"I ain't telling and don't go trying to be a detective about it either. Now let's go look through old evidence."

"Do you think we'll find something?"

"Only one way we can find out. Let's take a ride."

"THIS PLACE IS PRETTY BIG." Lucky eyed the building.

"Houston's big. The growth of the city has increased the crime margins." Jack opened the front door to the main office.

"Hiya, fellas." An older man stood behind a wooden desk that had seen better years.

"Smitty, haven't seen you in ages." Jack stuck out his hand.

"Yeah, you fellas don't come out here much since they built the new evidence storehouse. I heard it was a humdinger too. Only time I see some of ya is when you're working an old cold that's twenty years plus old. Is that why you're here?" He eyed Lucky, wondering who this pup was.

"Smitty, this is Dawson Luck. Lucky, this is Smitty. He's worked at HPD for, what, thirty-five years now, is it?"

"Yep, been here all my life, or at least it feels like that. By the way, Jackson, I'm retiring in six months, so's I won't be here much longer. Gonna go on a long, fishing trip."

"If anyone deserves to retire and go off fishing, it's you, Smitty."

"There are plenty of fresh cases to solve, so why are you boys out here?"

"Got an old case we're looking into, and we came to check out the evidence boxes."

"The people who are supposed to keep the place straight ain't worth a plug nickel, and I am just one man; sorry about that in advance."

"Sure, thanks, Smitty. Come on, partner; let's go wade through years of evidence boxes to find what we need."

They walked through a main hallway to a double door, and Lucky was chuckling because Jack was recounting a short Smitty story, but as he pushed open the double doors to the storage unit, his face fell.

"Holy shit, look at this place. Doesn't anyone *ever* come in here and straighten up?" Lucky might not do so well with people and diplomacy, but he was meticulous about order. Smitty was right. The place was a disorganized mess.

"Gawd dang, Jack, it's going to take us all afternoon in here."

Jack handed him a slip with the evidence case number on it. "Here, look for this case number. We better get started, or we'll be here until we have to head over to the club, and there goes date night for you."

That was all it took. Lucky grabbed the file number and went to work trying to locate the boxes. He didn't hear the end of Jack's Smitty story and didn't care. He started numerically, but that didn't work. Nothing was in order. Jack headed across the aisle to work; hopefully it would go faster that way.

Almost three hours later, they were dusty and grimy, but they'd found the boxes. Lucky had even straightened out some that were misplaced and misfiled on the shelves.

"Here, Luck, take those two boxes and I'll take these two. Go over there; there's a long table we can use."

"Is her car at impound, I mean, after all these years?" Lucky pulled on his latex gloves, and taking a small knife, he cut the red tape with the words *'Evidence. Do Not Tamper'* that sealed the boxes.

Jack dusted off the top of one of his boxes. "The reports say it's there. We can check it out. Let's dig through these boxes first, see what we come up with."

"You think the car could have prints inside?"

"I've thought of that, was thinking about that when we were out in Waller. You know something else, Luck? We should run Max Renner through the system; can't believe I haven't done that yet."

"I don't profile that much, but by the looks of him, I'd say he's had run-ins before."

"Me too. After we get back to HPD, let's look him up, see what pops."

Gloves on, Jack took his pocketknife out and cut the tape, sealing the box. Inside, he found the paperwork from the decedent's glove box. Items found in her car: an empty plastic cup, a street map of Houston. There was an umbrella, jumper cables, even the trash from the floorboards. The box wasn't full, so he moved to the next one. This box contained her purse and the contents of her purse, bagged and tagged.

Costume jewelry not listed and the shoes she must have been

wearing. Picking up the items, he looked at each of them. There was one imitation leather wallet; a compact, lip gloss, and a brush. Pulled out of the wallet was her driver's license and social security card. There was a small amount of cash found in her wallet, and a roll of condoms. The condoms had niggled at him, and now he knew why—they didn't belong to Celeste Mason. They were the property of a prostitute named JoAnn Cutter.

"Hey, here are her clothes in this box." Lucky began lifting out each sealed and bagged item. "Damn good thing this ancient storage is climate controlled, Jack; otherwise, this old shit would smell pretty crappy.

"Houston has tons of evidence. The new facility couldn't hold all the old evidence. It's why they left it here, and kept this building. So, what clothing do we have?"

Lucky ticked the items off as he removed them from the box.

"A blouse, a blazer, pants, a bra, and some scarves, but no underwear, Jack. That's odd."

Jack's head popped up. "Scarves, did you say scarves?"

"I did. Why?" Lucky looked at the clothing lying on the table. No bloodstains were visible on most of the clothing. He guessed she had been naked when she was killed. I mean, she was a prostitute, right?

"Why are scarves such a big deal?" Lucky's latex-gloved hand came up to scratch his chin.

"Because I recall Daphne telling me that this JoAnn woman liked the rough sex."

"That doesn't prove a thing. Why are you so thrilled?"

"Skin cells transfer by touch. Whoever was using them had to have transferred skin cells. Sex and sweating go hand in hand. What if they were used in tying her up? Whoever tied her up had a handful of the material. All of this happened in one night, so these scarves were never washed. Whoever handled them will have their touch DNA on them."

Lucky stared at the evidence bag holding the scarves. Jack might be right. This might be a goldmine of DNA. Problem was matching it to the right person.

"Hey and look here, I found the condoms. Six unopened packages." Jack held the bagged strip up. "They're all intact, at least in the wrappers. No telling what's left inside."

Lucky walked to Jack's end of the table. They were both quiet as they looked at the evidence bag that held the condoms.

"From what everyone said about Celeste Mason, the girl was shy where men were concerned. If she wasn't seeing anyone, why would she have condoms?"

"Well, Jack, my missing girl probably bought them in bulk. Look what she did for a living. That brings me to a question, Jack. How did your vic get to be the so-called boss? What did she do? Walk in one day and say, here's what I want to do. Have you thought about that?"

"I've wondered about it, and I have no answer, but someone knows. We just need to get someone to talk."

"I guess we just take this one box back." Lucky began boxing the evidence back up.

"After we sign out with Smitty, let's head over to the morgue. I want to drop the scarves off to Bennie."

Knee-deep into performing an autopsy, Bennie didn't hear him knock, so Jack pushed the door open and stuck his head in.

"Hey, Bennie, got a minute to talk?"

"Jack, sure, come on in, but gown and mask up first if you will."

"Can you get to a stopping point and come out? Do you mind? We'll wait in your office. This is a very private matter."

"Yeah, let me document something. I'll be right there." Bennie turned his masked face back to the cadaver on the steel table. He bent over, looking into a body, which sort of grossed Jack out but fascinated him as well.

Less than ten minutes later, a still gowned M.E. met them in his office.

"So, what are you two crime fighters up to today, and what can I do to help?"

Bennie sat down and grabbed the bacterial wash, pumped out a dab, and rubbed it with both hands, then repeated the same process.

Jack filled him in on the details of the cases they were working.

"I'm sure I don't have to tell you how sensitive this is. So you need to be the one who does the forensic work, not your techs. It needs to be kept quiet."

"Absolutely, Jack, without a doubt. It's not like the judge is going to volunteer his DNA. How will you get a comparison sample?"

"We'll figure something out. How soon can you get a DNA profile?"

"Jack, for Christ's sake, this is Houston. The crime lab is backed up, and everyone wanted stuff yesterday."

Jack opened his mouth, but Bennie interrupted him. "I'll put a rush on it, maybe get it back in a week, but it's not a guarantee."

"Yeah, I understand. But it's better than waiting for months."

"I promise, as soon as I have the report, you're the first call I make, Jack," Bennie said, as they were leaving.

"Thanks, Bennie, and uh, remember to keep this between us. Captain Yao is about to have a stroke over this situation."

"Yeah, I can only imagine the stress he's under. Okay, fellas, see you guys when I see ya."

In his heart, Jack knew that this was an explosive situation, but had no clue just how many bombs were fixing to go off.

23

"Hey, Jack, sorry, traffic was crappy, or I'd have been here an hour ago."

"No worries, Dawson, we all understand Houston traffic. So, I looked up Max Renner."

"What did you find?"

"He has a record, and I'm kicking myself for not looking him up sooner. Anyway, he moved to Texas from Chicago, Illinois. Scottie Buccella was also from Chicago, what about that?"

"It's a big place, Jack. What else you got?"

"Yeah, okay, Renner was part of a biker gang and got in some trouble. Was arrested on drug charges but the charges were dropped. He has an arrest on a battery charge, for beating the shit out of another biker in a club. Seems the charges were dropped by the victim. Musta been a rival gang, who the hell knows?"

"Maybe it stopped a biker gang war. Anyway, does he have incidences in Texas?"

"No. But the guy did a two-and-a-half year stint in Chicago for selling drugs to an undercover cop. Says here he had over five hundred grams of weed. That's a class three felony up there. So his prints are available. If we can get prints from the car, we can crosscheck them with Renner's."

"You think there are prints on the car that weren't found back then?"

"What I think is no one worked the case back then. So, yeah, if we dig hard enough and be creative, then maybe we find what we need."

"Alright, partner, it's worth a shot."

"Then let's get on it. You call vehicle impound, find out the space number. I'll call Vince Stoner and ask him to meet us out there."

They went to work. Twenty minutes later, it was set.

"The car is on the lot, at the back. I mean, it's way in the back." Lucky rolled his eyes as he leaned his head back. "Like twenty-five years in the back."

"Cheech said he'd dig up CSU's old reports on this case if he can find any, and he'll bring the files with him. He's meeting us there at two-thirty. I didn't give him details, but asked him to keep this field trip to himself."

"Involving more people could be a dangerous thing, Jack. The gossip could get back to Wolff. Until we leave, I'm going to see what I can come up with by Googling the clubs, all three of them. I want to see if any of them pops."

"Sounds good." Jack's mind was full of Daphne's story. The lies Jenna Berrie and Max Renner concocted. If he were a betting man, he figured Ralph Delvecchio lied to them, too. A high-ranking official was involved. Just how would this story end?

While Lucky dug into his search of the clubs, owners, past owners, or shareholders, Jack began surfing through the archives of Vice reports in Houston from 34 years back, looking for anything connected to any of the clubs. Maybe a report with Max Renner, Jenna Berrie, and JoAnn Cutter mentioned in passing, or even Skip, no last name.

"Whatdaya find in the clubs, Lucky?"

"I found the connection to the owners of the club, not much else though."

"You did? What connection?"

"The first owner of the Crystal Barrel was a guy named Gregory Staltzworth. He sold the building to Curtis Sutton. Later, his wife, Sara Sutton bought the land. Which is odd, they each owned a separate piece of the property. That transaction took place in '60. The Silver Moon, as it used to be known, was purchased in '64. Again, the mister owned the building and the misses the land."

"That solves one mystery at least," Jack remarked.

"What mystery is that?" Lucky looked up.

"Who Celeste's rich distant relative was. Sara no-last-name now has a last name, and it's Sutton." Jack sat up straighter and stretched his back.

"Archie Bowers was Sutton's kid. I remember her name as next of kin. Sutton was his last name. Sara's maiden name was Bowers; it was on the report but I had no idea it was the same Sara. Evidently, he was going by her maiden name. Makes me wonder if he was the intended target, and the lawyer was collateral damage." Luck furrowed his brow in thought.

"That's one thing we might never find out, pard. What about the topless bar, the Blue Marble?"

"From what I found, it was a new club. They built it and owned the building and the land. Then they took down the building and sold the land. It was an undisclosed sale to a no-name corporation. The no-name corporation who bought the land parceled it out to single buyers. There's not just one venue that covers that land now." Lucky leaned back, slumping a little in his chair.

"So, evidently Curtis Sutton kicks it from a heart attack, and the wife gets the buildings in her inheritance; now she owns the land and the buildings." Jack stopped to think for a second. "Then what, Mason gets the land and the buildings once Sara Sutton dies? This has to be how she ended up owning the clubs. A good question would be who started the gaming and prostitution business. My guess is she inherited the illegal shit from the Suttons who'd already turned the clubs into whorehouses and gambling dens."

"If we find this *not* dead woman, we can ask her. The SS Corporation sold the Crystal Barrel in '91 to Ralph Delvecchio and an unnamed partner."

"Yeah, that's what he told us, he and a silent partner own the place. What about the Silver Moon, does it say?" Jack tapped his pen against the desk.

"SS Corporation still is the listed owner, but doesn't list any names or shareholders. SS, you think that's Sara Sutton, Jack?"

"That would be my guess. She willed them to Celeste Mason. If Mason is supposedly dead, then who did *she* leave it to?"

"No clue, Jack." Lucky scratched at his chin and then glanced at his watch. "Hey, let's vamoose; Cheech will be standing there with his thumb in his ear wondering where we are."

"Hiya, Cheech, how are things in CSU?" Lucky asked as he stepped out of the car and stuck out his hand, and they shook.

"Business is booming. We're printing and processing more crime scenes than we can handle. Guess the bad guys are our job security. Hey, Jack."

"Were you able to dig up any old records?"

"Man, Jack, you get right to it, huh?"

"Hell, Cheech, this case is already pushing thirty-five years. So how's about we work on not adding on another year. You ready?"

Cheech held up his crazy CSU suitcase. "Lead the way, Jack, and by the way, I have some of the ancient files with me. We can compare notes when we're done."

Mason's car was in the corner, backed up to the fence. They all gloved up and Jack and Lucky watched as Vince Stoner, AKA Cheech, went to work. He dusted the steering wheel, the dash, the inside armrest—he dusted his ass off.

"All I got is two prints, Jack. And I really don't think they are usable." Cheech felt beaten. "I'm sure the car was wiped down. I mean our records have zero fingerprints, not even these two crappy ones." He was frustrated; he so wanted to help with this case.

"You mind humoring me?" Jack squatted near the driver's door.

"Okay, sure, what are you thinking?"

"Three places I'd like you to dust if you would."

"Where, Jack?" Cheech leaned over to see where Jack was pointing.

"There, where the seat lever is, can you dust that on the underside?"

He examined the area. It was small, but it was large enough to have a print. Cheech called himself a CSU operative, joking he could pull a print off a gnat's ass. He was determined to get something to help Jack.

"I can give it a shot. Do you think you'll find the dead girl's prints? It said in the files her fingertips were cut off, so there won't be any comparison prints."

"No, not her prints, whoever she is. This woman was short, only five feet one. If someone else drove her car, and that someone was say, right at six feet tall, they wouldn't have been able to drive without moving the seat back. CSU reports from back then stated not much blood spatter or brain matter was noted in the car. I'm guessing this information is some of the only factual information from back then."

"You might be right," Cheech nodded. "I've read some reports."

"If you notice, the seat is upright and close to the steering wheel. She wasn't killed here, she was dumped here. Someone moved her to the driver's seat, because she didn't drive her dead self to that vacant wooded area. Do you think they dusted here, Cheech?"

"I wouldn't know, but if they missed a print, and it's there, I should be able to pull one. I can also see if there's a print on this lever too." He pointed to the lever in the front, the control lever that moved the seat up.

"If he or she was taller, they'd have to move the seat back to drive and then forward after they moved her body."

"Give it a shot." Jack was covering all the bases, as in no stone left unturned.

Cheech started on the seat lever. He began dusting the dark area with a light dusting powder. His fingers were emotionally crossed. He wanted to find a print, any usable print.

"Jack, I think I've got something here, by George."

Reaching for the print lifting tape, he placed it where the print showed up from the dusting powder, smoothed it over, and then lifted the tape.

"Lucky, reach in my case, hand me one of those white print cards, would ya?"

Lucky handed him the white print card. Cheech pressed the tape to the card, and then he pulled up the tape.

"Uh-huh, Houston, we have fingerprints." He stood, looking at what he had. "It looks to be the tips of two fingers, see?" he pointed out. "I'd venture to say it's the middle and ring finger of the left hand. It's not a complete print. I'll see if Latents can work with it."

Without a prompt, even though space was tight, he got the white dusting powder on the small surface of the plastic seat lever which moved the seat backward and forward.

"Nothing here, and even if you get the part off and tried superglue fuming, I'm afraid all you'd get would be a smudge."

Jack and Lucky stared at the white card with the two partial fingertip prints. Now they had a real lead.

"Any other place you want me to dust, Jack?"

"See the seat belt? The pictures showed her seat-belted in. Someone had to click it locked. You think you can get prints–if there are any–here, and here? There could be prints on the underside of the seat belt clasp. This would be where the perp had to touch it to lock it in place." He pointed out to Cheech as Lucky poked his head in the front passenger window.

They both watched as Cheech repeated the process on the clasp.

"This area is too thin, let me try the back." With his gloved hands, he turned the metal clasp over. Taking the dusting powder, he dusted it on while the other two watched.

"There's something here, but it's a big fat smudge; no good, damn it," Cheech swore.

"Where else, Jack?" Lucky wondered where a print might have been the original CSU team missed.

"Let's get some tools to take the seat belt off, and you can take it with you. I'd like for you to use superglue fuming on them. It wasn't done because all the seat belts are intact."

Cheech looked like the Cheshire cat with all of his teeth showing. "Hell yeah, that's a great catch, Jack."

Back at the impound office; Jack put a request in to have the seat belts removed and sent to Vince at the CSU lab.

"As soon as the mechanic gets the seat belt off, I'll get it over to ya, Cheech."

"Thanks, Jasper, appreciate it, man." Jack waved.

"Say, Cheech, can you meet us up at that mom-and-pop diner, the one near Headquarters?"

"Yeah, I know the place. That lady, I think her name is Bernice. She makes a mouthwatering apple pie."

"Yeah, that's the one. We can get a bite to eat and go over the reports you brought and compare them to what we have so far."

At the small diner, they took a table at the back.

"My notes don't have any list of items that were printed. Not a rape kit either. It's strange though," Cheech said between bites of hot apple pie à la mode.

"What is?" Jack took a forkful of blueberry cobbler and chewed.

"I saw the pictures of the dead girl. Hell, I couldn't find any samples, swabs, nothing. She had a little hair left, but they did not preserve any of it. There were no files on the blood spatter, and to be honest, the reports are very sketchy. If you want my opinion—" he said as he put the last bite in his mouth, waiting for one of them to respond.

"Absolutely, Cheech, we'd like to hear what you think." Jack took another bite of the scrumptious cobbler.

"I'm not accusing anyone, but the medical examiner on the case," he looked at his file. "This Layton Conch was on the take. He covered up stuff, doctored the reports. A basic M.E.'s report is there, but the other extensive reports I typically see aren't. And these files were in a mess."

"Yeah, so were the files we have, and they're half-assed done."

"Look at this, I found it stuck in between reports." Cheech pulled a page out of his binder and handed it to Jack.

He read the handwritten note:

The medical examiner, Layton Conch, said no rape kit was necessary, or any testing to be performed on the pants or the scarves. If more items show up to be processed, immediately inform him.

"Who wrote this?"

Cheech shrugged. "No name and no initials. I'm sure whoever wrote it is long gone."

"It proves one point though. This was a cover-up and we need to pull the covers off." Jack pushed his empty dessert bowl to the side.

"Jack, I'll email you a scanned copy of the reports I have that don't match your copies. Sorry, guys, I hafta bounce, got a couple of things hanging in the wind at the lab I need to finish before I head home."

"Thanks, Cheech, you've been a big help."

Jack dropped Lucky off to get his car in the garage.

"I'll see ya in the morning, partner." Lucky saluted.

Keyed up over the fingerprints, he knew Cheech would get them to Latent Prints first thing in the morning putting, a rush on it. He had one piece of physical evidence with the prints, and he hoped the DNA was another piece. Now he needed to match the DNA once Bennie received the report back. His gut told him if he had to bet the farm, he was betting Troy Wolff's DNA was on a major part of the evidence.

All of this, the waiting and not knowing was giving him a tension head ache. Jack needed relief, he needed—he knew what he needed.

He drove over to Gretchen's side of town. He had no idea if she was even home. At least seeing her house, knowing it was a part of her might ease his tense nerves and stop the pounding in his head. He smiled. There were lights on in her house. He saw her shadow silhouetted in a window shade. She was home. Good. He was hoping she'd be glad to see him. Parking his truck on the street, he got out, walked to her front door and knocked.

24

Lucky was already on his second cup of jo when Jack walked into the squad office.

"Running late this morning, I see."

"I didn't much sleep last night, but hey, that's okay, I feel like I can conquer the world today."

"Jack, now dad gum you, here you are chipper again. Are you taking happy pills, or is it a woman, because, by golly, it's one or the other."

Luck wished he would spill, but Jack wasn't talking. Last night was just for him and Gretchen. Oh, it had not gone that far, but being near her, holding hands and kissing her, had eased his tensions, his headache, and his worries over this exasperating cold case.

"Okay, Jack. Today is another day. Hey, isn't that what Scarlett O'Hara said?"

"No, it wasn't. She always said, 'because tomorrow is—another day'."

"You've watched *Gone with the Wind,* Jack?"

"Uh-huh, with my mom years ago—and frankly, Lucky, *my dear,* I don't give a damn." He paused. "What you think?"

"We've hit a roadblock, Jack, that's what I'm thinking."

"I'm over the moon with what Cheech got yesterday. So why are you bummed out?"

"We have no live persons to talk to, except the ones we can't find. And the ones we've talked to are liars. Now what, buddy? We sit here with our thumbs up our—in our ear?"

"First, we get my murder book updated and your missing girl case updated with all of our new findings, concrete or not, because it's all we have. Then we look for this Skip fella. On my list is hunting for Jed Logan, and damn it, Celeste Mason, cuz the woman isn't dead. And we need the judge's DNA."

IT WAS THREE O'CLOCK, and 7-11 walked in.

"You guys goofing off I see," Jace Severson said, pulling out his desk chair and plopping down.

"What have you two been up to? Ya'll catch a hot case?" Xi Chang passed Jack's desk and grabbed his chair, rolling it over between the desks.

"Nah, we're working a couple of unsolved cases. Are you guys working one?" With Wolff's involvement, Jack steered the conversation away from their cases.

"Yep, caught one early this morning before the freaking sun was up."

"Oh, yeah, whatdaya catch?"

"A club owner got rubbed out, over there close to North Shore."

Jack's ears pricked up. "No kidding, what club?"

Jace picked up his notebook. "It's called the Station, some guy named Skip, Skip Johansson."

Jack glanced at his partner and gave him a slight head shake, as if to say, *don't say a word.* He saw Lucky's mouth open, then shut.

"So, what happened?" Jack leaned back in his chair, so interested he was quaking inside.

"They found this Skip fella dead at the side corner of the building. He took one shot in the head, execution style. The shooter used a nine mil. We found one casing," Chang began, and Jace took over.

"It was three-fifteen, and a bouncer was doing a walk around the building. After closing time, they always check for drunks, or people doing it in cars." Jace's eyebrows wiggled up and down.

Chang stepped in. "Scared the bejesus out of him when he shined his flashlight as he was rounding the corner—"

"He almost stepped on the poor guy." Jace finished his partner's sentence.

"They have live cameras?" Lucky asked.

"Yeah, they do and we haven't seen the feed yet. The parking lot is lit up but only in the center of the lot. There's not very much lighting on the back sides of the building, since no one is supposed to park there. There are two cameras, one on each corner of the building facing the parking lot. These cameras should give a clear shot of our perp walking toward the building. They have cameras at the very back of the building, too. But the problem is they face front, and the lighting is poor. Those cameras are the only chance to see the deed being done," Xi said.

"Did anyone see him leave with anyone?" Names popped up in Jack's head. Jed Logan, Celeste, maybe even Wolff, could be the perp.

Jace shrugged his big shoulders. "We questioned everyone who was still at the club, but no one saw him leave. Plus, no one heard a gunshot. Our shooter used a silencer."

"The staff said the guy didn't have any enemies. Everyone liked him. One of the bartenders said even though he was a few marbles short, he was a super nice boss," Xi said.

Jack knew it was the same Skip, the one Daphne had told him about. The odds of this happening were like a million to one.

The phone on Jack's desk rang. "Homicide, West."

"We'll be right over. Sorry, fellas, Lucky and I gotta go see a man about some fingerprints. Hey," he looked at both Xi and Jace, "keep us caught up with your case."

"Sure, Jack, will do." Jace Severson saluted him.

"Goofball," Xi muttered.

Jace wadded up a piece of paper and tossed it at his partner's head, missing him by a few inches.

Out of earshot, Lucky was excited. "Jack, man, what are the odds of this happening?"

"I'd say since we were trying to find a guy named Skip, who is associated with a bar, and the bar is connected to our cases a kajillion to one. That being said though, I never would've imagined your cold case and my cold case would be connected either."

"Was that Latent Prints that called?"

"No, it was Cheech. He said the superglue fuming yielded a print. He wants to show us."

"Whatcha got for us, Stoner?"

"Let's go to the lab."

The seat belt straps were hanging in an enclosed chamber with heat-resistant glass.

"They arrived late this morning."

Jack stepped closer to the glass window.

"Those white patches—are those fingerprints?"

"Uh-huh. Here, I'm going to take them out." Cheech gloved up and opened the chamber door. He removed the straps and carried them over to a workstation, and then he jacked the microscope to one-hundred times and peered into it.

"This is a usable print. Look, Jack."

He stepped to the side and Jack got a closer look. "That's a clear print."

"This strap has what appears to be three prints, see here?" Cheech pointed out two more prints on the underside as he turned the strap over. "That might be a thumbprint right here, on the outer side, forefinger and middle finger here." He pointed to the smaller, closer prints. "I assume the person grabbed the seat belt like this and then popped the tongue into the buckle to lock it."

"What I don't get is this—if she was dead, why seat belt her in?" Lucky took his turn to peer into the microscope.

"Killers can't always be perfect. If they didn't make mistakes, we'd never catch them."

Cheech was right. No one was perfect. Even the best of the best screwed up at least once, but never on purpose.

"This other strap, the one that goes around the waist, one print was picked up. This part is near the tongue. It's a thumbprint. The prints on the backside were just blobs. Sorry."

"Don't apologize, man. You got prints we can use. Will you send them to Latent Prints for us?"

"Sure. I'll ask Tori to call you ASAP."

"Now," Lucky stated after they left CSU, "we have something to look forward to."

"This, plus I'm hoping 7-11 gets a positive ID on the man who shot Skip Johansson. Nothing is that random, Lucky. I think it is connected. However, it could've been a robbery gone sideways, but I just don't see that, or I don't wanna see it."

Lucky agreed. It could just be a coincidence.

THERE WERE two notes on Jack's desk when he got to the office the next morning. One was a message from Tori in Latent Prints to call her after nine, the other was from Xi Chang, and it simply read, 'Jack, stay at the station until Jace and I get there, Xi.'

It was right at 8:30.

Patience wasn't a virtue Jack had right now, so he sent Xi a text— *I'm at the station, won't leave till you get here—just get here.*

We'll be there in about five, was Xi's reply.

"Morning, Jack." Lucky slumped into his chair. "Any news?"

"Tori, in Latents, left me a message, wants me to call her after nine. Xi left a message on my desk. It said to stay at the station until they get here."

"Wonder what Xi wants?"

"Not a clue. He said he'd be here in about five. We need a solid lead with those prints." Jack's nerves were on edge.

"Me too, I—" Luck was about to say something when Xi Chang opened the door, poking his head in.

"Hey, Jack, Luck, the captain wants to see all four of us. Jace and I are headed to his office now."

"I've called you all here because we've had too many out of the ordinary events happen in the past few days." Captain Yao was silent for a moment; staring at them. "Gentlemen, I've been in law enforcement for going on now twenty-four years. I've seen a helluva lot of shit. The word coincidence is not a word we use in law enforcement often."

The captain leaned into his desk, propping his elbows up. Clasping his hands together, he laced his fingers together forming a steeple. Laying his closed lips against the fingers forming the steeple, he sat, thinking.

No one said a word. The captain unclasped his hands and sat back.

"Chang, Severson," he addressed them first. "Almost two months ago, I assigned West and Luck here, each a cold case. Their cases unpredictably intersected and are connected. One is about a missing prostitute and the other an unsolved murder of another woman. This twist of fate rarely happens. I've asked them to keep the case information hushed because of the names which have been intertwined with their cases."

Captain Yao then turned his attention back to Jack and Dawson.

"7-11 told you about the murder they caught early yesterday morning. They went through the club's surveillance video last night. The camera caught the perp walking up to the front of the club. He took out his cell phone and three minutes later, this Johansson walked out. They are talking and walking to the side corner. They stand there for all of eight minutes. The perp takes a gun out of his inside coat pocket and shoots the vic once in the head and he casually walked away. It was not a robbery; it was a murder, execution style."

The detectives knew this was a cold-blooded killer and what ran through all their heads was one question—*why?*

Captain Yao let this sink in for a few seconds before he spoke up again.

"Jack," Yao addressed him singularly. "You told me about the conversation you had with Daphne Walden's husband the day you were out there getting her story, you remember?"

"Yeah, I remember, Cap, but what does this have to do with 7-11's case?"

"Here's a picture of 7-11's perp. Recognize him?"

Jack stared at the picture. His mouth dropped open, his ire rose, and his insides boiled. He handed the picture to Lucky.

"Who is this?" Dawson Luck stared down at a picture of a cold-blooded killer.

"Son of a bitch, it's Harvey Walden." Jack's jaw muscles clenched. The conversation he had with the man called Harvey Walden played back in his head. *He hadn't wanted her to tell her story, let sleeping dogs lie. You can't change the past. It's her life story, not mine. It was her last request to him. He already knew the story, and he'd said with conviction this was her life story, not his.*

"Who is this man? I mean the real man, not the sad sack husband I met?" Jack stood. He wanted to pace, but there wasn't room.

"His real name is Harvey Walden—Buccella, Jack. Walden is his mother's maiden name. He wasn't using the last name Buccella, but it popped when we did a background check." Yao looked up at him.

"And sit back down, hurts my neck to talk to you when you're standing."

Jack sat. He was fuming; that bastard played him.

"Xi and Jace went out to his place last night to bring him in for questioning, but he was gone. Jack, the house was empty."

"I guess she died then, or he wouldn't have left. That was what, almost two and a half weeks ago. He told me then that Hospice was coming in a couple of days. She was in bad shape. Chances are it didn't take long for her to die. Was there a For Sale sign on the property?" Jack's jaw twitched as he clenched his teeth again.

"No, but the place was cleared out. The house, the garage, and the shed were empty. All the guy left in the buildings was an echo," Jace said.

"I'm betting, knowing she was dying, he was already prepared to skedaddle, had it all arranged, that bastard." Jack wasn't just mad, he was mad as *hell*.

"Is someone going to tell me and 11 here what's going on?" Jace Severson spoke up. "Xi and I feel like we're walking into the middle of a movie and have no clue what the plot is about."

"Jack, did you hear from Latents?" Yao asked ignoring 7-11's request to catch them up on what the deal was.

"Yeah, I'll be back; gonna call Tori right now."

"While you're gone, we'll get 7-11 caught up."

Jack went to the squad room, knowing if he saw his reflection in a mirror, his ears would be firecracker red, with smoke steadily streaming out. God, he was pissed. He had been standing three feet from the man, Harvey-fucking-Walden-fucking-Buccella two weeks ago. How was he related to Scottie Buccella, and why had he whacked Skip?

Jack snatched up the phone and called Latent Prints.

"Tori, this is West in Homicide. It's after nine. Whatdaya got for me? ...Email it to me with an attachment. Thanks, I owe ya." He was ready to hang up, but she said something else.

"Yeah, yeah, a dozen tamales from Garcia's; then you're paid in full. Is that it?"

The email popped up, and he printed the attachment. Back in the captain's office, Jack took his seat. Then he told them what Latent Prints had found.

25

Three cases, two 34 years old, one brand new, not even 48 hours old. What was next?

"Captain, what's our next step?" Jack folded the paper in half with the Latent report on the fingerprints and put it in his pocket.

"Here's what we are going to do. Xi, you and Jace get an arrest warrant written up and go after Buccella. Put out a BOLO, then contact Central Patrol and have them help you. Find that bastard. Report back to me later or sooner if you get something."

"Yes, sir, Captain, we're one it."

Davis Yao reached into a drawer and pulled out a bottle of antacids, shook three out, and chewed. His stomach was on fire, and his head was about to split wide open. Jack and Dawson waited for him to chew and swallow. Jack felt bad for him. The captain had ulcers. Because a so-called respected judge for Houston was involved, new ulcers could be on the horizon.

"Judge Wolff, I'm sure, has heard the news about Skip, and if he hasn't, he will. Bad new travels faster than light. There's not a doubt in my mind Wolff doesn't know who Skip is. Get Wolff's DNA. Do it without his knowledge, but get solid proof the DNA is his. Take pictures and then take the stuff to Bennie. Tell him I said, put an 'I wanted this yesterday' rush on it."

Dawson Luck got up to leave, his hand on the door, Jack on his heels.

"Jack."

Jack turned around. "Yes, sir?"

"Get a tail on Delvecchio. I don't care what you tell them or who you get, just make it happen. Before you plan on a way to get the judge's DNA, get a warrant for this Max Renner, have someone pick him up."

"Because Max Renner might object to being brought in, I'll get the Violent Task Force to pick him up. And Delvecchio, you mean Ralph Delvecchio, from the Crystal Barrel?"

"That's the one."

"Why, how is he involved our cases, Cap?" Lucky asked him.

Captain Yao's stomach gurgled again, and he closed his eyes as the fire in his gut blew in and then out, before he spoke.

"This is a royal mess and don't ask me how I found out. I've got my sources. Ralph Delvecchio and Troy Wolff are related. They're cousins. Delvecchio owns the shithole club, but before then he was a bartender. My bet is he worked with Skip Johansson at the Crystal Barrel. And I have a hunch he knows Harvey Buccella. I'm also betting he knows your dead girl ain't dead, Jack."

"I'm not sure we can take any more surprises, Captain."

"Well, all I can say is if we don't get a handle on things, we could have another murder case on your hands."

BACK AT H.Q. Dawson Luck started on the warrant for Max Renner, while Jack called Mava at the courthouse. Lucky was glad she flirted with Jack and had a crush on his partner, because Jack was going to have to woo her into giving him, as inconspicuously as possible, the judge's schedule.

"Hey, Jack, who we gonna ask to tail Delvecchio while we're on the judge?"

Jack took two seconds to think about it and grabbed the phone. "Hey, glad you answered. Does Vice have anything big going right now? No? Can you and Sparky do me a favor, come up to six? I have a sensitive issue to discuss."

"You gonna get Rick and Sparky to help? That's a brilliant idea."

It took less than an hour to update Rick Tormo and Katherine Sparks.

"Here's his home address. Tail him, and since you guys are dressed like you are, I'm betting you can blend in at the hole-in-the-wall tonight," Jack pointed out matter-of-factly.

Rick Tormo wore shabby jeans and a red t-shirt with black skull and crossbones, and underneath the words, Shark Bait in black lettering. He had on worn-out black motorcycle boots, an old green John Deere ball cap, with a three-day scruffy beard working.

Katherine Sparks, his partner, a feisty woman, at about five foot four, dripping with attitude. Nicknamed Sparky, she could handle her own with the boys in Vice, not taking crap off anyone. Most of the fellas wondered why she wasn't nicknamed Taz, as in Tasmanian Devil. Katherine wore less shabby looking jeans that hugged her hips. She'd stuffed her pant legs into black biker boots. Wearing a pink shirt with a picture of a donkey and the words, Kiss My, above the donkey's hindquarters. The white ball cap she was wearing had her auburn-reddish ponytail pulled though the back hole and in black lettering across the front it said, Bite me—I bite back.

"We've been roaming the Fifth Ward. I have to keep up my image, Va'to." Rick let out a low gangster laugh, and then, just as Lucky took a drink of his tepid coffee, Sparky grabbed her crotch, pretending to hock up a loogie, and in a gruff voice said, "Me too."

Lucky spewed his coffee everywhere. It even shot out of his big nose.

"What the—hey!" Jack spurted out when he saw Sparky jump out of the way of the spray of coffee, and Rick doubled over in laughter. Lucky was coughing, and his face had turned a nice shade of pink. Spewing coffee from his mouth was one thing, but out of his nose, in front of a woman, that embarrassed the piss right outta him.

"Man, Sparky, I wasn't expecting you to grab your, uh, do what you did. Hell, warn a guy not to be taking a drink before you pull a stunt like that."

Lucky wiped his face and then began mopping up the coffee he spewed on the corner of his desk and all over his paperwork. "Crud, I'll hafta redo this freaking paperwork."

"Hey, Lucky, I'm sorry," she said with a little chuckle. "Here, I'll help you."

"Don't worry about it, Sparky. He doesn't even let me near the paperwork, and I'm his dang partner. He's almost too anal about it."

Rick had a huge grin on his face. His partner made him laugh and Katherine Sparks put all his other partners to shame. She was a powerhouse, dedicated detective.

"Jack, we'll keep you posted if anything vital comes up, and Lucky, I'm sorry I made you spew coffee on your paperwork, but hell, I've already warned you guys that there's no telling what I might say or do." Sparky patted Lucky on the back. "See ya later, dude," she said in the gruff voice, her eyes full of mischief, and focused on Lucky.

Lucky opened his mouth to comment, but thought better, so he shut it.

JACK HANDED the warrant for Max Renner over to Sargent Zach Pappert, affectionately known around the squad room as Pappy.

"Pappy, this is a big man, an ex-biker gang member from up Chicago way. His biker friends could be at his place. They work on their bikes out there occasionally. I can't say who you'd be up against if they're out there, too."

"Don't sweat it, Jack, we'll be prepared. You say this guy lives in Waller, Texas? Who'd wanna live out there in BFE?"

Dawson Luck nodded. "Same thing I said when we were out there questioning the dude."

"I'm positive Jenna Berrie will be right behind you when you haul him in. It would be in her best interest if she came here on her own. She has been lying to us, and I'd like to question her again."

"Thanks for the heads-up, Jack. We have two other warrants to serve, and then we'll head out to get your boy. I'll get DePaul, Felix, Tenney, and Knots. When your big dude sees my bigger dudes, he will brown his tighty-whities. I don't think he'll resist too much. My guys eat bikers for breakfast."

"Yeah," Lucky said, "they *are* the American dream team—add in Gordo, and they can be the defensive line by themselves. Men made of muscle and brawn, grit and power."

"Makes me wish I was a younger man." Jack grinned.

Pappy agreed. "Yep, to be young again would be wonderful, but not dumb again. I'll text you when he's in custody at the station."

"Good deal. Tell Captain Yao you put him in an interview room, that way someone can check on him every so often."

"What about the woman? If she follows, where do you want her?" Lucky spoke up. "Put her scrawny ass in an interview room. Maybe that will scare the truth outta her."

"Okay, will do." He gave them both a salute wave and headed out to gather his team.

"I like ole Pappy and his team, Jack. They're the good guys."

Jack, for one, was glad those monsters were on their side.

"Mava told me he has a lunch meeting at one-thirty at Quattro's over off Lamar Street. Have you heard of the place?"

"Yeah, but I've never eaten there. Isn't there a parking garage across the street and several parking lots behind that area on the corner of Dallas and Austin Streets?"

"Yeah, and we'll hit the parking garage. It's twelve-thirty, so let's head that way. Grab the digital camera with the zoom. We can drive-thru somewhere and get lunch, then find a place to sit and stake him out."

"Good idea. My stomach thinks my back has caved in. I'm starved."

"Dawson, man, you're always hungry. Stop at the vending machine; grab some chips and a candy bar or two. We might be tailing him for a while. I'll grab a couple of bottles of water."

They drove through a Jack in the Box, and Lucky hooted. "I can't believe you picked Jack in the Box, *Jack*."

"Shut up, I like their sourdough jack and the curly fries. What are you going to order, bottomless pit?"

Fueled by fast food, Jack pulled the unmarked car into the parking garage across the street from Quattros. He drove around until he found a parking space on the fourth level.

"This'll work. We can go over to the edge there." Jack pointed.

"And unless he is looking right at us, he won't see us. We can use these square pillars to stand behind, and we'll be less visible to onlookers. Besides, who looks up these days? Everyone has their eyes glued to their phones even while they're walking."

"Good point, Jack. Everyone has their head in their phones these days."

Jack grabbed the camera and his soft drink, took off his suit coat, and opened the car door. It was hot. Hell, it *was* Texas. Both men rolled up their shirtsleeves. Walking to the back of the parking level, Jack peered over the side.

"Lucky, let's move over to the left. More, better view of the front doors of the restaurant."

"It's one-fifteen, Jack; he should be showing up pretty soon. One thing I've learned about the judge, he's very punctual, or habitually early."

Jack pulled the camera up to his face and zoomed in on Quattro's. "This camera has a helluva zoom; it'll pick up a blackhead on his nose."

"There he is." Lucky gestured with his head. Sure enough, there was Judge Troy Wolff, walking alone up the sidewalk.

"I wonder who he's meeting. I wish I had coerced that outta Mava." Jack clicked a few photos of him walking up and into the door of Quattro's, alone.

"It's funny, now that we know what he has hidden in his past, you wonder what he's still up to."

Jack's gut clenched. "That's it, partner."

"What's it?" Lucky shot Jack a sideways glance.

"If he was into that stuff back then—dominants and submissive, with bondage and this S&M shit—what's saying he still isn't into the same thing now?"

"At his age, Jack, now with a wife and grown kids? And he has a grandkid or two. Not to mention he's a judicial figure. Shit, he hands out sentencing. As it is right now, knowing what I know, I can't stand the thought of him handing anyone a life sentence, with or without the possibility of parole, not even a sentence of ninety days in county. It makes me sick."

"Uh-huh, it makes my skin crawl too. We've had to have him sign off on warrants, to search and seize and to arrest the very type person I feel he is—lowlife."

"You see anyone familiar at all, someone he'd be meeting with?" Lucky's eyes scanned the area.

"Nope, not a soul, not many pedestrians out right now either, and no one's gone into Quattro's in the last half hour." His eyes were trained on the entrance to the hotel.

"One-thirty on the dot. Bet whoever he's meeting is already in there. Maybe we'll see them leave together."

"Okay, now we wait, and uh, sweat." Jack huffed out.

Two and a half hours later, their shirts were stuck to their skin with perspiration. Lucky had gone back to the unmarked car and retrieved the two bottles of water, tepid, but at least the water was wet.

"Cripes, Jack, it's straight up four. A two and half our lunch. This is ridiculous." Lucky stretched his back, popping his neck to work out the kinks in both his back and neck from standing and peering over the concrete wall of the parking garage.

"Must be very important business or they're sharing some brewskis and shooting the damn bull. No one has walked in or out of the doors to Quattro's for the last hour." Jack focused the camera again, watching the doors.

"Maybe it wasn't business."

"How do you mean?"

"Quattro's is in a hotel. You think he got a room and is uh,"—Jack trailed off, his thoughts headed in another direction.

An 'aha' moment hit Lucky.

"He's meeting someone in the hotel, not in the restaurant. You think he's stepped it up from the no-tell-motel to a posher place to have his tête-à-têtes?" Disapproval dripped off each word Lucky said. "He's been in there long enough to meet someone, eat and leave, and if he walks out alone, we may never find out."

"Unless—nah, never mind," Lucky didn't complete his thought. "You mean, see who's signed in, rented a room, or eaten lunch?"

"That's what I was thinking, but this isn't like that place off Southwest Freeway. All Occasions Motel. Wasn't that the name?"

Jack pressed his lips together to keep from laughing, and he emitted a slight soft snort.

"I was thinking about the proprietor at All Occasions, that Tully Cranston fella. If the judge was to show up there, the old man would put up a sign saying Judge Wolff rented a room here. That old guy would love the publicity."

"Yeah, what is gonna happen when this all comes out? What kind of publicity will he get then? I'm betting it happened in a room at that ratty hotel."

"I'm sure you're right, Luck. The old man, Tully, said he didn't have any idea how far back his records dated. He has them stored in his son's barn, about thirty years' worth. Said he wasn't a neat freak or organized, and after seeing his front desk and the paperwork there, I can attest to that. Besides, he said the rats in his son's barn had destroyed a lot of boxes. If we have to, we can go get them for someone to go over."

Lucky gave an involuntary shiver. "Rats and barns, uh-uh, Jack, not me. Besides, who would have used their real name?"

A big laugh escaped Jack, and being in the garage it reverberated. He took a step back so he wouldn't be seen hanging over the edge.

"Lucky, you'd lose your lunch if you had to see paperwork so mistreated, as anal as you are about ours. Hey, look, there's the judge, he's on the move."

Lucky peered over and saw him as Jack took a few pictures. The judge was alone, his suit coat draped across his arm, his tie was off, and stuffed into a pocket.

"His tie and coat are both off. So I'm guessing it was one helluva lunch." Lucky's lipped curled up on one side in a sneer. He had no respect left for the man called Judge Troy Wolff.

"Let's head out. I know what car he drives." He placed the cover back on the zoom lens and headed toward the car. Without a word, Lucky followed.

IT HAD TAKEN them thirty minutes to get through the traffic that had bottlenecked on Interstate 10 toward the Loop. They had followed the judge on his route home, and at first Jack had been disappointed that they had nothing to show for their afternoon. That was until the judge made a pit stop. Camera at the ready, they had taken the pictures as the judge sat and ate at, of all places, the same Antone's he and Lucky stopped at when there were in this area. This was a sure sign to both of them he didn't have lunch at Quattro's; it was a different type of lunch meeting altogether.

Jack shot several pictures of him sitting alone, eating a sub, a bag of chips, and drinking a soda. The best part was watching him drink that soda without a straw, and the pictures proving it was the judge. Jack zoomed in on him when he took a drink and set the plastic glass down. Then he widened the frame to capture the entire table. Not only would his fingerprints be on that plastic cup, but his DNA too—perfect. With the zoom lens, Jack saw who was managing the counter, and he busted a gut.

"Call Antone's number, partner, ask for Viola. She's working the counter. Tell her we are on a secret mission, and we will be stopping by to get some food. Tell her Jack said not to clean off any tables until we get there."

Could they get any luckier—Viola—she was an aspiring detective who dreamed of being an FBI agent, like the *Untouchables*. There was one major problem though: Viola was in her sixties. However, she turned out to be the break they needed.

An hour later, Jack's phone chirped as a text came in. Opening his message, he read: *Secured Max Renner in interview room 5. You were right, Berrie woman followed, put her in interview room 2. Yao knows. Pappy.*

Jack glanced over at Lucky.

"Pappy has Max Renner at the station. Jenna Berrie followed."

"Good deal. You think we have what we need?"

"I think we do," Jack said.

26

Max Renner sat in interview room number five. He was not a happy camper. This was the mother of understatements.

"He wasn't a very cheerful person when Pappy brought him in," Yao said, as they watched the monitors for both interview rooms five and two. "We calmed him down, so we could uncuff him."

"Did he say anything or lawyer up?" Jack studied Max Renner on the monitor. He was a big man, or he appeared to be bigger in the small interview room.

"Nah, says he has no clue why he's here and has nothing to say. It's what they all say, right?" The captain always found that comical, but true.

Jack looked at the monitor of Jenna Berrie sitting in interview room two. "What about her?"

"All she asked was if she was under arrest. We told her no, you came to the station on your own. She wanted to be in the same room as the Renner fella. Pappy told her it was the standard protocol and not to argue with him."

Yao nodded to the screen that showed Max Renner, who was

now standing and stretching his big treelike neck, and then he walked over to the door and put his ear to it.

"Alright, Jack, go in there and get him to tell you something. Even if you don't get him to talk, we have his prints, and we have two stories, albeit from a dead girl and a demented cop. But if you have to, hell, lie to the scum bag. Do whatever you have to do to break the biker bastard."

"I'll do my best, Captain."

The latch to the door of interview room five slid open, and Max saw the doorknob twist. Jack West entered first, and his partner was right behind him.

"Take a chair, Mr. Renner." Jack took a chair and squared it around to face Max. Dawson Luck took the other chair, pulled it back by the door, sat down, folded his arms, and without uttering a word, he just glared.

"I shoulda known you were behind my being here. I done told you everything I could. How many ways can I tell ya? I don't know nothing more than what I already told ya." Max ran his hand over his bald head. Sweat had beaded on his forehead, and the black t-shirt he was wearing showed signs of sweating. The interview room was relatively cool. Jack saw right away Max was under stress.

He set down a thick folder and a tape recorder. Max stared at both.

"I'm aware of what you've told us, but we'll go over it all again, and Mr. Renner, I'd advise you to tell the truth. I—"

Max cut him off. "I *have* told the truth. Should I make up some fucking lies so you'll leave us alone?" His fist pounded the table as he slightly rose from his chair.

"I'd advise you to keep your cool in here, or I'll be forced to cuff you to your chair, understand?" Jack's eyes narrowed at the big man.

"I'll do my best to try." Max lowered his somewhat raised buttocks back solidly to the chair, his face losing the red angry hue.

"Your rights have been read to you, is that correct?"

Max nodded.

"Are you willing to talk to us on your own accord?"

Again, Max nodded.

"Okay, what was your job at the club, Crystal Barrel?"

"Bouncer."

"Did you work any other bars that were owned by SS Corporation?"

"Yes."

"Mr. Renner, or should I call you Max?"

"I'd prefer to be called Sarge, but seeing how you told me before you needed to use my official name because this was effing official business, I guess Max is fine." The big man stretched his legs under the table, crossed his arms over his big barrel of a chest, squinting his eyes in anger.

Jack thought that was a little better, a whole sentence this time, and not just a one-word answer. This was progression.

"Tell me, how did you get the nickname Sarge? Were you in the army?" Jack needed the big guy to relax, so he tried a little casual chit-chat.

"No, it was my rank in the biker's gang I used to ride with when I lived in Chicago. And let me repeat that, I *used* to ride with; don't no more."

"So, talk to me about that night. I—"

Max cut in on him. "I'd like to cooperate, but—"

Jack held up his hand. "Let me finish, then you tell me how much cooperation you're willing to give. Deal?"

Max Renner shot him a piercing stare, and his brows furrowed. The muscles in his jaw were visibly flexing. He looked over at Dawson Luck, and he gave him an evil eye, never adjusting his legs, feet, or unfolding his arms.

"I'm listening, Detective."

"First, I just want a yes or no to the next two questions. Okay?"

"Yes. Now, what's the second question?" The big bald man was being a smart-ass.

"Touché, Max. No one can say you don't have a sense of humor now, can they? And that's not the second question. Question one—are you familiar with a man named Skip Johansson?"

"Yes."

"Question two—how about a man named Harvey?"

"Harvey who?"

"Walden."

"No, never heard of a Harvey Walden."

Jack studied the man's face. "Okay, Skip Johansson, what's your relationship with him?"

"We worked together; he bartended, I bounced."

"You stay in contact with him?"

"Nope, we lost contact. He moved over to another bar, and I stopped bouncing. I guess I haven't seen Skip in over thirty years. Man, I ought to try contacting him. I liked the guy." Sarge let out a long exhale. Remembering his past brought back happy and distressful memories. He had liked Skip, goofball, naïve Skip.

Jack pulled out the photos of a murdered Skip Johansson, aware Sarge had no idea Skip was dead. He laid the pictures face down.

"What's this? A lineup for me to pick from?" Max shifted in his seat.

Jack's mouth was set in a straight line, his hand resting on the stack of pictures.

"I'm afraid not."

Sarge sat up straight, pulling his long legs up from the stretched-out position, and he placed his palms flat against the table.

"What's this about?"

"See for yourself."

Sarge pulled the stack of photos toward him. His eyes never left Jack's face, and without looking, his hands turned the stack over, then his eyes moved to the pictures. A sharp intake of breath, the blood rushed from his face.

"That's Skip. Oh my God, who did—why—what the hell?" He viewed the next picture, and then he shoved them away not bothering to look at the rest.

"Why would someone want to kill Skip? He was a sweet guy, goofy, but he wouldn't hurt a flea."

Just by his initial reaction, Jack realized this upset him. He scooped up the pictures and put them back in the file.

"That's what I was going to ask *you*. Why would someone want Skip dead? Some bad things happened back then, and don't sit there and tell me you don't know a damn thing because you're lying." Jack's voice boomed, bouncing off the walls of the interrogation room.

"None of what you think you know had anything to do with Skip Johansson. That's about all I have to tell you. As for saying anything else, Detective West, I've nothing to say." Max was again being hard-core.

Jack had expected this. "Skip wasn't involved, or that's your story, but with him being dead, I can't ask him." He laid the manila file on the table, scooted his chair up, and leaned in.

"You are simply the opposite. You were there; I've got the proof."

"Proof of what?"

Jack's eyes bored into the man's eyes. "Your fingerprints, Max, that's what I've got."

"My prints, on what? I think you're bluffing your ass off." The big guy slouched in his chair with cocky confidence.

"The girl they found dead, you remember, Celeste Mason? I'm sure you recall that night, don't you?"

"Just what am *I* supposed to recall? I wasn't freaking there."

"My partner and I took a trip to the old evidence storage to see what had been collected at Ms. Mason's murder scene. It bothered me because the dead woman's wallet had no pictures, not a damn one. I inspected the worn-out plastic sleeves and if you held them just right, you could see faint imagines of colors, where pictures had once been. Thing was, I just didn't think about it until later."

Max said nothing, and Jack went on.

"Forensics has improved over the past decade, and it improves daily. Two things which have improved in the last two-plus decades are the collection and testing of DNA, and, Max, fingerprinting technology. Nowadays you can damn near get prints off any type of substance. Things such as wood, metal, cloth, paper, plastic, and silk. Even articles with a distinct pattern or ridging can be worked with, and prints can be found that are basically invisible to the naked eye."

Renner held up his palms in a gesture of okay, *so what?* "What does any of this have to do with me? I ain't involved in any of that."

"It concerns you a great deal since we found your prints, or should I say several of your prints, on the wallet supposedly belonging to Celeste Mason, and the seatbelt straps in the victim's car. I have a question for you, Max. Did you give Celeste Mason the pictures out of JoAnn Cutter's wallet, or did you toss them? Which was it?" Jack's eyes never leaving the bald man's face.

Max Renner's face fell, and he paled, but he stayed silent.

"Max, do you need me to repeat the question?" Jack's deep baritone voice resonated in the interview room.

"I heard you the first time, Detective."

"I recall the second trip we made to Waller—you said you weren't initially in that room, then you didn't finish what you were saying. Jenna admits to being at the door. She claims all she thought she saw was feet on the bed, but wasn't sure whose feet they were. If you don't recall saying that, I can play the tape back. Well?" Jack sat back and crossed his arms.

Sarge continued to be the man of stone. His silence was infuriating.

"Tell you what. You're already under arrest for either killing that woman, and if you didn't, I have you on conspiracy to cover up a murder. I'm going to book Jenna on obstruction of justice. You can both go to prison. Am I getting this through your thick skull?" His fist hit the table with a thud.

"Leave Jenna outta this. She did what she was told. She wasn't involved in what was going on."

"So Max, tell us, what was going on?"

"Are you willing to leave Jenna out of this if I cooperate?" Sarge clenched his jaw so hard Jack swore he heard a tooth crack.

He locked eyes with the big man. He had nothing on Jenna he could make stick, but Renner didn't know that. Besides, he was fishing for a whale. Jack wanted to nail the judge's sorry ass to the wall.

"I want the damn truth about that night. After you talk, I'll see about a deal for Jenna. If you cooperate, I'll put in a word for you with the DA. Do we have a deal?"

Max Renner nodded in agreement. He'd do it to protect Jenna, and he hoped like hell the system showed him some leniency.

Jack started the recorder, and Renner told them what had happened that night at the All Occasions Motel.

When he was finished, no one said a word. The silence made Max uncomfortable, so he broke the unbearable quiet that filled the interview room.

"Like I said, I wasn't there when it happened. They told me we needed to help a man out. I had no idea that she was dead until I got there. No one told me shit until it was over."

Jack was trying to read him. Was he downplaying his part, or was he telling the truth? His tone sounded genuine when he admitted he had no idea what went down initially. All of this did not erase the fact that he facilitated in the cover-up.

"Nobody ever talked to me about that night. Here I was working at her bars, and no one ever questioned me about her, or who wanted her dead, nothing."

"Cops on the take shoved it all under the rug. No one wanted answers back then. Tell me something, Max. Do you believe Celeste Mason and Jed Logan could have perpetrated this?"

Sarge's massive shoulders jerked up in a small shrug. "Not sure. Celeste was getting death threats, and she needed to disappear. I knew Wolff; he was a regular customer for the girls, and he was into that crazy, dangerous sex. Jenna told me about it, and I made her quit hooking. When she told me what he made her do, I was mad enough to kill the bastard. I'll admit it, when his balls were in a sling, I didn't care, and I enjoyed having something to hold over his high and mighty head."

"Are you blackmailing the judge, Max?"

Max let out a raunchy belly laugh. "Are you kidding me? If I were, I'd be living somewhere else besides BFE Waller. Listen, I had no idea they intended to use JoAnn as a body double. I told you already, I wasn't in on the plan. God, man, I have my own worries, and I didn't want trouble with the law either."

"Where is Celeste?"

"I have no idea. All I have is a phone number, I swear."

"I'm going to need the number. Would you be willing to be a witness for the state?"

"Are you leaving Jenna out of this?"

"I have to tell the DA the entire story, but I think she's basically safe. You, though, I can't tell you for certain if the DA will work a deal or not. That's not my decision. What I can do is tell them you cooperated fully. You understand?"

Sarge bobbed his head a minute, thinking about it. Lucky for one wondered what he was thinking about. This was a deal of a lifetime and he better jump on it.

"Deal, then."

"Good. Now, you recall the woman, Daphne Walden?"

"She was Jenna's friend, not mine. She and Jenna worked together at the Blue Marble. I worked at the Barrel, uh, Crystal Barrel, full time. There's not much I know about her except I heard she died."

"Did you know her husband?"

"No, never met him. When we moved to Waller, I was trying to put all that business behind us." A certain pain filled his eyes. "Guess no matter what you have in your past it always catches up to you. What's the next step, Detective West?"

"Right now, I need to talk to Jenna. Tomorrow I'll call the DA's office to get someone over here to see what sort of deal we can arrange."

Jack nodded at Lucky, then turned back to Max. "I'm going to let you go on your own recognizance tonight, and if you run, I swear I'll find you. After that, I'll go after Jenna and she'll be charged with accessory after the fact. Are we clear?"

"Yeah, crystal."

"Good. I'll call you tomorrow and give you a time to meet with the assistant district attorney."

Without another word, Jack and Lucky left Max Renner in interview room five, alone.

27

"I wonder how the search for Buccella is going." Lucky stood at the interview room monitors as they watched a morose Max Renner, sitting alone, his cocky confidence gone—a man who was now contemplating what his future would be, or if he even had a future.

"I hope they find that SOB soon. We need to check out the phone number Sarge gave us. I'm betting it is a burner phone. At least it's a number more than we had yesterday. Alright, let's go see if we can rattle Jenna Berrie."

Jack opened the door and walked in, Lucky right behind him. He set down a bottle of water, a thick file, and his tape recorder, and then he pulled his chair up to the end. Lucky pulled a second chair back toward the door, taking up the same stance as he had with Max Renner.

"Sorry we've kept you waiting, Ms. Berrie—may I call you Jenna?"

"Uh-huh, yeah. Is Sarge okay? He's still here, isn't he?"

"Yes, we—"

"Please, please don't put him in jail," she whimpered.

"He's not in jail, yet. Max told us about that night. Now it's your turn to answer some questions."

She brought her hand up and swiped a tear from her cheek.

"I'll tell you what I can."

Jack turned the tape recorder on.

"Do you-"

She butted in on his question, not letting him finish. "Can I smoke in here, because I need a cigarette?"

"Sure, I'll—" Jack started, but Lucky got off his chair first.

"I'll go get an ashtray." In a short five seconds, he came back with an old flat metal ashtray.

"Tha-thank you." Jenna pulled the ashtray closer.

Lucky said nothing, not even you're welcome, and he took his place again, assuming the same posture as before.

Jenna tapped out a cigarette. Her hands were shaking as she tried to light it, so Jack held the lighter for her as she steadied her hands. Inhaling a long drag, she closed her eyes, held it for a minute then turned her head to the side and exhaled.

"I'm ready, Detective."

The cigarette soothed her shaky nerves, as she took a second long drag.

"Do you know Skip Johansson, or Harvey Walden?"

"Yes, both of them."

"How are you acquainted with these men?"

"Skip bartended over at the club, uh, Crystal Barrel, and Harvey worked for the Blue Marble. He was married to Daphne."

"Jenna, Max said he never met a man named Harvey. Why would he say that? If Harvey worked at one of the clubs she owned, he should have met him, at least once. Why would he lie?"

"He *didn't* lie. Sarge didn't work at that club, and he had no reason to go there. There were tons of people who worked the clubs, and we didn't hang out with everybody. Harvey came onboard a year before Celeste died. Once I quit hooking, Sarge stopped working at the Silver Moon and worked full time at the Crystal

Barrel." Jenna took a couple more long drags and tapped the ashes off her cigarette.

"Jenna, let's not lie to one another. We both know she's not dead. I figure Celeste is still somewhere in Houston. Don't play me, it won't work. No more lies."

His eyes focused in on hers. Jack didn't blink. Jenna held his stare for half a minute before she blinked, then turned her eyes away. Her head bent and she stared at the worn, metal, discolored ashtray as she tapped her cigarette against the flat rim again. The room, so silent one could almost make out the sound of a hiss as her cigarette burned down, little by little.

"It's your dime, Jenna, so I'd advise you to talk."

"Fine, Celeste is not dead. What has that got to do with me? I mean, I did nothing wrong."

"Tell me about that night. What happened?"

Jenna bit her bottom lip to keep it from quivering, large tears formed, remaining on the front of her eyes, like oversized watery contacts. She blinked, sending two single raindrop size tears cascading off each cheek. Taking one last drag of her burned-up smoke she crushed what was left of it, and inhaled.

"Sarge asked me to bring Celeste's car and a bag of her clothes to AO, uh, All Occasions that night. Don't ask me what time it was, all I can remember was that it was late, after midnight."

"And?" He prompted her.

She stared down at the table as she spoke. "I got there and parked her car, grabbed the bag of clothes, got to the door and knocked. Sarge opened the door, and as big as he is, he had the doorway blocked, so all I saw was feet on a bed. I never saw who the person was. And to tell you the truth, I thought the woman was passed out drunk. How could I've known she was dead?"

Tears cascaded down her face, dropping onto her nose and falling to her upper lip.

"Tell me what else you saw, everything, the entire truth, and remember, no lies. That will be your saving grace."

"Even though Sarge had the doorway blocked, I heard Jed and Scottie talking. Sarge took the bag from me and when he moved, I got a glimpse of another man."

Jack leaned in, hands on his knees, his eyes following her eye movement, not letting her break the gaze he had locked on her.

"Jenna, this other man—who was it?"

The woman ducked her head to break eye contact and said a name; however, she said the name so low even the recorder couldn't have picked it up.

"You'll have to repeat your answer, Jenna, I didn't hear you, and if I didn't, then the recorder didn't either."

"I, uh, ahem—" She cleared her dry throat, picked up the bottle of water, uncapped it, took a drink, recapped it, and set it down.

"I said I saw Troy Wolff."

"What was he doing, Jenna?"

"He was on the floor in the room, half-naked, and passed out cold."

"You did excellent. Now, Jenna, I have some pictures for you to see and they're not pretty. I'm positive this will upset you, and I'm sorry for that." He opened the file, and took out the pictures, placing them facedown.

Jenna eyed him as she pulled the pictures toward her, sliding them to turn them over. She turned the top photo over and her hands shot up to cover her mouth to hold her scream in.

"God, no, that's Skip. Who did this to him?" She pushed the pictures away with such force they shot off the table. Lucky bent to retrieve them, and handed them to Jack.

"Harvey Walden did this."

Her face went ashen. "Why, why did he do this?"

"That's the sixty-four-thousand-dollar question we all have. Did you ever know him by another name, Jenna? Did Daphne ever tell you about him?"

She took her hair in between her fingers and twisted it. "If he had another name, she didn't say. Daphne was private about their life."

The woman was lying, damn it. Jack took the pictures and sifted through them and found the picture of Harvey, putting his gun to Skip's head.

"Jenna, Harvey is a cold-blooded killer."

He laid the picture in front of her, stabbing at Skip's dead body with his finger.

She averted her eyes, and her body convulsed with tiny jerks. Jack felt the table vibrate as her body shook. He looked up, and she was unashamedly sobbing, both hands covering her face.

"Skip was a sweet guy. He was immature, but he was nice to all the girls. He-he-he was a goofball, a fun goo-goof-goofball."

"What did Daphne tell you about Harvey? Tell me what you know, Jenna, tell me for Skip."

"All she told me was he had been in trouble in Chicago and that's why he moved to Texas. When I talked to her last, she told me he was closed-off. He was selling the house and had moved stuff out or was throwing it out. Daphne was afraid he was planning to commit suicide. She begged him not to do it, to live until his death came naturally and to honor her life by keeping his. He told her he wasn't ready to die, not yet, because he had business to attend to."

"What business? Did she tell you? Did you ask her?"

"No, she didn't, and I didn't ask. Daphne had a coughing fit and began coughing up blood, and had to get off the phone. That was the last time I spoke with her. She died three days later."

Jenna's brows came together in a sharp V, and her face took on tangible anger. She hadn't even gotten the chance to say goodbye.

"I am sorry, Jenna. I liked Daphne. She was full of spirit and a little bossy. And, back in the day, she was a damn hot-looking woman."

Jenna only half-smiled, because she knew being mad would not bring her friend back.

"She was all of those things, and a helluva canasta and poker player."

"One last thing, Jenna, do you know where Celeste or Jed Logan are?"

"No, I don't. Sarge has a number to reach them. He just told me. I hadn't seen her since the day before that all happened, and that night was the last time I saw Jed. And that's the truth, so help me God." Jenna crossed her heart. "Detective West, am I going to jail?"

"I can't say for sure."

"What about Sarge?"

"Depends on what kind of deal he cuts with the district attorney, but they might be lenient."

"Can I cut a deal too?"

"It's something we can talk about when the time comes, if it does."

Leaving her, Jack and Lucky headed to the monitor room.

"We'll cut both of them loose, and then I'll call the ADA in the morning to set up a meeting."

"You think he'll run, Jack?" Lucky yawned. It had been a long day, and it wasn't over yet.

"No. I think he knows I'll hunt his ass down no matter what. I think Skip getting bumped off spooked them."

"Okay, what about Wolff? We have some evidence, so how do we move ahead with that?"

"Getting an arrest warrant for Wolff will be a very touchy subject," Jack said. He pulled out his phone.

"I'll call Bennie; ask him to meet us at the lab early tomorrow."

Lucky arched his back, raised his arms, stretching. "Gonna call the wife."

Lucky stepped away for privacy while Jack dialed Bennie Guay's number.

The medical examiner answered on the third ring.

"Bennie, its Jack West. Sorry to call you this late. Can you meet us at the crime lab early tomorrow morning, seven-ish? We have something to compare the touch DNA with."

Bennie tried to stifle a yawn. "Sure, see ya then, thanks."

Jack hit end call.

After letting Max Renner and Jenna Berrie leave, Jack and Lucky had just stepped into the squad room when the door opened behind them, and 7-11 dragged in.

"Hey, you guys are still here." Jace plopped into his chair laying back in a slouch and closing his eyes.

"We figured y'all were at home comfy in your beds by now." Xi took his seat and kicked his feet onto the desk.

"No sighting on Buccella?" Jack was busy clicking his keyboard. "Nada, but Central Patrol is still out looking," Jace ended with a yawn.

"Did you get any good information out of that Max Renner or his woman, Jenna Berrie?" Xi stretched his arms over his head, letting a wide yawn escape.

Jack gave them the skinny on Max and Jenna and their stakeout on the judge.

"You took pictures of him at Antone's, and he didn't eat at Quattro's? What the heck was he doing at the Four Seasons then, having an *um'chicka'bowow*?" Jace tried to say that with a straight face, but didn't pull it off.

"That, my friend, is a damn good question." Lucky smirked; it pissed him off.

"Who knows what he was doing? I know he wasn't eating a late lunch, or he wouldn't have stopped at Antone's for dinner. But guess who was working the counter today?"

"Was it Viola, our resident wannabe FBI spy?" Xi Chang rolled his eyes, and a huge laugh burst out of him.

"Yep, it was Viola. God bless her. Hey, you guys, I think it's been a long day, and we should all go home. Let's start fresh in the morning. How about it, fellas?" Jack got up, clicked his computer off, and stretched.

"I like your idea, Jack." Lucky was more than ready to end the day.

"Xi, if the warrant squad finds our boy Buccella; text me, I'll be here pronto." Jack wanted that man's head on a platter, on a spear, or in a box, just any way he could get it.

"I forgot to ask you if you'd heard from Rick and Katherine in Vice. They check in or what?" Jace stood and pushed his chair under his desk.

"I wasn't expecting to hear from them until the morning, unless they had news that couldn't wait. It's close to midnight, and they're staking out Delvecchio. Since he's at a bar and they're undercover, they may close the place down, observing." Jack yawned. "If Rick or Sparky get a lead, or something significant, one of them will text me. See you guys in the morning, I'm out of here." Jack did a hand wave in the air as he walked to the door, headed to the back stairs and to the garage. He was bushed, he needed sleep, and tomorrow was another day—well damn, he was Scarlett O'Hara, after all.

28

"So, you took these pictures of him at Antone's with this glass?" Bennie took the evidence bag with the red plastic glass which had Judge Troy Wolff's DNA on the rim, and his fingerprints, should they need them later in the case.

"And the best part was there were no other customers in the restaurant. Lucky called her and told her we were on a secret mission and to not clear off any tables until we got there."

Bennie grinned. "Good ole Viola, the resident FBI agent-in-training, or spy, or CIA agent. She's a hoot."

Everyone associated with the HPD knew Viola and her dream of being FBI, CIA, or a detective.

"I'll put a rush on this, but it might not get back for more than a week." Bennie scrunched up his nose and bobbed his head. "I have a buddy; I'll call him and tell him it's vital that we get this back soon as he can. It's the best I can do, Jack."

"We understand the backlog the labs have, but whatever you can do to speed it up would be appreciated."

Back at the station, he began cross-referencing the phone number Max Renner had given him for the Mason woman.

"Hey, it's about time you got here. I thought maybe you guys were getting extra beauty sleep," Lucky joked as 7-11 walked in, one behind the other.

"Yo! So, Central Patrol turned over the hunt for Buccella to the warrant squad, and Sargent, Leo Loomis, texted me. They spotted our guy but lost him, damn it." Chang was disappointed.

"At least they spotted him. I thought maybe he had jumped ship and headed to Mexico."

"You have any luck with the phone number?" Jace rolled his chair back and propped up both feet on the trash can under his desk.

"You'd freaking think it would be simple, but ain't nothing easy these days. Jack's been cross-referencing the number, but shit, nothing's popped," Lucky responded, to Jace.

"Let me try. What's the number?"

"Here, knock your socks off, Xi." Jack reeled off the number.

"The girl's name is Celeste Mason, right?"

"Yep, and the man's name is Jed Logan."

Xi typed and clicked away while Jack, Lucky, and Jace watched and listened to the keys clacking as he skimmed over a site, then he clicked and typed some more.

"If she wanted to disappear, she's not using her real name, and him—this Logan fella—he didn't disappear, no reasons to change his name," Xi said, burying his head into the computer.

"She had to have changed her name." Dawson Luck stood up, walked over to Xi's desk, and watched over his shoulder as he worked.

"Well, the woman is not using her name because I've seen zero Celeste Masons, and zero Celeste Logans, her age." Jack stopped to think. "What would she be calling herself these days?" Jack was mumbling to himself.

"She might've made a new name outta her old name like an anagram." Jace nonchalantly stated as he wheeled his chair over to Xi's side of their two desks to watch him work.

Jack jotted her name on a notepad and began working it out.

What anagram would she use if she used one? It took him about five minutes.

"It can't be this easy, can it?"

"What can't be that easy, Jack?" Lucky raised his head up and looked over at Jack, as did Jace.

"You said something about an anagram, Jace. Her first name is Celeste. With her first name I came up with the name *Steele*, as a last name."

"That's a damn common name, Jack," Xi said as he stopped clicking and raised both arms to stretch.

"That would be her last name." Jack analyzed what he had written. "Her first name would be Sara."

"But Jack, the last name on your anagram is missing the C in her name," Xi pointed out.

"Okay, how about Sara C. Steele?"

"Why Sara, Jack? What does that have to do with her?"

"Sara Sutton was Mason's only living relative, and she left the clubs and the funny business to Celeste when she passed."

A light bulb went on over Lucky's head, figuratively. "Hell yeah, Jack, SS Corporation—Sara Sutton, Sara Steele, that's brilliant."

Xi used that name and went to work. In less than twenty minutes, Jack, Jace, and Lucky heard Xi say, "Bingo, we have a winner."

Jack went and stood behind him, peering over his shoulder.

"Thanks, Xi. That would have taken me all day." He jotted down the address and stuck the paper in his pocket.

"Now what, we go see her, or what?" Back at his own desk, Lucky wondered what was running through his partner's head.

"What I want is a confession about what happened in the hotel room that night. As a bonus, I'd like to hear her say she ordered the hit on Scottie Buccella."

"Jack," Lucky said looking at his watch, "you gonna call the ADA?"

"Jonell Simone? Why are you calling her?" Jace looked from Lucky to Jack, then back to Lucky for an answer.

"Max Renner wants to cut a deal and hopes he either stays out of jail or gets very little jail time. Plus, he told us he'd testify for the State."

Jack dialed the DA's office and asked for Jonell Simone. He didn't go into detail on the phone but talked her into canceling her afternoon because it was highly urgent. If he was yanking her chain, he'd pay dearly, she promised. He was damn glad that fireball was on their side.

Jack called Max Renner. Jenna answered.

"Uh-huh, I'll tell him, two o'clock, yes, Detective West, we'll both be there."

Jack knocked on his desk. "That's set."

The next call would be to see what Rick and Katherine had found out. Picking up his phone, as he dialed, the squad room door opened and Sparky walked in.

"Howdy fellas, ya'll look busy," she joked.

"Hey, I was fixing to call up to four. How did it go last night?"

"Place is a major dump, Jack. What a shithole. We nursed a beer, played pool all night, staking the place out." She grabbed an extra chair and pulled it up between Lucky and Xi's desks.

"So, what about this Delvecchio dude; or the place, get any vibes, see anything at all interesting?"

"Criminitly, Jack. One freaking question at a time, would ya? Here's the skinny. This place is running girls, we're sure of it." She held up her hand before Jack or Lucky made a peep. "Wait, let me finish, please."

They were all ready to ask her a thousand questions.

"Rick saw a few of the girls in the club last night that we've been watching over by the truck stop. It's about six miles west off I-10."

Yeah, they all knew the place.

"A few of those truckers came to the bar looking for a cheap piece. We recognized some regulars. The truck stop's been a regular gold mine for the prostitution industry. There's a thirty-five dollar a night no-tell-motel three blocks away, and they might even have an hourly rate, who the F knows?"

"Vice set a sting up over there?"

"We're working a case over there, Xi, not to bust the girls, but to find out who's running them. It's not your usual run-of-the-mill operation. It's bigger than one pimp running a few girls. What we want is the man at the top that is making all the decisions."

"So, you think this bar is connected to this?"

She bit her bottom lip when she looked over at Jace. "We think so, but can't confirm yet. We watched several of the girls with the men. It was obvious they were hooking, but we just let it happen. Rick saw at least three different girls go up to this Delvecchio dude, hand him some cash, then he would hand them a napkin. We're sure it either had a name or a number on it." A sad looked passed over her face.

"How women can stoop to this level has always stymied me. I saw two of the girls head to the restroom, so I followed them and parked myself in one of the stalls to listen. These chicks are lunatics, and if they're dead one day and you're working their homicide, I won't be shocked."

"Why, what were they talking about?" Jack's ears tingled, and his gut lurched.

Katherine Spark's lips curled in disgust. "S & M and that bondage crap, with handcuffs and other scary shit. They were laughing about it."

Lucky looked at Jack. "Are you thinking what I'm thinking, that maybe Wolff frequents this place?"

Jack's face went grim. "Well, Delvecchio and Wolff are cousins. They could share the same sick fetishes. Remember what I said. If he was that way before, chances are he is still into all the other nasty shit related to that kind of behavior."

"Leave this alone, Jack, and let Vice handle it. Because, one, it's what we do, and two, it's more than just the girls." Sparky got up and pushed the chair back. "Look, fellas, this is stuff we need to handle. I came to thank you for getting this crappy bar, the Crystal Barrel, on Vice's radar. You've given us a tremendous lead, so we got it from here."

"Spark—" Jack began, but she raised both palms up and stopped him.

"Jack, listen to me. There's more at stake here. A year's worth of work for Vice. You getting us involved and giving us this Delvecchio dude was a huge break." She gave him a hard stare, moving both hands to her hips. "It's so much more than hookers, Jack. And we're after the big kahuna. We've discussed the possibilities of your Delvecchio being part of the top tier. So, leave it alone." She pushed the chair back against the wall.

"Hell's bells, Spark. I don't want to mess up Vice's work, but you and Rick better damn well keep us abreast of what's happening. You realize what we're dealing with." He stood and put both palms flat on his desk top, leaning in and staring at her.

"We will, we will. If anything pops, I'll call you myself, I swear."

"Alright, Sparks, I'll hold you to that."

"You bet, Jack." Katherine Sparks waved and went out the door.

"Hey, Jack, think we should get someone to stake out the address we have for Sara C. Steele, the improved former dead girl, Celeste Mason?" Lucky looked across the desk at him.

Drumming his fingers on top of his desk, he didn't answer. "Jack, I asked you if—"

His hand slapped the desk in a loud *thawaap*, repeating it with the other hand, and then both hands like a drumroll.

"I've got a damn idea."

"Well, you want to tell us, or are you gonna keep playing the drums on your desk? A plain old, hey guys, I got an idea without all the sound effects would work, pard."

AT ONE O'CLOCK, the ADA walked into the station. Jonell Simone was a top-notch attorney. Placing her in the role of ADA was a wise decision. She was tough; she never gave up and never backed away from a tough case. Jack respected her tremendously, even though she had come from the other side. Years ago, Jonell had worked in the public defender's office, which was not always friendly with any cops on the force in any department.

"Good to see you, Jack."

"Yeah, Jonell, it's good to see you too. Are you ready to hear an unbelievable story?"

"I've heard them all, Jack. Give it your best shot."

He began the story, and her jaw dropped open in a *shut the front door* look, more than once.

"Holy crap, Jack, this *is* unbelievable. Never in my life would I imagine Troy Wolff—I mean, I would never have thought him to be, well—that type of guy, or have that sort of sexual lifestyle. This behavior boggles my mind."

"Believe me, Jonell, it boggled the shit out of mine."

"Okay, let's get down to the basic facts. Here's what you don't have, Jack. No eyewitness and no proof your dead girl is this JoAnn Cutter and not this Mason woman. Crap, let's tick this list off, Jack." She looked at him, and he opened his mouth to speak, but she held up one finger. "Let me talk. I let you, now it's my turn."

"Okay, Jonell, talk."

"First, we need proof a hit was ordered for the shooting on Richmond Avenue for the attorney and the Bowers man. If the missing prostitute, this Cutter woman, was the only witness, and she *is* dead, pardon the pun, that's a dead end. Homicide Detectives Ian Simpson and Pete Bullard were supposedly on the take, but there is no evidence to support this statement.

"There is also no way to prove Bullard killed Randy Simpson. Ian Simpson admits he executed Scottie Buccella, on the boss's orders, and he helped Bullard cover up his son Randy's murder. The problem with this is the old man has dementia. Not a star witness for us, Jack.

"Next we have a missing prostitute, who everyone says is the dead girl in your case and the dead girl, this Mason woman, is not dead, and to top it off, she is the boss in this whole cluster-fuck.

"You got all of this information from Daphne Walden, an ex-prostitute dying of lung cancer. Problem is, we cannot call her in because she died. Xi and Jace get a homicide, caught on camera, of a man executing a club owner named Skip Johansson. This is the same Skip Johansson who told Daphne about Wolff, and what he did that night at All Occasions Motel. Our cold-blooded killer is none other than the dead prostitute's husband, Harvey Walden, whose last name is really Buccella, and he is related to the guy Scottie, who Ian Simpson executed. Did I cover it all?"

"That about sums it up, Jonell." Jack kept Ralph Delvecchio and what Vice was working on to himself. There was already way too many working parts to this situation.

"God, Jack, this sounds like a complicated drama, a made-for-the-big-screen movie or one of those who-done-it miniseries. Where's the evidence proving your dead girl is this Cutter woman—"

Jack cut her off. "Now that you're up to speed on the cases, let me update you on our progress in getting proof."

Her forehead shot up. "Alright, you have my attention, I'm listening."

Jack gave her an account of the stakeout on the judge, the trip to Antone's, the fingerprints on the wallet, and the seat belts.

"DNA, huh? You can't argue with that, or fingerprints. Wow, Jack, getting the DNA off his cup was a very smart move. The judge can't deny he was there or that the cup wasn't his since you have pictures to back up your evidence. But why do you need his DNA? What do you have to match it to that connects anything to anything?"

"We have the scarves from evidence lockup that were found with the dead girl. Bennie did a Touch DNA test—and he put a rush on the cup for us. He said the report should be here by tomorrow afternoon. He knows a man who owes him a favor."

Jonell's mouth opened, then closed and opened again, but she said nothing. She sat in a state of disbelief. It was so quiet Jack heard his watch ticking. The scene felt frozen on pause.

As if someone had hit play, Jonell moved, and her mouth opened and words came out.

"You say this counter person at Antone's, uh, Viola, would swear an oath that the judge was there, and she saw him drink out of that cup?"

"She was, and she would testify, I guarantee it."

"Okay, let's see." Jonell tapped her pen against her notebook. Find this Mason woman, Jack, then—"

"We found her. She's going by a different name. We have a phone number and an address, and—"

Jonell's eyes widened. "You did?"

"Yeah, it's a long story." It was craziness, because who would ever believe they'd done it with an anagram?

"Let's talk about a few things first. I don't think there's much we can do about the Randy Simpson killing. I mean, even if we had real proof, not the ramblings of a dementia-ridden man, it wouldn't matter. Bullard died, I heard."

"Yeah, he died last year, and the kid Randy is dead. Leaving it alone is fine by me. Even if we proved Ian Simpson whacked Scottie Buccella, what difference would it make? Simpson's pretty much at death's door, and couldn't withstand a trial."

Jonell did a sideways shrug and crinkled her nose on one side.

"That's fine with me. I can sweep it under the rug. There is one thing though."

"One thing?" Jack wondered what he left out.

"Finding this Mason woman will prove she's not dead. But how are you gonna prove the dead girl was the Cutter woman? Maybe it isn't her?"

"Ah, that one thing we have, Jonell. I have a witness who saw the dead woman and can identify her. There are two witnesses who saw Troy Wolff in the room that night with the dead hooker. The best news is they aren't dead."

"Really?" she asked, giving him a suspicious look.

"Uh-huh, and I have a plan." Jack went into detail about Max Renner, and his plan.

"Jack, it might work. I mean, what other shot do you have at a confession?"

"None, this is it. And I'm ninety percent sure Renner will help us, but he's going to want to strike a deal. I'm more than certain he'd like to bypass jail, but—" He stopped to look at her.

"But, but what, Jack?"

"If Renner gets her to admit to ordering the execution on Richmond, we'll have her on this, and maybe he can get her to admit to the Cutter woman's murder, or at least the set up to get her killed. *But* we still have the judge to deal with. Are you up for this and the consequences we might face?"

"You're damn Skippy I am. Houston doesn't need a man with moral turpitude handing down sentencing or representing our city. Even if it wasn't murder, it's still manslaughter. Accident or not, Jack, he's responsible for telling the truth. Christ Almighty, he was a lawyer representing scum just like him. It makes me wonder how much he bent the law back then. Now here he is, a judge, doing God knows what, even now. I feel sorry for his wife and kids. This is going to tear them apart."

"Then let's do this and let the dominoes fall. Let's go see if Max Renner's here."

29

"Max, stop fidgeting. I can't get this taped on if you keep squirming."

Art was exasperated. The big man was squirming and sweating and the tape wasn't adhering.

"You sure about this, Detective West? What if she doesn't tell me anything or gets suspicious?"

"Relax, Max. Just get her talking. It's a chance we have to take. The team will be around the corner. If anything goes south, we're on it. Besides, you're huge. She's a tiny woman."

"Yeah, well, tiny women can hold guns, and I ain't ready for that."

When he said that, Jenna's eyes bugged out and her hand flew to her mouth to cover her audible gasp and Max turned his head.

"Hey, don't worry, she ain't gonna pull a gun on me, she trusts me, Jenna."

"Lots of stuff could go wrong, Sarge. Be careful, please."

"Sure, baby. Detective West is gonna watch my back, right, Detective?"

"Absolutely, if anything out of the ordinary goes down, we're busting in." Jack looked at Jenna, and she studied his face. Not once had Jenna ever trusted a cop, but she trusted Jack.

"Max, here's the button, just press it and it will engage the microphone." Art poked him to get him to pay attention. The big man wiped the sweat off his hand and took the small square box.

"Put it in your pocket. My team and I will be in a van around the corner. As soon as you get to the front door push the button. We'll be listening to everything."

"That's it?" He looked at Art.

"Easy-peasy, my man, that's it."

"Jack, we're going to set the van up, and then we're headed to the address. When do you expect you'll be there?" Art Walsworth checked his watch.

"We'll be twenty minutes behind you, and Art, man, thanks for your help."

"Why're you thanking me, Jack? We're all on the same team."

"I guess because you and your team are doing this, no questions asked."

Art slapped him on the back. "Jack, you're a strange man. Me and the boys in Tech never get the full story; we do as we're told."

Lucky, Xi, and Jace all made comments as Art left. Art got a "Thanks bud, we owe ya, man."

Jace waved, adding in, "See ya on the other side."

Art rolled his eyes.

THE TECH VAN parked around a corner on a side street, two blocks from the target address.

"Jack, it's Art, you read me?"

"Yeah, Art, we read you loud and clear. We're about a mile out on the north side. 7-11 will be coming up from the south end."

"Roger that."

Jack drove past the house, did a U-turn, and then he eased the car up and pulled over. He had a clear line of sight to the front of the residence. Only one street led you into the neighborhood from the main road. This was an advantage because there was only one way in and one way out of the vicinity.

He clicked on his radio. "Art, Lucky, and I are in place. We're across the street, two houses down from the target address."

"Roger, we're ready to rock and roll once your man gets here."

"Guys, this is Jace. We're northbound on the main street. There's a short driveway on an empty lot, and from here we can see anyone approaching from both ends of the street. Where's Renner?"

"Lucky texted him. He'll be here in less than ten."

The clocked ticked, yet time felt like it stood still as they waited. "Jack, our guy's coming up the street. He just turned into the community."

"Copy that, Jace, we see him."

"You ready, Art?"

"Absolutely, Jack, we're set to go."

Jack and Lucky watched as Max Renner pulled his truck up, turned off the engine, cut the lights, and sat there, not moving.

"What's he waiting for, an invitation?"

"Give him a minute, Lucky. He's trying to gear up."

They watched. Max didn't move.

Dawson Luck's hand was on the car door.

"Wait, Luck, he's getting out."

"Good thing, I didn't want to have to yank the dude outta his truck."

"I don't think that would have been an issue, pard. The guy's a tank, you're a bicycle. Max would crush you."

Dawson Luck snorted. "Yeah, well, this bicycle packs a mean Glock."

Max walked up the walk and to the front porch, put his hand in his pocket, and pressed the button on the remote. Everyone was listening in now.

"Testing, one, two, three." He glanced back at Jack's car and got the thumbs-up.

Max rang the doorbell; Jack and Lucky ducked once the front door opened.

"Sarge?"

"Yeah, it's me. Long time no see, Celeste."

Narrowing her eyes, she stood there looking at him. Suspicions filled her head.

"Uh, you gonna let me in or what?"

"Where's Jenna? She with you?"

"Nah, she's at home, back in Waller; I'm alone."

Jack could barely see the woman; Max was so big he was blocking their view. He got a glimpse of her face when she peered around Max and looked at the street. It was dusk, and harder to see. Celeste saw Max's truck; no Jenna.

"Fine, come in. Then tell me why in the hell you're here." Sarge walked in, and she closed the door.

"He's in the house," Jack reported to the others. Now it was all up to Max Renner.

"You look good, Celeste."

"Thank you. Alright, Max, you didn't come all the way out here to tell me I look good, so just what are you here for?"

"We just gonna stand in this damn long entryway and talk? Jesus, Celeste. I haven't seen you in, what now, almost twenty-eight years, and this is the welcome I get?"

"Oh, dear, where are my manners?" Hostility oozed from her lips. "Don't get an attitude. For once in your life be polite."

"For once in my life, what the fuck does that mean?"

"We both know you can be a bitch. You can't deny that, now can you?"

A rather bitter laugh escaped her. "You're right, I can."

She led him down a long hallway, past one closed door and into a nice sitting room.

"Take a seat and then tell me why you're here. After you're done, I need you to fucking leave."

Sarge looked around. "Nice place. Must be nice to live in a place like this."

"Yeah, it's nice. Okay?" She stood in the door way with crossed arms, waiting.

"Jed here?"

"He's upstairs."

"He gonna come down?"

"He can't."

"Why not? Are his legs broken?"

She walked over to a chair, sat, expelling a huge sigh. "He can't because he had a stroke two weeks ago."

"Sorry to hear that. How bad is it?"

"Bad. The right side of his body is weak. He has a hard time with his speech, and he has a very hard time remembering things. Why are you here, Sarge? To ask us how we are? You could've picked up the damn phone for that, so?" Her bitchy attitude was back.

"Skip's dead."

"Well, you could have called to tell me this. Did he have a heart attack or what?"

"Yeah, someone put a bullet in his head. It was like a heart attack. It made his heart stop beating." Max's eyes never left her face as he watched her reaction.

Composed and unmoved, she was a stone. He had been right all these years. The woman was heartless. He'd admired her back then. No petty girly emotions, a business woman who ran a profitable business. Now he saw her as a cold, self-centered bitch.

"When did it happen? Who killed him?"

Ignoring her, he asked her another question.

"Anyone tell you that Daphne died too?"

"No, no one told me. Someone put a bullet in her brain?"

"She died from lung cancer. What the fuck, Celeste. Plenty of people died on your watch, but some people died, as nature planned it, when it was their time to go."

"Died on my fucking watch? So what; none of that has anything to do with you."

"Is that what you think? Well, it's come back to haunt me and Jenna. I called you to tell you HPD had reopened your damn murder case, and this is how you say thank you? Cops have questioned Jenna, me, and there was one more person who had a story to tell."

"Oh yeah, who, cuz I can't think of anyone who would talk?"

"She did, and she died, that *she* is Daphne, one of your girls."

"The ramblings of an ex-hooker. Christ, don't make me laugh."

"She found out you weren't dead. Skip let it slip. Simpleminded, sweet Skip, he told her. What you did was sign Skip's death warrant. You killed him."

"How did I do that? I didn't put a gun to his head."

"He was the one you sent to get Scottie out to that drive-in that night. Scottie thought he was meeting you and he trusted Skip. Hell, everyone trusted Skip. He set it up for you, and you sent the cop, Simpson, out there. Tell me I'm wrong."

"Scottie had to be whacked. He was dangerous. He knew I wasn't dead, but I was still getting death threats. I found out he was the one who had been sending them. It was him or me. Sorry about Skip, but I can't raise the dead. What does his murder have to do with me, anyway?"

Sarge ignored her question.

"It happened before, too. Someone was a threat to you, and you'd order their death. It was easy for you."

"Jesus, now what are you blathering about?"

"Richmond Avenue, ring a bell?"

"Why do you want to talk about this now, Sarge? Are you trying to clear your conscience because mine is clear enough? Roger was a slime-ball and Archie was a time bomb. Don't forget that you were the one who pulled me out of the way when the car almost crushed my legs. If you recall, that was Roger's doing; he hired those thugs.

How about when Archie and that bitch JoAnn held me at gunpoint? You forget about that incident? I could've been dead then, and we wouldn't be having this goddamn conversation. So yeah, they needed to go, both of them. Scottie was happy to do it for me. He wanted to have it to hold over my head."

Celeste moved in her chair but did not get up. She was so pissed off her voice had cracked and she had to wipe the spit off her chin.

"Jesus, woman, no reason to get your panties wadded into your crack."

"I've known you, Sarge, almost forty years now. If it were anyone else sitting in that chair asking me these kinds of questions, I would get a gun and shoot them in the face. So, I'm going to ask you again why this matters any longer." Her hands on the arms of the chair had balled into tight fists.

"Jenna is afraid to leave the house to even check the mail, and I want to make sure the killing stops with Skip. Celeste, I never asked you nothing back then. Maybe now, after over thirty-four damn years, someone can tell me the motherfucking truth before I croak. There is only one person left alive that can answer my damn bloody questions, and that's you. That's why I'm here."

She leaned back into the plump, comfortable armchair and closed her eyes. Her past flashed like an in-color cinematic film. Without opening her eyes, she spoke.

"All right, Sarge, what else do you need for me to explain?"

"JoAnn—what happened to her that night? Before I got there?"

She sat silently, her eyes stayed closed. She guessed Sarge needed closure for a past life.

He was about to reach over and shake her out of her so-called trance when she spoke.

"I had enemies. I needed to disappear, as in I needed to be dead. Scottie never controlled things; even you knew that back then. Yes, I set JoAnn up. It was a plan that we, Jed, Scottie and I, worked out. Hell, we weren't even sure if it would work, but it did, beautifully.

Jed was aware of JoAnn's S&M fetishes. She was a scary maniac with her sexual ways, and so was he back then.

"Who is he?"

"Damn it, Sarge, you were in the room for the aftermath, so you know it was Wolff. Jesus, let me finish so you can get the hell outta my life. Scottie wanted JoAnn gone because she witnessed the shooting on Richmond Avenue. Jed hated her, and she was the perfect body double for me. We told her to dope his whiskey up with more than a normal amount of coke. I told her to get crazy with him, and Jed told him to go overboard with her. He did, she did, and he killed her. It was an accident, but we hoped—" She opened her eyes and looked at him.

"Then you had him in your pocket, and I helped cover up your evil. Is he still in your pocket?"

"Not like before, but if I need him, he complies. I have proof to crush him."

"Did you know Daphne was married?"

"No, I didn't. Who was she married to?"

"Harvey Walden."

"Yeah, good for her, or it *was* good for her, I guess." Celeste was tired; this little unexpected visit was draining her.

"You don't remember Harvey, do you?"

"Why should I? Who is he?"

"He used to work for you. He bartended at the Blue Marble. That's how him and Daphne met."

"So many people came and went, and he was only a stupid bartender. They were a dime a dozen."

"Like Randy Simpson was, am I right?"

"Jesus, are we going to discuss all my sins? Haven't I confessed enough for one millennium?"

"Nah, you just answered my question. By the way, Walden wasn't Harvey's real last name. Walden was his middle name or his mother's maiden name."

She shrugged her shoulders. "So, he used his mother's last name, it happens."

"Nope, don't think that was the reason. You asked me a question earlier that I didn't answer."

"What was that?" Her voice uninterested. She didn't care. She wanted him to leave.

"Who killed Skip Johansson—I never answered you."

"Well, who killed Skip?"

"Harvey Walden—Buccella."

A sudden jerk and her eyes opened in alarm, and her face went pale. *Did he say Buccella, as in relation to one Scottie Buccella?*

30

The information spilling out of her mouth was more than they had expected.

"Man, who would have guessed she would sing like a canary, Jack?"

"Not me, I thought he'd have to pry the information out." Jack's cell phone chirped.

"West. You're sure? What was rented? Thanks, man."

"What's up, bud?"

"I had an alert put out on Daphne Walden's credit cards. She just rented a Silver Nissan Versa forty-five minutes ago."

"A trip from the grave. Smart move, Jack."

"Jace, you copy?"

"Roger. What's going on, Jack? Are we moving in now?"

"No. You guys be on the lookout for a Silver Nissan Versa. Newer model will have a sticker on the back window—Airport Car Rental."

"Who's driving it?"

"My fat pain-in-the-ass and your cold-blooded killer: the one and only Harvey Buccella."

"You're joking?"

"No, and don't stop him. Let him come this way because he's coming for her. Move in with caution once he turns into the subdivision. Roger?"

"Oh yeah, we copy."

Celeste speaking again grabbed their attention. "Sarge, I'm tired and I need to check on Jed. Are we done now?"

"I suppose so. You gave me the answers I came for. I have one last question for you though."

She stood, looking at him, angling her head toward the door.

"One last question? Haven't you asked me enough questions already?"

"Yeah, maybe, but what're you going to do?"

"About what?" She huffed walking to the door leading to the front hallway, wanting him to follow.

"When Harvey Buccella comes calling? He's not coming to talk to you, you know, don't you? I mean, what're you gonna do, call the police and tell them he's coming after you for calling in a hit on one of his relatives? Mob families are tight; of all people, you should know that."

"He doesn't know it was me. How could he?"

Sarge's laugh was bitter. "You believe that, don't you? You of all people should know how loose-lipped hookers are and how much their johns talk back. Fantastic sex, a great blow job. You mix all of this with drugs and booze, and those girls got the men to tell them anything. Harvey Buccella bartended for you at The Blue Marble. Understand what I'm saying? How many of your top-notch whores worked there, huh? He knew who, what, and why, but then Daphne came along. They fell in love and she didn't want to lose him. She begged him to wait it out, thinking maybe he'd let it go. And he did, for more than thirty years. I shouldn't say this because I want nothing on Jenna's head, but—"

Jack looked at Lucky. "You realize this is a message to us, right?"

"Yeah, I get it. Now he's telling the truth. How nice of him. Are you going to do anything?"

"No, Lucky, I'm going after the big fish, because the minnows are cooperating."

"What would be on her head?" Celeste had had enough of this game of twenty questions.

"She knew who Harvey was. Daphne told Jenna everything. She knew about Harvey, and about Scottie, even about Skip's part. Jenna knew once Daphne found out she was dying of lung cancer, Harvey would be out for revenge. Even after all these years, he never forgot. I've had to live with Jenna for these past thirty some odd years while she's been scared to death waiting for a bullet to the head, because she knew too much. Enough to get her shut up permanently."

"Well, she's not dead and neither am I. I won't spend the rest of what years I have left being afraid, either. Now, just leave me in peace."

"I wanna see Jed before I go, be the last chance I get. I've known him longer than I've known you; at least give me that."

Sarge didn't budge; he brought his bulgy arms up, crossed them, and took a stance that said *I'm digging in.*

"He won't like you seeing him this way, but if that's what it takes to get you the hell out of our house, then fine. Damn it, you can go see him."

Jace radioed in. "Jack, silver Nissan headed your way. He just turned onto her street. Xi is circling around the block and we'll come up the back way."

"We see the car. He's about six houses away. Art, you copy?"

"Yeah?"

"Call for patrol back up, 10-40, no lights, no sirens. Tell them to go to the end of this street and one street south. Block it off. No one in or out, copy?"

"Copy, Jack, I'm on it."

"Jack, he stopped, one house away, and he's out of the car. We have him on the Skip Johansson's murder, shouldn't we—?"

"No, we're not doing anything yet, Lucky."

"Man, as soon as she opens that door, he's gonna shoot her in the face, I—"

"No, he won't. Skip was a petty job, all he ever did was lure Scottie out to the abandoned drive-in. Buccella is planning on taking care of all persons involved, even Ian Simpson. She's different, though. She was top dog, and he's going to want to discuss this first, and then kill her. Besides, he doesn't know Max is there."

Lucky feared another murder was about to be committed while they sat and watched.

Jack's eyes never left the front of her house as Harvey rang the bell. The door opened and Jack didn't see her flinch until she realized who he was.

"Jack, units en route, will arrive in five minutes."

"Roger, Art. Jace, where are you?"

"Two houses behind you, came up without lights. We coasted in."

"Okay, vest up, we're going in."

"Jack, are you—"

"Look, Lucky, I want the bastard for several reasons. Mainly cuz he popped Skip, and part of me wants him cuz he played me. This way we get her, and we have more on him. Not just murder, but we can add in attempted murder, because he intends on killing her."

"Then let's make sure he doesn't, and get going. Xi and Jace just walked up."

"Here's the plan. He knows my voice, so Lucky, you stand front and center. Jace, Xi, and I will flank the sides. When she opens the door, I'm banking on Buccella to be behind it, holding a piece on her. Give her the sign to be quiet, and then say something like, sorry to bother you, but I want to know if you take the paper, or some shit like that. Hold this note up telling her keep the door unlocked. Come on, guys, let's rock-n-roll and get this job done."

Lucky rapped on the door.

"Were you expecting company?" Buccella arched his brow.

"No."

"We're going to the door together, get rid of whoever it is, or they can die with you."

Opening the door just enough to see who it was, Harvey stood behind the door, his gun aimed at her. Seeing a detective in Kevlar, her mouth dropped open, but no sound came out. Lucky held one finger up to his lips, shaking his head, and held the note up for her to read.

"Sorry to bother you, ma'am, I'm soliciting new customers for—"

"We already take the paper, but thank you." She cut him off, shutting the door, pretending to lock it.

Harvey nudged her with the barrel of his pistol. "Good, now go back into the other room."

A gun at her back, she walked ahead of him to the front room.

"Sit." He waved the revolver at a chair.

"Let's talk about my cousin. His name used to be Scottie; you remember?"

"Yeah."

"So talk." Harvey didn't sit, his revolver never leaving her face. "Fine, but can you point that fucking gun somewhere else? Jesus, I'm sick of men pointing guns at me."

"Yeah, well, none of them ever pulled the trigger. I'm thinking your luck is about to change."

Lucky opened the front door, Xi behind him, Jack behind Xi. Jace covered the door.

Jack motioned for Xi to move right and Lucky left. The hall was wide and long enough to creep up the sides to the doorway leading into the front living room.

A squeak sounded, and Jack looked up toward the staircase that led off of the hall. Sarge had set his foot on the first step. He signaled for him to back it up, then with another gesture to stay put.

If this hadn't been such an intense moment, he would have

laughed at the look on the big bald man's face. The one thing Sarge hadn't expected was to see HPD detectives decked out in Kevlar with guns drawn. Sarge picked his foot up and inched back. Lucky and Xi were waiting for his next call. Jack moved up next to Lucky and made a hand signal to wait and listen.

"Celeste, are you going to talk, or do I just shoot? What's it gonna be?"

"So, Harvey, you used to bartend for me at the Blue Marble, is that right? Huh, I don't remember you. Seems you make a piss poor impression on people. Not very memorable, are you?"

"That's how you expect to get out of this, Celeste, by insulting me? Jesus, Daphne was right, you are a nasty bitch. Nothing about you is impressive."

"You married a whore. What does that say about you? You too hard-up to get a decent woman, is that it?"

"Jesus H. Christ, my trigger finger is itching."

Her voice exuded strength, but she was putting up a front as she popped out of her chair.

"Yeah, well, I'm not sure what's stopping you then, scratch it."

"Hell, Scottie had a thing for you. He never wanted you dead."

"Well, his threat letters told a different story. Besides, it wasn't personal, it was business. Of all people, you being a Buccella, you should know that. Shit, Harvey, didn't you ever see *The Godfather*?"

"Yeah, but the Buccella motto is an eye-for-an-eye. And this *is* personal. I'm here to demand my pound of flesh, a hundred and ten pounds of flesh. Stand up, now."

Xi motioned to Jack. He had eyes on Harvey. The man's back was to the doorway. Jack gave the go-ahead. Xi and Lucky moved in, and Jack hung back, out of Harvey's sight.

"Drop the gun, Buccella," Xi called out. Harvey stepped toward Celeste. His left hand reached out, and he grabbed her by her right arm, swinging around behind her. He took a step back behind the chair, his pistol pointed at Celeste.

"You shoot, I shoot, I don't give a donkey's dick whether I live or die, but she needs to die." His words strained as he tried hard to contain his anger. If he let his anger get the best of him, he would lose his edge.

"It doesn't have to end this way." Xi raised his revolver and aimed it straight at Buccella. One thing Harvey did not know was that Xi Chang could hit the freckle off a gnat on a fly. He was more than just damn good; his marksmanship was superb.

Lucky inched to the left. Xi stood to the right, and Jack leaned in and had a visual on everyone from his position at the door opening. Jace had stepped in further and was standing inside the front door, ready to move in if needed.

"You two stop," Harvey warned as he put the gun to her head.

They were right. He didn't want to die today. He wanted to get back to Chicago and let the family know he had vindicated Scottie's death. Afterward, he'd let the chips fall where they may. He no longer cared.

Jack stepped into the doorframe. "Daphne would want you alive, Harve."

"Detective West, nice to see you, or maybe not, in the spot I'm in."

"Drop it. It's over, Harvey."

"No, Jack, it's not. People hafta pay up for the past. She's the last one who owes, and I expect my payment with her blood. Hell, I'm not even going to kill the old cop who shot him; heard he's about dead, anyway."

Harvey pushed the gun harder to her head, causing her to wince.

"What if I tell you she is going to get hers, and live to be sorry about it sitting in prison?"

"Oh yeah, and how will that make me feel any better?"

"We have it all. It was taped. Her part of JoAnn's death, Scottie's execution the hit over on Richmond. We even have the story on Randy Simpson's so-called accident. Man, we have all that and more."

Her eyes narrowed as she trained them on Jack. "What the hell are you talking about?"

"Max was wired. We heard everything. You're going down for all of it, Miss Mason." Jack took another step into the room.

Sarge had set her up, that motherfucking rat. The reservoir of hate she had built up over the past thirty-four years burst, and she transformed into the cold-hearted, evil bitch she really was.

"*Sarge, you bastard, Sarge!*" she screamed at the top of her lungs, "*get your motherfucking ass down here now!*" She had enough power in her heated state to pull away from Harvey, who hadn't expected this, and lost his firm grip on her arm as she wrenched away.

This gave Xi Chang just enough space to get a shot off, hitting Harvey Buccella in the right shoulder. His body took the full hit, and his right arm flung out, pistol still in hand. Dawson Luck moved in a flash, lunging toward the man, pushing the chair Buccella had been standing behind, knocking him off balance.

Celeste tried to dash out of the room, but Jack grabbed her by the arm, subduing her, just as Sarge hit the last step on the staircase.

"Stay there, Max, don't move until I say you can," he instructed.

The detective was holding a gun. Sarge would not move, let alone breathe. With one quick movement, Jack grabbed his cuffs and cuffed Celeste's hands behind her back. Then he pushed her toward the room she had darted out of so he could assess the situation.

Harvey Walden Buccella lay with his face to the floor and Dawson Luck was trying to hold him down. The injured man was bucking like a wild bronco while blood pooled under his right shoulder.

"It can't end this way, motherfucker, let me up. I swear I'll kill all of you, but her first."

Spit was flying as he screamed and thrashed about. Lucky wrenched his right arm twisting it to get the man to stop bucking. The shot in the right shoulder had not stopped him from resisting. Jace had his other arm; bending it back to the one Lucky had twisted so they could cuff him. Even after getting his wrists cuffed, his legs and feet were thrashing about kicking and flaying wildly. Jace took his cuffs and Xi's cuffs cinching the man's ankles. Harvey ultimately stopped fighting because the cuffs on his ankles were biting into his flesh.

Xi called for an ambulance, and for patrol backup, which he knew were close.

"Sarge, you can move now." Jack walked a cuffed Celeste Mason out toward the front door.

Her eyes held a cauldron of hatred. "You—you rat bastard, you're in just as deep as I am; you were there, and you covered it up."

"I might sit in a cell for a while, but that one incident is all I had a part in. You're on your own for all the other shit. I planned nothing. Just like JoAnn and Skip, you used me as a patsy. The only difference is I'm alive." Sarge turned to address Jack. "Is it okay with me going upstairs? Jed's up there alone, and until you get someone out here, I'll stay with him."

"Sure, Sarge, I'll have to get someone from Social Services out here, but until I do, you can stay."

Jack was no longer worried about Sarge. In the end, the big bald man had done the right thing.

"Thanks. I appreciate you trusting me, even though I don't deserve it." He turned back to Celeste. "Don't thank me. I ain't doing it for you. I'm doing it for Jed. He might have bent the law some back in the day, but he was a decent man before you hooked your claws into him." With that, Sarge took his leave and headed upstairs to take care of an old friend.

31

Buccella was in the ambulance, cuffed and pissed. Jace decided it was in the best interest of everyone that he rode with him to the hospital and had one of the patrol cars follow for support once the transfer from the ambulance to hospital occurred. The medical staff would have to knock his ass out before the doctors could even think about working on his injuries.

Celeste Mason was in the second patrol car, verbally cursing Sarge out as loud as she could, and Jack wished like hell she would shut up. "Take her to central booking, Jeffers. We'll be right behind you once when we're done here. Get her printed, take her pretty picture, and then put her in a holding cell."

"Will do, Jack, see ya in a few." Patrol Officer Jeffers climbed into in his car and drove off with a screaming bitch in his back seat.

"Jack, I'm heading to the hospital. I'll give Jace a ride back to H.Q. The shot to Buccella was a through and through. They ought to have him patched up so we can transport him to Booking. We'll see what the doc says."

"Sounds like a plan, Lucky. Xi and I will stay here, cordon the area off until the OIS team gets here. I'll call the captain, get him out here. They can get yours and Jace's statements later about the details of the shooting."

"Good, deal, see ya later."

Xi Chang scanned the room, shaking his head. "Jeez, Jack, I hate OIS investigations and relinquishing my gun. Crap, I haven't been involved in full-out shooting in five years."

"Xi, it was a clean shoot, we all saw it, and I wouldn't worry."

FOR THE LAST EIGHT HOURS, non-stop, he'd questioned Celeste Mason, had Art Walsworth get the tape copied for the DA's office, and called in a favor to Social Services. His contact would send someone out to pick up Jed Logan and get him transported to a local nursing home. He let Max Renner and Jenna Berrie know the ADA, Jonell Simone, would be contacting them. If they skipped town, all bets were off. He assured them he'd find them. Once he did, he'd lock them away so long they'd never see each other again.

The doctors patched up Buccella's gunshot wound. They had to sedate him to treat him. When the sedation wore off, he became a wild man again. They had to shackle him, hands and feet. Hell, at one point Jace was ready to get the white coat with buckles. Once the hospital released him, he was booked and placed in the county jail.

Captain Yao and the OIS team came out, assessed the crime scene in an officer-involved shooting, and had CSU out to process the scene. Xi gave his statement, relinquished his firearm to Captain Yao, who had clapped him on the back and told him not to worry. Jack gave his account of the shooting, and then explained where Jace and Luck were. The OIS team went to the station a little later, took their statements, and left.

Jack dropped onto his bed at 3:00 a.m. He was mentally and physically exhausted. It had been a damn busy night and with this much going on, one thing was for sure—the lid had popped open, and the worms were spilling every which way. And these worms were talking worms. The news would hit, and Judge Wolff would hear. If he hadn't been so dead tired and had his warrants ready, he would have gone to the judge's house and hauled his ass in. Jack was ready for tomorrow so he could end this case.

COFFEE IN HAND, he made his way into the squad room; surprised to see Lucky, Jace, and Xi already there.

"You guys spend the night here?" Jack asked.

"I've been here since five-thirty; figured I had paperwork to get started on, and I have the warrant for Wolff ready to go, waiting for a signature," Lucky said.

"Yeah, I told Lucky I'd help with the paperwork since our cases are connected. Besides, I'm going to be desk-bound until the OIS team clears me to have my firearm again."

Xi's gun was like another arm on him, and he felt unbalanced.

"Hey, partner, you'll be packing again soon. It won't take long to get it sorted out." Jace stayed optimistic.

"You helping Lucky with the paperwork would be better than him ending up with me or Jace, cuz we aren't close to being as proficient or anal as you two birds are."

"Thanks, Jack. I guess that'll have to do for now." Xi picked up a stack of blank reports, sifted to the one he needed, and dug in to keep his mind off the shooting investigation.

"Jack, any ideas yet on who you'll ask to sign the warrant for Wolff?"

"Gave that some thought this morning, Jace, and I think Judge Carlson is who I'm going to approach."

"Yeah, I don't think she'll waiver on it. Jack, I've heard her and Wolff don't always see eye to eye. Didn't she blast him in the paper once about a case he presided over?" Xi Chang looked up from his paperwork.

"She did. It was right before you and Luck moved to Houston.

The case concerned a massive weapons charge. Some lowlife selling guns to illegals, not just a few guns either. Several assault rifles, Uzis, a load of semi-autos with the serial numbers filed off, and Judge Wolff overruled the sentencing when he shouldn't have. It was the man's fourth offense. Prior to this charge, the same dude was arrested for possession with intent to sell to a minor, aggravated assault, and a burglary charge. Wolff was the presiding judge for every case. On every damn case all the perp got was a slap on the wrist, and Wolff was taking heat about it."

"Yeah, I remember that," Jace spoke up. "The guy was a three-time loser. This dude should have been tossed in the can as a habitual criminal on his third offense. I'm thinking he was pulling in favors for the Mason gal back then. Or it might have even been Scottie Buccella."

"Well, one thing I know is, Judge Nora Yorke-Carlson will be thrilled to sign the warrant, get him disbarred, and jailed. She can't stand the bastard."

Jack was positive Judge Yorke-Carlson wasn't corrupt; he'd bet his last dime on this.

"What's the plan, Jack? I have a gut feeling it ain't gonna go well with Wolff." Lucky wheeled his chair between his and Xi's desk.

"So?"

Jack tipped his head back and stretched it from side to side, popping out the stress kinks.

"I say we get him at home, not at the courthouse; too much can go haywire there. You and me, we go in and try to reason with him. He's gonna fight it, say he can't go to jail, ain't safe, he'll get shanked. We tell him we'll keep him segregated."

"What if—and I'm just saying what if here, Jack—he fights it, he ain't going, he'll die first?" Lucky looked hard at Jack.

"Like he shoots himself in the head?"

"Yeah, that's what I'm thinking."

"Lucky has a point, Jack. Man's been a respected official figure in

Houston for years now. No way he's gonna want to be in one of Houston's jails." Jace looked over at Xi. "Don't you agree, 11?"

"They're right. Hell, he might've already shot his brains out."

"I'm telling you he doesn't have the guts. He likes to dominate, in the courtroom and evidently in the bedroom or motel room or whatever, but he's a coward, or that's how I see him."

"Well, coward or not, we have to bring him in, and I'm sure it ain't gonna be a party."

The door opened and Captain Yao stuck his head in the room.

"Jack, a word, in my office please."

"Sure." He got up and shrugged to the other guys, then headed to the captain's office.

"What's up, Captain? Everything okay?"

"Have a seat. Great work last night. It was a long night, but it went smoothly."

"That's not why you called me in here, Davis. What's up? It's something cuz I see it in your face."

The captain nodded absently. "Courthouse called this morning. They told me Wolff didn't make it into his chambers. He had an eight o'clock hearing, and never showed, plus no one can reach him. Our media relations phones have been ringing insanely. There are also a few gawking reporters in the lobby, not from *The Chronicle* or *The Sun*, but from some cheap rag magazines. Word is out and shit's rolling downhill fast. Chief Pratt's already sent word to get this tied up and quieted down to an inaudible murmur. What's the plan? Are you going in after him or sending the warrant squad, what?"

"I'm going in, Lucky and me. We were discussing it when you stuck your head in. I sort of figured he was going to lie low, not leave his house."

"Yeah, he's there, so I already knew he didn't go to the courthouse."

"You did, how?"

"Hell, after last night I knew word was going to get out. I put a detail on his house, just for, well, you know why. His kids are grown, so it's him and the wife at home. A taxi picked her up, so my detail called in a unit to follow her. She went to the airport. Jack, guess he's sending her away. I don't know if she knows what all of this is about. But they've been married for over forty years. Women are smart, but who knows?"

"You think he's barricaded himself in, waiting for the National Guard to come busting in?"

The captain inhaled deeply. Leaning his head back he blew out air, and looked at Jack.

"No, I think he'll *off* himself, that's what I think, so he can die as a *haunted man.*"

"Cap, he's a coward. I don't think he has the guts. He's been hiding behind his law degree and his black robe, and he's a narcissist. To be honest, Lucky and I think he's still in the sex game—S&M shit and the works."

"Jack, I suggest you get over to his place, find him. We need him alive so we can legally prosecute the bastard. I don't want a dead man whom the town might make a martyr out of. Is the warrant signed and ready?"

"Judge Carlson should be at the courthouse now. Mava said she has a case at ten, and she expected her at eight-thirty." It was 8:45.

Captain Yao looked like he had aged ten years.

"Hey, Davis, we'll get him, and then we can call *The Chronicle,* have them send Tessa Coy over. She'll do a great job spinning this vulgar, bizarre story. The main thing is, she will downplay it, keep the crappy stuff out, and focus on the real facts. I've never known her to write like the shitty tabloids do. She'll do the force and the city proud."

"Yeah, ya think?"

"She'd better, or I'll never call her again for the scoop."

"Blackmail, Jack—" Davis Yao snorted, "I like it."

"Good Lord, Jack, I thought Judge Carlson was going to either pee her panties or break out in song and dance. She hates Wolff."

"I guess she knew something wasn't right even way back then. Could be she followed his less-than-honest career."

"Hey, is Yao's detail still on the judge's house?"

"Yeah, he sent word for them to stick around in case it gets crazy." The judge's house was luxurious—even the bricks, and the glass looked expensive—and it was in an affluent, quiet neighborhood. Affluent neighborhoods were taking a beating. First, the Stegwig murders, now this. Guess having money did not mean a thing, could not save your life or keep you out of jail.

Yao's detail sat across the street. The four of them all did a silent head nod acknowledgment.

Jack's boots and Lucky's shoes clicked on the concrete drive. Any other noise heard might have been the faint chattering of a squirrel. He hoped to avoid screeching ambulances and the sounds of police sirens, jarring the neighborhood into a frenzy.

Jack rang the bell, and they waited. No answer, no nothing. He rapped on the door harder.

Dawson Lucky yelled, "Judge Wolff, we need to talk."

***

Troy Wolff heard the bell and the knock, then he picked up the finest bourbon money could buy and poured another tall glassful. He drank the entire glass without stopping to breathe. Then he poured another, setting the glass down, no longer caring whether a coaster protected the cherry wood desk.

The pictures were out, scattered on his desk. Like before, the colors were quite vivid. With closed eyes, he relived the memory of the fantastic sex and the night which haunted him. What she had allowed him to do. It had all been unbelievable, and the warm feeling behind his zipper started spreading, just as it always did. What a fantastic piece of ass she had been. Damn it, he was getting a hard on. Thirty-four years later and he had never stopped dreaming of her.

No other woman ever gave him that much pleasure. God knew he had his share of women—hell, he was still searching for a woman like her. Once you have had that kind of sex, it gets into your veins. You cannot stop, or at least he couldn't.

The dungeon—his favorite place—now he would never go again. It was over. He did not give a rat's ass about the wife, just his kids, and the one grandkid. Last night, he had written them all a goodbye letter and mailed them out. Then he sent his non-fucking, sexless wife off to Florida to see her mother. She'd been his meal ticket only.

He picked-up his fifth glass of the finest Kentucky bourbon and a picture of the dead hooker with him lying on top of her. Lifting his glass, he said, "Here's to you, JoAnn, your fine sweet-ass pussy was the best I ever had." He chugged the drink, then poured another half glass. Sitting back in his big executive chair, he stared at the revolver he'd laid out on the desk.

"Jack, try the door."

The doorknob turned, it was unlocked.

"Don't call out. It'll spook him," Jack said in a low whisper.

"Leave your gun holstered. I don't want him to feel threatened." Motioning for Lucky to go to the right, Jack went to the left, clearing each room they entered, working their way toward the back. The house was massive. Lucky passed through the formal dining and into a dream kitchen, walked out the second door, and heard Jack's voice.

"Judge Wolff, here you are. Detective Luck, we're back here, in the judge's office."

Lucky followed Jack's voice down the hallway.

"Hey, Judge, everyone's been wondering where you are," Lucky said, eyeing the revolver on his desk. He shot a look at Jack.

"Judge Wolff," Jack began, but Wolff cut him off.

"No, not anymore—" His speech was slurred, and Jack saw the bottle of bourbon on his desk and the empty glass.

"Ain't judgish anymore," he slurred his words. "Just plain old Troy Wolfffff—" he ran together a long string of *f*s.

While Jack had his attention, Lucky undid the strap on his holster and eased his gun out.

"Detective Luck, I may be a little drunk, but I ain't smashed yet and I ain't blind either."

"Yeah, I know, Judge. But what say I take the gun off your desk? Since you've been drinking, we don't want anybody to get hurt." Lucky took a small step toward the desk, gun in hand, but not aimed at Wolff. Jack had Lucky in his peripheral vision.

"*No.* It's my gun, gonna need it here in a minute. My life's over now." Picking up the half-full glass of bourbon, the man chugged it, and picked up the bottle to pour another.

"Drinking will not give you a steady hand, Troy. Why not hand me the bottle and let Lucky take your gun? This way nothing bad can happen."

"Lookie, Jack, it already did, but it was a fuckin' accident, it was. I didn't know I was pulling them damn scarves so hard. God damn it, that woman was the best piece of ass I've ever had. She was also a lunatic, like me. Shit, I didn't want her dead—I wanted to keep fucking her."

"Okay, I get it, it was an accident. But what you're doing now ain't necessary." Jack stepped up to the desk, slowly. He hoped he was appealing to the drunken side of Wolff, the not quite rational side.

"Jack, I ain't stupid. Hell, I'm a judge, and I know the laws, backward and backward. I mean forward. Besides, my torrid life will be splashed in the news; can't have this happen, nope. My darkest secret aired out for the public. No, Jack, if I can't have it all, then I'd rather be dead."

Lucky took another step, but Wolff saw him, and his hand

covered the revolver on the desk. A drunken judge and a loaded revolver didn't make for an ideal situation.

"Troy! You know how it is. You'll get a fair trial, and maybe we can keep some of this information sealed. But you know we have to do our job; haven't you told us this for years now?"

Wolff's head whipped around. "Yeah, well, I never thought I'd be one of your zhobs, Zach—I mean, jobs, Jack," he slurred his words.

Lucky took another calculated step toward the desk, wondering if the judge's reflexes would be impaired because of the alcohol in his system. It didn't matter; he was going take the chance. It could be his last chance before Judge Wolff picked up the gun and pulled the trigger.

Troy Wolff's reactions were near choreographed as his right hand slid over and his middle finger looped around the trigger guard. He pulled it toward him, and in one swift motion, he had the gun up, aimed at Lucky.

Lucky put his hands up, still holding his gun in his right hand.

"Whoa, give me the gun, Troy, before someone gets hurt."

"Back off then." He sounded sober, although Jack knew he wasn't. Lucky took a quarter-step.

Wolff had the gun up, his eyes not veering from Lucky's, and with his left hand, he picked up one of the pictures, but didn't look at Jack as he spoke.

"See, here is the proof, but I'm telling you it was a goddamn accident. God, I have paid all these years for being a fucking patsy. They controlled me, don't you see?"

"Then let's go with this for your defense. Maybe you can beat the rap."

"Jack, stop. I know what you have. You think I don't hear things? The city of Houston will crucify me, and you know what the worst part is?"

"No, Troy, you fucking wanna tell me, or do you wanna tell the dead hooker what the worst part is? Jesus, Troy, you think it's all about you, you bastard." Jack's voice got louder with every word he said, which surprised Wolff; he wasn't used to *anyone* ever screaming at him, and he jerked his head around to look at Jack.

Lucky took this opportunity and lunged toward the desk. Taking a sidestep, his left hand swung over to the judge's right hand, the hand he had propped on top of his desk holding the gun. For a man who had been drinking, his reactions were swift. Pulling the gun out of Lucky's reach, he pointed to where Jack was standing.

Time slowed to a crawl; so slow everything was in slow motion and it felt surreal.

Lucky's left hand hit the judge's desk in a loud *thawaap*. Wolff's body turned to the left. Pulling his arm back, he moved the hand holding the gun across his body, keeping it out of Lucky's reach. Jack sidestepped to his left, getting out of the line of fire in case the gun went off. Hell, a drunk was holding it.

This threw Lucky off balance; he began toppling over the desk, knocking over the half-empty bottle of bourbon. His hand slid across the top, sending eight-by-ten photos flying off the desk, hitting Wolff in the right elbow, sending the revolver upward toward the ceiling. Lucky's gun bounced against the judge's desk as he tried to keeping his balance. The chambered round in the judge's pistol went off.

The gunshot put it all back on real time and at regular speed. Jack, who had been moving out of the way and to the left of the desk, reached for his gun. Lucky had hit the floor, but not before half his upper body had crashed into Wolff, dumping him over in his chair.

"Lucky, you hit?" Jack couldn't see if he was or not and had no idea who shot what or who.

"No, and I didn't get a shot off either. That was from his gun. Find Wolff's gun, Jack, I'm okay." Lucky hauled himself off the floor.

Jack stepped around to the back of the chair which had dumped a drunken Troy Wolff over, who was now laying with the left side of his face smashed to the floor. Wolff wasn't moving. Squatting, Jack checked for a pulse. He was alive.

"Troy, can you hear me?"

A drunken voice sounded out. "Oh crap, I shot myself." He had pulled the trigger, and how he had shot himself in his left knee was anyone's guess. Paramedics had Troy Wolff strapped on a gurney, and as the gurney wheeled by, he stuck his right hand out and grabbed Jack's arm. The detective looked at his arm, then at the judge's face.

"Jack, I would've loved to have been a man like you; a good man with morals."

Jack didn't say a word as he pulled his arm from the man's grasp. He looked up at the paramedics. "Get him out of here."

The Next Day

THE CAPTAIN HAD SUMMONED Jack to his office. As usual, when he walked in, Captain Yao was on the phone, and he pointed to a chair for him to take a seat.

"Uh-huh, she will. Sure, Chief. I'll have Jack sit with her, go over all the details. He's in my office now, I'll tell him. Yeah, we'll talk later." Captain Yao hung up with the chief of police. "How are you, Jack?"

"I'm doing okay, a little tired. The last few days have been nonstop."

"You heard me tell the chief I'm going to have Tessa Coy come over, and you and she will go over the details of the cases. Tell her I want to see her article before it goes to press. No argument, or I'll get the chief and the mayor involved."

"Sure, Davis. Oh, and Bennie called this morning. All the DNA results are in."

"Well?"

"The touch DNA off the scarf and the DNA on the cup from Antone's are a match. It was him."

"One more piece of concrete evidence, Jack. The man's going away. Even if back then it was an accident, he covered it up, or at least let them cover it up, and he didn't say a word."

"Wolff had some of the most damning evidence himself. The pictures we confiscated at his home. Don't know where the originals are. I'm sure he was being blackmailed in some manner."

"Guess it won't matter any longer. One thing I don't want leaked out, shared, or otherwise talked about are those pictures. Just keep them under lock and key. Some freaking scandal magazine will splash them all over Houston if they get them. Hell, all over Texas. Houston's gonna be rocked enough by this. Don't need to add pictures to the story."

Jack sat back, crossing one leg over the other. "Yeah, this turned Houston on its ear alright."

"Hell, Jack, we've survived floods and hurricanes, and eventually this will die out and be a faded memory. But what Homicide did, what you and your team did, well, I gotta say, in all my years it's never been done before."

"What's that, Davis?"

"Solve three cold cases and a new murder, all at the same time. At least that's all we'll report. We're going to close the case on the Scottie Buccella murder as solved. Ian Simpson will die in his own personal hell in that old folk's home. As far as Bullard's part in the alleged killing of Simpson's son, we're leaving that as it is—a one-car accident. Homicide has a record that no other homicide team has ever accomplished. The chief is busting his damn buttons over this."

"Thanks. We were all just doing our jobs. But, it feels damn good."

"You said Wolff said something to you when they wheeled him away. What was it?"

"Huh, he said he would've liked to have been a good and moral man like me."

"Jack, hell, I'd give my right nut to have twenty men just like you."

"That means a lot to me. Thank you, Davis."

"Jack, take a few days off. You and Luck won't draw a case unless it is necessary. Relax and be ready to come back refreshed."

"Sounds like a good idea, Cap, think I'll do that."

PEACEFUL, it was nice. He sat on the concrete bench decorated with angels and sat the paper bag next to him. Looking at the headstone, he spoke.

"Cole, sorry I've missed our visits for a few days, but I was covered up with work. You've been in my thoughts always, and I know you know that."

Jack leaned back, closed his eyes, and inhaled the fresh air, smelling the freshly cut grass. A few birds chirping were the single sounds he heard. Opening his eyes, he smiled at the headstone.

"You know, bro, we never had a beer together. I wasn't old enough to drink before you—well, you know."

Reaching into the bag, he pulled out two cans of Miller High Life; he popped the tab on the first one, then he stood up and set it on the small ledge of the headstone, leaning it against the empty flower vase.

Sitting back on the bench, he took the other beer and popped the top.

"Remember last time I was here I told you I'd have a surprise for you? Well, Bro, this is it, our first drink together."

Jack lifted the beer up, looked at his big brother's headstone, and said, "Here's to you, big brother. Cheers."

LOOKING FOR MORE?

READ ON FOR AN EXCLUSIVE LOOK AT *LETHAL LIAISONS*, ANOTHER JACK WEST NOVEL.

LETHAL LIAISONS - PROLOGUE

The scream was ear-shattering, echoing throughout the empty house. The woman's face turned green and her stomach lurched. She was going to vomit. The man did not make a sound. He grabbed his wife and pulled her back from the doorway. Brenda walked behind them, chatting up the home's amenities, and the shriek jarred her to the core. Her mouth opened, but she felt paralyzed. Seeing a dead body was not on the real-estate listing flyer.

Fifteen minutes earlier

"It's over our budget. Why are we looking?"

"Honey, it's been on the market for over sixty days. They might lower the price."

The couple parked in front of the house for sale. Mathers' Realty offered the property. A metal sign planted in the owner's yard, Al Mathers, middle-aged black man, in the top right corner and underneath the agent's name, Brenda Cochran, and her phone number.

A compact silver sedan pulled up.

"We aren't obligated to buy. We're just looking." Her husband opened his door.

"You'd better hope I don't love it. I'm tired of disappointment."

"Hey," the real estate agent called out. "Good to see you. Y'all ready? I just need to get the key out of the lockbox and we'll be on our way."

"Goodness, it's cold in here. What do they have the thermostat set at, minus ten?" The female client shivered.

"That's odd. I showed this house day before yesterday, and it hasn't been shown since. I remember setting the A/C at eighty. No sense in wasting electricity on an empty house." Brenda Cochran stepped to the left hallway, into the front sitting room, and looked at the thermostat.

"Someone has this set at fifty-eight degrees. Good gracious!" The agent moved the temperature up and turned to her clients. "I think you're going to love the back of the residence. There's an oversized family room with a rock fireplace, and it's set off an enormous kitchen. Let's head back, shall we?" The agent followed the female client, letting her lead the way. Walking over the threshold, five steps in, her heart leaped into her throat and her scream loud and ear-piercing. Her husband yanked her, pulling her backward, nearly ripping her arm out of the socket. Brenda, busy chatting up the house froze in place.

Her hands flew to her mouth, not able to utter a sound. In a state of shock, no one moved, or breathed, all eyes upon the scene before them. Time ceased to move, and their feet were like cement shoes.

"We have to call the police." Brenda Cochran backed out of the room.

"I've got to get outside because I'm going to be sick." The client's face turned various shades of green. She felt her stomach lurch.

They called 9-1-1 then stood outside on the front lawn waiting for the police. Brenda Cochran's hands were shaking. She never smoked in front of her clients, but today she needed a cigarette.

"Sorry," she said sticking the lighter to the end, firing up, and taking a long drag.

"No worries. If I had a fifth of whatever, I'd be chugging it right now." He pulled his wife closer to his side.

"You don't have to stay. I'm the realtor; I can give the police the information." Her hands shook as she lifted the cig to her lips.

"We'll stay. They may want to talk to us too. I'd like to get it over with now and not deal with it later."

When the police officers walked in, they found a middle-aged black woman on the floor. Blood pooled under her right side. Her body face up, eyes closed, her arms bent at the elbows. Each of her hands placed low on her stomach, one on top of the other. Her legs were straight out, her ankles crossed. It gave her a peaceful, sleeping look. The makeup, not the shades a black woman would wear.

Officer Jeffers stepped back. He did not need an ambulance—he needed Homicide, the Crime Scene Investigators, and the medical examiner.

Detective's Xi Chang and Jace Severson, Team 7-11, were next in line on the Homicide table.

LETHAL LIAISONS - CHAPTER 1

Sweat rolled off his face as the salty Pacific Ocean air clung to his skin, as well as the sand he'd kicked up during his run. Stooped over, huffing, Jack West finished his morning run, and it felt good. Sprinting on the sand required more force than running on asphalt, thus making his run more of a challenge; he had challenged himself for the past five days. His calf muscles were sore as heck the first couple of days.

Stretching his legs, Jack extended his arms upward toward the sky. He would make time to work out, stay healthy, and get in better shape back home. Turning, he looked at the ocean. No breaking waves, just calm at this time of day. Vacationers coming alive as the day broke. He felt at peace.

Jogging back to where he'd started, he scanned the paradise he had been in since last Tuesday. Today was the last day of his vacation in beautiful Maui, Hawaii. A place with waters as blue as the sky, and one word came to mind: Utopia. Here you would find white sandy beaches and waterfalls for the explorer or the average Joe.

Breaking waves for the surfer. Gigantic banyan trees in Maui were pieces of God's artwork. Jack thought the banyan trees resembled giant octopuses on steroids and out of control. Some looked like alien forms from a far-off planet in the outer galaxy.

Colorful flora he had no name for sans the bird-of-paradise and the yellow hibiscus. Banana trees and coconut trees lined the island. Maui, Hawaii an exquisite place, he mused, taking the stairs leading to his room two at a time.

Opening the door, he smiled at another lovely thing Hawaii had —the one he had loaned to them for the brief time he would be there —Gretchen Benson.

Leisurely lying in bed, she turned when she heard the door and smiled. "Good morning, cowboy."

Jack walked to the bed, leaned in, and kissed her. They had been together for two years, and he never grew tired of kissing her whenever he had the chance.

"Did you enjoy your run this morning?" She reached to hug him. "Gretch, I'm sweaty, sandy, and yucky. And I smell."

"We can fix that."

Gretchen climbed off the bed and grabbed his hand. Smiling she led him to the rock shower with the double bench seat and the rainfall shower head. In less than ten minutes, Jack stood kissing her under a cascade of water. Her hands roamed his back and his muscled arms. In one swift motion, he lifted her, soaking wet, carried her to the bed, and laid her down, her giggling the entire time.

"Gretch, you're a funny woman, laughing when I'm trying to swoop you up in a serious seduction."

Jack lowered his head and took her lips. Gretchen knew what that kiss meant. He lowered his body next to hers, and she willingly complied.

Their relationship had passion and mutual respect. Neither had ever said, I love you, to the other. Jack wanted her in his life, yet he never looked past the here and now. He lived each day, one by one.

Once they were satisfied, they lay together, a sheet covering them, and Gretchen rolled up on her side to look at him.

"Jack, you're an amazing guy."

"No, I'm not. I'm just a fellow from Houston, Texas, visiting Maui, Hawaii with a gal too good for him."

"Jack West, I mean it. You're an incredible man who still has good left in him. From some of the most horrendous acts of violence you've seen and the stories you've told me, and I can imagine the ones you have left out. You're a gentle lover and a caring man."

Jack never thought of himself as gentle or caring until he met her. Over time, their relationship blossomed. He trusted her, and she trusted him. They had fun and their physical chemistry, off the charts, as in explosive. Yes, he had demons. The job as a homicide detective would never leave a man scar-less. Somehow, he could suppress the dark side of the heinous things he had seen. He never wanted the evil parts of his life to touch her or interfere with what was going on between them.

"Jack?" She caressed his bare arm.

"You've been the amazing one, Gretch." He turned his face toward hers. "You've taken a back seat to my job, gone days without seeing or hearing from me when I've been knee deep working a case. You've tolerated my irritated moods or my disappointment when it wasn't going well. And you've never told me you thought my job is too dangerous, or suggest I get into a safer line of work."

Gretchen tucked her head under his arm and rolled up closer.

"Jack, you have a very hard job, and my complaining won't make it easier for you. You had this job before us. I knew what you did for a living. I have no complaints, Cowboy."

He relaxed, pulling her closer. "I'm glad. What makes me unhappy is—" Trailing his words off, he began caressing her arm.

"Jack, what makes you unhappy?" Her words muffled as she turned her face to his bare chest, giving him butterfly kisses.

"Going back to Houston and leaving paradise and jumping back into reality."

"Well," Gretchen said, as she pulled her naked body up over his, letting the sheet slither off, and her hair cascade over his bare chest.

"Let's be the volcano Hawaii never knew existed on their islands and let's explode." With a sexy giggle, she pressed her lips to his.

Regular airport hubbub and the rush of frantic passengers wiped out the tranquility of the last seven days.

"Back to reality, huh?" Gretchen scowled.

"Yep, but I can live on the memories of the past week with a smile. Not to mention the million and one pictures you took."

Gretchen rolled her eyes. "Sorry, couldn't help myself. Maui is gorgeous. I love memories in pictures. It helps me recreate the experience."

"I know, Gretch. Let's get to baggage claim and get the hell out of George Bush's Airport."

Once all of her luggage was set in the house, Jack held her in his arms at the front door.

"Gonna be weird tonight, sleeping in my bed without you," he whispered in her ear, nuzzling her neck.

"Yeah, but I'll see you soon I hope."

He left her standing there as he headed back to Deer Park, watching her wave goodbye in his review mirror until she faded out of sight.

The flight had been direct from the Kahului Airport in Maui to the George Bush International Airport in Houston, non-stop. There was a time difference of five hours, with Texas five hours ahead. He felt like he had lost ten hours, not just five. It was nearly 7:00 p.m. Wednesday night, but he was still on Maui time and it felt like 1:00 in the afternoon. Halfway unpacked, he showered, made a sandwich, grabbed a beer, and sat in his favorite recliner. At 9:15, he scanned through the local television channels searching for news. Gone for eight days, counting their return day. He figured some news would be noteworthy, because it was Houston, after all.

Channel KHOU-11 was showing the weather forecast. Crud, he had missed the news. Clicking over to Fox 26 Houston, he got the weather again. No news. Flipping from channel to channel, he found nothing worthwhile to watch. He turned off the television and turned on the radio.

It was 10:30. He hadn't realized how tired he felt until his eyes closed for more than a minute. He would take a short catnap, then get up and finish unpacking.

The clock on the table illuminated in the darkness, and he adjusted his vision. Three-thirty. Wow, he'd slept for five hours in his recliner.

Yawning, he stretched then headed to his room. Flopping on his bed, he missed Gretchen's body next to his.

———————

"Jack, glad to see you made it home in one piece. Wow, you got a great suntan, dude. You could blend in with the locals in Mexico." Lucky grabbed Jack's outstretched hand.

"It's good to be home, but I needed a relaxing vacation."

"My wife's jealous. She wants to go to Hawaii now, thanks."

"We had a magnificent time, and it felt like paradise."

"How's Gretchen?"

"She's wonderful." Jack's face beamed.

His so-called chipper moods had driven Dawson Luck crazy. He had badgered him for a few months, and then Jack let him in on Gretchen.

"I knew it was a woman. I just had no clue who, you rascal. You're as lucky as I am. I mean look at me, and then you see my beautiful wife. I understand why the fellas call me Lucky, even though my last name is Luck." He chuckled.

Dawson Luck had transplanted from the Arizona Police Department. Not a tall man at just five-foot-nine, with enormous feet and an enormous nose. His eyebrows were bushy and thick and looked like a unibrow. Jack thought he should take up waxing. When he frowned a certain way, it resembled a black caterpillar wiggling along his forehead. His odd unibrow had not prevented him from getting a gorgeous wife.

How he had had the incredible fortune of marrying a goddess was beyond any of their comprehension. As one of the other detectives had said, "It's gotta be because of his enormous nose, or his giant feet."

"Coming back on a Thursday, smart move, Jack, especially knowing we weren't gonna be first up for this weekend."

"Yeah, I knew I'd be dealing with jet lag."

"I hate to tell you this, but they changed the schedules. We're stuck with being on call tonight and tomorrow night," Lucky said.

"That stinks. So, partner, what's been going on with the Houston crime scene for the last eight days?"

Lucky got Jack up to speed and then told him he needed to finish some paperwork he'd been assisting Robbery with.

"7-11 catch a break yet?"

They'd caught a fresh case, right before Jack went on vacation, involving a woman found murdered in an empty house in the Fourth Ward. Their investigation was ongoing.

"No, it's been mostly dead ends, but they're still digging."

The story of how 7-11 became 7-11 still floated around the station. Anytime they had a new employee the most popular question asked was, why do you call them 7-11? I don't get it? Then the explanation was necessary.

7-11 were Xi Chang and Jace Severson. Chang's first name a Chinese name, and looked like the Roman numeral XI, thus spawned the nickname, Eleven. When partnered with Jace Severson, Severson close enough to be seven. One fellow dubbed them 7-11, and it stuck.

"So, do they have a person of interest at all?" Jack hated unsolved cases that ended up stuck in cold case files—no justice ever served.

"Well, they haven't completely ruled out the husband yet. His motive is a big life insurance payoff. I got caught up helping Gilly in a robbery and haven't seen 7-11 much in the past six days." Lucky continued typing a report he needed finished.

Chang and Severson's investigation had been ongoing for close to three months. Jack heard snippets, but he and Lucky had their own murder to work. Their five-month investigation of a teen murdered in a park by a rival gang finally solved. They'd started the grueling task of gathering all the evidence to give to the district attorney.

Three days later, the files sat on the DA's desk. Then the twenty-year-old charged with the crime hung himself in his cell. Now no trial needed. It irritated the crap out of Jack. The killer took the cowardly way out.

The loved ones of the dead were cheated out of proper justice. Jack made damn sure to get the reports tied up before Destination Maui. As soon as the 5:00 whistle had blown, he had too.

"Lucky, gonna go talk to Chief Yao. Be back shortly."

"Sure, Jack, he'll wanna see ya since you've been on vacation, lollygagging. You earned the time off, bud. We all need to escape from the mayhem and chaos, and get back to the good we've missed doing the job we do."

Dawson Luck was being philosophical. Jack never knew Lucky had this side to him, and he agreed fully.

"Jack, hey man, nice to see you're back. You look great for an old fart," the COD said, reaching across the desk to shake hands. It used to be Captain Yao, now it was Chief of Detectives Davis Yao.

"I'm rested and ready to get on it and put some criminals behind bars." Jack took the chair across from Davis's desk, askew with papers and files. "You look snowed under, Chief."

"Nah, it's just HR paperwork, working on evaluations, your basic unexciting work. How was Hawaii? You think Gretchen's the one?" He fired off the second question before Jack could answer the first question.

"Hawaii was a fantastic, beautiful place, and about Gretchen, well, I don't know, Davis. We'll see how it goes."

"The chief of police is still bragging on the homicide department and Judge Wolff's case. He says nothing for weeks, and then something happens like that one-year sting Vice worked. They break up an immense prostitution ring and some second-tier drug runners, and the chief is bragging again. Lord Jack, a S & M sex dungeon in Houston. Who knew one even existed?"

"Not me, Chief."

"I guess it shocked the hell outta me when Vice found it, and in a damn dive bar, too. It's, well, I guess I'm just an old stuffed shirt."

"Lucky was right. The Crystal Barrel was more than a shithole dive. Ralph Delvecchio and his silent partner being Judge Wolff still shocks me. Wolff had been a prime customer of his own dungeon. It makes me sick. As far as you being a stuffed-shirt, hell that makes me one too. I've never understood that kind of fetish, and never will."

"Well, since that was where the prostitution ring was and the dungeon got raided, that's thrown Wolff into the spotlight, again. Jack, people taking pictures of that crap is even more obscene. It's something I don't understand."

"I think our ex-judge relived the experience in photos, while he, well, no other way to say it, beat off."

"It definitely put his name back in the news. He should be happy he gets to hide in his protected jail cell. The man still makes me want to upchuck. But regardless of that, Chief Pratt is proud of Homicide. He's still busting at the seams since we closed four cold cases at one time and took down a judge with no morals."

"Well, Davis, it's time to move on, get some more solid work done, cold or new cases. Put those nasty bastards behind bars. Clean our city up. We have a helluva department, all of us fixated on the same goal, to make Houston safe."

"It is okay to take some credit, Jack. There is no harm in admitting you are an outstanding detective. If not for some of your gut instincts, we would overlook things. You have done an impressive job with Dawson, too. Even though he was a three-year detective in Robbery when we got him from Arizona, he's learned a lot from you, Jack. Give yourself some credit."

"I have to give the credit to Frank Windom. God rest his soul. He drove me and molded me. Glad I had him as a partner, learned a lot from him. I still miss him."

"Okay, Jack, sorry I can't talk more, but I have at least three evaluations to finish. Go check in with Captain Brooks, no matter how much you might not want to." The COD knew how the detectives felt about the new captain. Damn. Brody Brooks. Jack and his fellow detectives would like to kick him out on his ass.

AUTHOR'S NOTE

Word-of-mouth is crucial for any author to succeed. If you enjoyed *Twist of Fate*, please leave a review online—anywhere you are able. Even if it's just a sentence or two; it would make all the difference and would be very much appreciated.

Thanks,

Deanna

ACKNOWLEDGMENTS

I would like to thank the following people for their help and support:

To Thomas Faught, thank you for devoting your time from the start to finish as my beta reader, and putting up with all the faux pas. To Sharon Jaeger, thank you for all of your wonderful help on this second printing edition and for your EYES. Sharon, your love of reading crime novels has been a tremendous blessing to me; thank you.

To Seth Colten for taking time to 'school me' on fire arms, thank you.

Finally, to my family who never thought I was crazy for following my dream.

A special thank you goes out to another dear friend. We have never met in person because he lives in Dublin, Ireland; fellow author, Robert E. Kearns. Ed, thank you for your ear, your advice, and for your moral support, keeping my spirits uplifted. If I ever get the chance to visit Ireland, I promise to look you up.

ABOUT THE AUTHOR

Twist of Fate—A Jack West Novel is the official debut novel for Deanna King. Deanna lives in Texas with her husband Travis.

Made in the USA
Middletown, DE
01 November 2022

13822814R00217